Existential Therapy

CW00408016

In 1958 in their book *Existence*, Rollo May, Ernst Angel and Henri Ellenberger introduced existential therapy to the English-speaking psychotherapy world. Since then the field of existential therapy has moved along rapidly and this book considers how it has developed over the past 50 years, and the implications that this has for the future.

In this book Laura Barnett and Greg Madison bring together contributors from both sides of the Atlantic to highlight issues surrounding existential therapy today, and look constructively to the future whilst acknowledging the debt to the past. Dialogue is at the heart of the book, the dialogue between existential thought and therapeutic practice, and between the past and the future.

Existential Therapy: Legacy, Vibrancy and Dialogue, focuses on dialogue between key figures in the field to cover topics including:

- historical and conceptual foundations of existential therapy
- perspectives on contemporary Daseinsanalysis
- the search for meaning in existential therapy
- existential therapy in contemporary society.

Existential Therapy: Legacy, Vibrancy and Dialogue explores how existential therapy has changed in the last five decades, and compares and contrasts different schools of existential therapy, making it essential reading for experienced therapists as well as for anyone training in psychotherapy, counselling, psychology or psychiatry who wants to incorporate existential therapy into their practice.

Laura Barnett is an existential psychotherapist working as therapist, supervisor consultant, and trainer in the NHS, and in private practice. She is the editor of *When Death Enters the Therapeutic Space: Existential Perspectives in Psychotherapy and Counselling* (Routledge, 2009).

Greg Madison, PhD is a chartered psychologist and psychotherapist in London and Brighton. He is also a Focusing Coordinator and teaches internationally on postgraduate university faculties in Europe and North America. He is the author of *The End of Belonging* (2009) and other texts.

Contributors: Laura Barnett, Betty Cannon, Havi Carel, Mick Cooper, Erik Craig, Emmy van Deurzen, Tamás Fazekas, Linda Finlay, Roger Frie, Maurice Friedman, Eugene Gendlin, Judith Hassan, John Heaton, Keith Hoeller, Alice Holzhey-Kunz, Alfried Längle, Greg Madison, Donna Orange, Simon du Plock, Kirk Schneider, Ernesto Spinelli, M. Guy Thompson, Les Todres.

'This is a "must have" book for everyone interested in existential therapy. The coverage of authors and topics is extensive and deep. Read it as a celebration of and guide to all that has happened in the field since May et al.'s "Existence" in 1958. I wish May, Laing, Bugental, Binswanger et al. were alive to see what has sprung from the fertile seeds they sowed. The void still stalks human destiny, but here are ways to confront it.
Thomas Greening, PhD, Professor of Psychology, Saybrook University

This text is the most prominent landmark in the field since May, Angel and Ellenberger's 1958 classic, Existence. When reading the chapters of these prominent existential therapists and thinkers, you rediscover the unique value of the existential contribution to the field of therapy and the urgency of this approach for our present situation as human beings.
Bo Jacobsen, Professor at the University of Copenhagen, Psychologist, and author of *Invitation to Existential Psychology*

Daunting in its scope and engaging in its style, *Existential Therapy: Legacy, Vibrancy and Dialogue* is a rewarding experiential and intellectual encounter with the past, present and future of existential psychology. This must-read for students and therapists alike is guaranteed to captivate the imagination and satisfy the intellect.
Pat Ogden, PhD, Founder/Director, Sensorimotor Psychotherapy Institute

This highly ambitious volume manages to successfully hold together many divergent perspectives in a coherent dialogue of philosophical ideas and practice dilemmas that is truly vibrant and provides the reader with the best overview of existential therapy that has been produced to date.
Paul Smith-Pickard, PhD, former Chair, Society for Existential Analysis

This book is a tour de force that under one cover discusses the main current approaches to existential therapy, and does so in a highly interesting and engaging way. History, theory, dialogue, meaning, life and death, and the future are all discussed in an illuminating way. It is a wonderful book for both students and practitioners to gain a greater understanding of current existential approaches from an integrative perspective.
Leslie S Greenberg, Distinguished Research Professor, Department of Psychology, York University Toronto, Ontario, Canada

Advancing Theory in Therapy
Series Editor: Keith Tudor

Most books covering individual therapeutic approaches are aimed at the trainee/student market. This series, however, is concerned with *advanced* and *advancing* theory, offering the reader comparative and comparable coverage of a number of therapeutic approaches.

Aimed at professionals and postgraduates, *Advancing Theory in Therapy* will cover an impressive range of theories. With full reference to case studies throughout, each title will

- present cutting-edge research findings
- locate each theory and its application within its cultural context
- develop a critical view of theory and practice.

Titles in the series

Body Psychotherapy
Edited by Tree Staunton

Transactional Analysis: A Relational Perspective
Helena Hargaden and Charlotte Sills

Adlerian Psychotherapy: An Advanced Approach to Individual Psychology
Ursula E. Oberst and Alan E. Stewart

Rational Emotive Behaviour Therapy: Theoretical Developments
Edited by Windy Dryden

Co-Counselling: The Theory and Practice of Re-evaluation Counselling
Katie Kauffman and Caroline New

Analytical Psychology
Edited by Joe Cambray and Linda Carter

Person-Centered Therapy: A Clinical Philosophy
Keith Tudor and Mike Worrall

Psychodrama: Advances in Theory and Practice
Edited by Clark Baim, Jorge Burmeister and Manuela Maciel

Neurolinguistic Psychotherapy: A Postmodern Perspective
Lisa Wake

Constructivist Psychotherapy: A Narrative Hermeneutic Approach
Gabriele Chiari and Maria Laura Nuzzo

Lacanian Psychoanalysis: Revolutions in Subjectivity
Ian Parker

Gestalt Therapy: Advances in Theory and Practice
Edited by Talia Bar-Yoseph Levine

Existential Therapy

Legacy, Vibrancy and Dialogue

Edited by Laura Barnett and
Greg Madison

Routledge
Taylor & Francis Group

LONDON AND NEW YORK

First published 2012 by Routledge
27 Church Road, Hove, East Sussex BN3 2FA

Simultaneously published in the USA and Canada
by Routledge
711 Third Avenue, New York NY 10017

Routledge is an imprint of the Taylor & Francis Group, an Informa business

British Library Cataloguing in Publication Data
A catalogue record for this book is available from the British Library

Library of Congress Cataloging-in-Publication Data

ISBN: 978-0-415-56433-5 (hbk)
ISBN: 978-0-415-56434-2 (pbk)
ISBN: 978-0-203-14765-8 (ebk)

Typeset in Times by Garfield Morgan, Swansea, West Glamorgan
Paperback cover design by Sandra Heath
Printed and bound in the UK by TJ International Ltd, Padstow, Cornwall

One repays a teacher badly if one always remains nothing but a pupil.
(Nietzsche)

In gratitude
To those pioneer and other existential therapists who preceded us,
In hope, and curiosity
To those existential therapists who will follow us.

Contents

Contributors

Laura Barnett (co-editor) is an existential psychotherapist working as psychotherapist, supervisor consultant and trainer in the NHS, and in private practice. She has contributed articles and chapters on existential theory in practice and edited *When Death Enters the Therapeutic Space: Existential Perspectives in Psychotherapy and Counselling* (Routledge 2009).

Betty Cannon, PhD is the author of *Sartre and Psychoanalysis* and numerous articles and chapters on existential therapy. She serves on the editorial boards of three existential psychology and philosophy journals. She is Professor Emerita of the Colorado School of Mines and Senior Adjunct Professor at Naropa University. She is president of the Boulder Psychotherapy Institute, which offers training in Applied Existential Psychotherapy.

Havi Carel, PhD is Senior Lecturer in Philosophy at UWE Bristol and also teaches at Bristol Medical School. She is the author of *Life and Death in Freud and Heidegger*. Her book *Illness* was shortlisted for the Wellcome Trust Book Prize. She has edited *What Philosophy Is* and *New Takes in Film-Philosophy*. She is currently leading an AHRC-funded project on the concepts of health, illness and disease.

Mick Cooper, DPhil is Professor of Counselling at the University of Strathclyde. He has written, co-written and co-edited a wide range of publications on existential, person-centred, self-pluralistic and relational approaches to therapy, including *Existential Therapies*, *Essential Research Findings in Counselling and Psychotherapy*, and, with Dave Mearns, *Working at Relational Depth in Counselling and Psychotherapy*.

Erik Craig, PhD has been teaching and practising Existential Psychotherapy for over 40 years. He has written and edited for several psychological journals, including special issues of *The Humanistic Psychologist* on Daseinsanalysis (1988) and Existential Psychotherapy (2008). He is a past president of the Division for Humanistic Psychology of the American

Psychological Association and of the International Association for the Study of Dreams.

Emmy van Deurzen, PhD is founder of the School of Psychotherapy and Counselling (SPC) at Regent's College and the New School of Psychotherapy and Counselling (NSPC), both in London. She is also founder of the Society for Existential Analysis and its journal *Existential Analysis*. She is the author of numerous books and articles on existential therapy which have been translated into over a dozen languages.

Tamás Fazekas, MD, PhD combines careers as paediatrician, Daseinsanalyst and philosopher. He is the author and co-editor of a number of books on psychotherapy, including, in English, *The Need for Psychotherapy* (Shaker) and has contributed articles on paediatrics. In 2004, Dr Fazekas founded the Hungarian Daseinsanalytic Society.

Linda Finlay, PhD is a practising integrative–existential psychotherapist. She also teaches psychology and writes educational materials for the Open University (UK), alongside offering mentorship/training on the use of qualitative research methodology. She has published widely. Her most recent books include *Relational-centred Research for Psychotherapists* (co-authored with Ken Evans) and *Phenomenology for Therapists*, both published by Wiley-Blackwell.

Roger Frie, PhD is a philosopher, psychoanalyst and clinical psychologist. He is Associate Professor of Educational Psychology and Human Development at Simon Fraser University, Vancouver, and Faculty, William Alanson White Institute, New York. Recent books include *Psychological Agency: Theory, Practice and Culture*, and *Psychotherapy as a Human Science*, with Daniel Burston.

Maurice Friedman, PhD is Emeritus Professor of Religious Studies, Philosophy and Comparative Literature at San Diego State University and co-director and founder of the Institute for Dialogical Psychotherapy in San Diego. He is a world-renowned expert on Martin Buber, has written prolifically on Buber and on Dialogical Psychotherapy and taught at numerous universities. He is the recipient of three honorary doctorates and various awards for his writing.

Eugene Gendlin, PhD is Emeritus Professor of Psychology at the University of Chicago and founder of the Focusing Institute. He was founder and editor of the APA clinical division journal, *Psychotherapy: Theory Research and Practice*. He is the author of numerous articles and books, including *Focusing* which was translated into ten languages. He is the recipient of a number of awards for his development of experiential psychotherapy.

Judith Hassan, OBE is Director of Services for Holocaust Survivors and Refugees for Jewish Care. She is a trained social worker and for more than 30 years has pioneered specialist therapeutic services for Holocaust survivors and refugees. She is consulted internationally on the subject of war trauma. She was awarded the National Care Awards Lifetime Achievement in Care in 2007.

John M. Heaton, MB, BChirg is a psychiatrist who has been practising psychotherapy for some 40 years. He worked with R. D. Laing in the Philadelphia Association and was Chair of the Training Committee. He was editor of *Existential Analysis*. He has written four books including *The Eye: Phenomenology and Psychology of Function and Disorder* and *The Talking Cure: Wittgenstein's Therapeutic Method for Psychotherapy* (2010), and numerous articles.

Keith Hoeller, PhD is the Editor of the *Review of Existential Psychology & Psychiatry, Studies in Existential Psychology & Psychiatry*, and of numerous books. He is the translator of Martin Heidegger's *Elucidations of Hölderlin's Poetry* (2000). In 2002 he won the Thomas S. Szasz Award for Outstanding Contributions to the Cause of Civil Liberties. He is currently writing an intellectual biography of Thomas Szasz.

Alice Holzhey-Kunz, PhD, philosopher and daseinsanalyst, is President of the Society for Hermeneutic Anthropology and Daseinsanalysis and co-founder and co-president of the Daseinsanalytic Seminar in Zurich. She has published three books and numerous articles on daseinsanalytic theory and on a new dialogue between psychoanalysis and existential philosophy. She was co-editor of the new edition of selected works of Ludwig Binswanger.

Alfried Längle, MD, PhD (psychology) is founder (1983) and president of the International Society for Logotherapy and Existential Analysis (Vienna), a scholar with over 200 publications, who worked closely with Viktor E. Frankl. He is professor of psychotherapy at Moscow's HSE University and Klagenfurt's psychological faculty. He is the recipient of two honorary doctorates and three honorary professor degrees.

Greg Madison, PhD (co-editor) is an existential psychotherapist, chartered psychologist, independent academic working in the UK and internationally, and the author of numerous articles. He is a country co-ordinator for the Focusing Institute, an accredited mediator, and a practitioner in private practice. Currently he is developing experiential–existential trainings across Europe and pursuing special interests in the experience of home, especially for those who live cross-culturally.

Professor Donna Orange, PhD is training and supervising analyst and faculty at ISIPSe (Istituto di Specializzazione in Psicologia Psicoanalitica del Se e

Psicoanalisi Relazionale, Roma); Faculty and Supervising Analyst, Institute for the Psychoanalytic Study of Subjectivity, New York. She is author of *Emotional Understanding: Studies in Psychoanalytic Psychology* and of *Thinking for Clinicians: Philosophical Resources for Contemporary Psychoanalysis and the Humanistic Psychotherapies.*

Professor Simon du Plock, PhD is Head of the Post-Qualification Doctorates Department and Director of the Centre for Practice-Based Research at the Metanoia Institute, London, where he leads research doctorates in psychotherapy in partnership with Middlesex University. He is a Foundation Member with Senior Practitioner Status of the BPS Register of Psychologists Specializing in Psychotherapy. He lectures internationally on existential therapy, and has edited *Existential Analysis*, the journal of the Society for Existential Analysis, since 1993.

Kirk J. Schneider, PhD is a leading spokesperson for contemporary existential–humanistic psychology. He is current editor of the *Journal of Humanistic Psychology*, vice-president of the Existential–Humanistic Institute, and part-time faculty at Saybrook Graduate School. He is also a Fellow of the American Psychological Association. Dr. Schneider has published over 100 articles and chapters and has authored or edited eight books.

Ernesto Spinelli, PhD is professor of psychotherapy, counselling and counselling psychology. He is an international trainer and theorist of existential analysis, as applied to psychology and psychotherapy and, more recently, the related arenas of coaching, facilitation and conflict mediation. Ernesto is Director of ES Associates, an organization dedicated to the advancement of psychotherapy, coaching, facilitation and mediation through specialist seminars and training programmes.

M. Guy Thompson, PhD is a psychoanalyst and author of more than 100 books and articles on phenomenology, psychoanalysis, and schizophrenia. He is a member of numerous psychoanalytic organizations, including the IPA, the Philadelphia Association, and the Psychoanalytic Institute of Northern California, where he is a training and supervising analyst. He serves on the editorial boards of various journals.

Les Todres, PhD is a clinical psychologist and Professor of Qualitative Research and Psychotherapy at Bournemouth University, UK. He is the author of *Embodied Enquiry: Phenomenological Touchstones for Research, Psychotherapy and Spirituality* and numerous articles and chapters. Current research interests include older person care, mental health and quality of life.

Series preface

This series focuses on advanced and advancing theory in psychotherapy. Its aims are: to present theory and practice within a specific theoretical orientation or approach at an advanced, postgraduate level; to advance theory by presenting and evaluating new ideas and their relation to the particular approach; to locate the orientation and its psychotherapeutic applications within cultural contexts, both historically in terms of the origins of the approach, and contemporarily in terms of current debates about philosophy, theory, society and therapy; and, finally, to present and develop a critical view of theory and practice, especially in the context of debates about power, organisation and the increasing professionalisation of therapy.

This volume is a welcome addition to this series – and, indeed, I am delighted that the editors, Laura Barnett and Greg Madison, approached Routledge and myself to consider this book for the series. It is a welcome and worthy addition as it not only fulfils the brief of the series but does so in a way that is true to the spirit of its subject. The book acknowledges and stands as a tribute to the legacy of existential philosophy and thought; it reflects the resonance – as its subtitle suggests, the vibrancy – both of this legacy and of present thinking with regard to existential therapeutic practice; and, consistent with an important aspect of the method of existential therapy, a significant amount of the book has been written – and, of course, edited – through and in dialogue. The editors have engaged, and, at points in the book, literally engaged with an impressive array of authors who reflect current and advanced thinking in this field.

I received the manuscript just as I was about to set out for a tramp or long, three day walk – on the Milford Track on the South Island of Aotearoa New Zealand. I decided to take the first half of the manuscript with me, and read it in the evenings we spent in the huts along the track. The book complemented the vastness and remoteness of the setting, and certainly enhanced my thinking about existence, existentialism, and existential therapy, an appreciation which remained as I completed reading the manuscript on my return to city life. I commend the editors, and recommend it to readers – wherever they read it.

Keith Tudor

Acknowledgements

We wish to thank all the contributors to this book for their thoughtful and inspiring words, and for their willingness to engage with our numerous questions and comments.

Our gratitude also goes to the editorial team at Routledge, whose swift responses and friendly, flexible approach have been a pleasure to work with and allowed us to think more creatively about the book.

And finally we would like to acknowledge the encroachment this book has made on our private lives and thank our respective partners, families and friends for their support and patience.

Introduction

Laura Barnett and Greg Madison

In 1958 in their book *Existence*, Rollo May, Ernst Angel and Henri Ellenberger introduced existential therapy to the English-speaking psychotherapy world. Its international list of contributors comprised the foremost existential therapists of the day, including Ludwig Binswanger, Rollo May and Eugene Minkowski; the book became a 'manifesto' of existential therapy for the twentieth century.

The following year, at Medard Boss's invitation, Heidegger travelled to Boss's home in Zollikon, Switzerland to teach a select group of psychiatrists. Thus, the first of the 'Zollikon Seminars' was born, from which a fruitful dialogue developed further between psychotherapy and existential philosophy. That same year, the Annual Convention of the American Psychological Association in Cincinnati hosted the Symposium on Existential Psychology which brought together the most eminent humanistic and personality theorists of the day – Gordon Allport, Rollo May, Abraham Maslow, Carl Rogers, and so on. Maslow's paper 'Existential Psychology – What's In It For Us?' reflects the spirit of excitement and curiosity that this new approach to therapy aroused. A selection of the proceedings from that symposium was published two years later under the title *Existential Psychology* (1961).

Fifty years later, while *Existence* has remained an important work of reference, the time is ripe for a new book that can offer a 'manifesto' of existential therapy for the twenty-first century. Indeed, the map of existential therapy has changed considerably since 1958: it has spread further across the globe, new 'schools' offering different perspectives have arisen and its impact on the therapeutic profession has increased.

'Manifesto' is not meant here in any normative sense: there has never been one unique way of being an existential therapist, let alone of *doing* existential therapy, and it is certainly not the aim of this book to try and put forward an existential orthodoxy (which would be a contradiction in terms). It simply wants to gather together the personal dialogues of some of the most influential existential therapists of the day, and a few newer voices, with a view to exploring topics of interest, highlighting some of the issues that surround therapy today and looking constructively to the future, while acknowledging our debt to the past. To celebrate the influence and vitality of the existential tradition in contemporary psychotherapy, this book offers, side by side for the first time, expressions of its diverse strands: the American schools (existential–humanistic and existential/contemporary psychoanalysis), the diverse emphases of the vibrant 'British School' including the Philadelphia Association, and the long-standing continental traditions of Daseinsanalysis and Logotherapy. The book also includes essays on major thinkers in the field such as Szasz and Gendlin. What can be said to unite all these various forms of existential therapy is a focus on the client's whole existence as being-in-the-world and a phenomenological approach to exploring that existence. This involves, on the part of the therapist, an abiding awareness of our ontological givens (those charac-teristics of our human-ness, such as our mortality, which we cannot evade) and how they enter the individual's experience of being alive. It also entails a non-deterministic view of human existence and a non-pathologizing way of being with clients that seeks to avoid the position of an expert dispensing interpretations.

The words 'legacy, vibrancy and dialogue' of the title express the book's aim of reflecting on existential therapy's past, its present situation and the future, as these interweave with one another and give rise to further ques-tions and reflections. While there is no doubt that the historical dimension of this book has captured the imagination of many of our colleagues, this is more than simply a celebratory 'anniversary book': such books can have a tendency to be hagiographic about its pioneers, eschewing of reflection and self-criticism, and complacent about the future.

Legacy, as we originally conceived it, stood for the debt which existential therapy owes to those pioneering existential psychotherapists featured in *Existence*, as well as the many others who helped make existential therapy what it is today, in all its diversity. 'Legacy' also expressed existential therapy's debt to Husserl and to the existential philosophers whose thought underpins its practice, from Kierkegaard and Nietzsche to Heidegger, Sartre and Merleau-Ponty, but also to those philosophers (existential and other) whose thought, though less embedded in the teaching of existential therapy, are of importance to us as we reflect on our own existence and that of our clients.

Yet legacy can also be seen as a key concept for existential thought and therapeutic practice. Our 'thrownness' and the 'givens' of existence are our lot – what has been handed down to us, the legacy we have received. Indeed, much of our work as existential therapists involves helping our clients to reflect on their legacy: helping them gain awareness of their freedom to view it from different perspectives and change those things that are in their hands to change, while learning to acknowledge and accept those aspects of their legacy that they cannot change.

This reading of legacy in the therapeutic setting echoes the philosophical concepts of 'repetition' in Kierkegaard and Heidegger, Nietzsche's *amor fati*, Sartre's view of a person's relationship to the dead in their 'necropolis' (1996: 587) and Derrida's '*héritage*'. These all develop themes of personal freedom within the context of our personal and/or societal inheritance, and the possibilities for renewal and creativity that this legacy (*Erbe, héritage*) offers: 'In one's coming back resolutely to one's thrown-ness, there is hidden a handing down to oneself of the possibilities that have come down to one, but not necessarily *as* having come down' (Heidegger 1962: 435; 383).

Vibrancy refers to the present vitality of existential therapy, and the way it resonates with the anxieties and hopes of today's times. Vibrancy, for our clients and ourselves, is also about learning to open ourselves to resonating with others, with nature, social currents, and the world around us.

Dialogue is also at the heart of existential therapy: indeed, two of the distinguishing characteristics of existential therapy are the dialogue it involves between philosophical reflection and therapeutic practice, and its dialogical approach to the therapeutic relationship. We trust that the view of existential therapy as a dialogue of experiential depth with the other – whether client, colleague, philosophical text or theory – will emerge strongly from the pages of this book.

Dialogue is at the heart of this book: half the chapters are in the form of a dialogue between authors. There are also, behind the scenes, our own dialogues, as editors, with individual contributors and those serendipitous meetings between contributors' ideas which dialogue in us; and the dialogue between us, Greg and Laura. We started off as almost total strangers to each other and have met only twice in the course of its composition, at a Society for Existential Analysis conference, yet our emails to each other have gone from the purely logistic to personal reflections on life, work and death. While this may sound of anecdotal interest only, it is an integral part of this book – it is not simply that nail-biting is far less stressful when done *à deux* and humour best when shared. Had either of us undertaken this book alone, the result would doubtless have been worthwhile. We feel sure, however, that it would not have been as exciting as the present offering: for the cross-fertilization of our different ideas, characters, interests, life experiences and even genders through dialogue has, we believe, significantly shaped this book. (An interesting topic for research?!) Finally, dialogue includes your own dialogues as readers.

Selecting contributors has felt a divisive process, as sadly we could not include all those whom we would have wanted to see represented. In addition, there are three therapists, Anthony Stadlen, Thomas Szasz and Irvin Yalom who, much to our sadness, felt unable for various reasons to accept our invitation, but whose voices, however, can still be heard, even if indirectly: Stadlen, through his learned replies to our behind the scenes consultations; Szasz in Keith Hoeller's chapter; and Yalom through the roundtable that closes the book.

After much deliberation, we took an editorial decision to confine ourselves to UK and US therapists, with the exception of Daseinsanalysts and Logotherapists. This has meant excluding contributors from important centres across the world, whose voices we would have liked to have heard – from Eastern Europe, the Baltic countries, Russia, Scandinavia, the Hispanic peninsula, Latin America, Australia. We hope that this current offering will now spur someone into offering them a channel of expression.

Book outline

In the first two chapters, Dr Eric Craig and Professor Roger Frie remind us of the historical and conceptual foundations of existential therapy. This is followed by two chapters that take their starting point in Heidegger's legacy: Dr Alice Holzhey-Kunz and Dr Tamás Fazekas' chapter which offers us two perspectives on contemporary Daseinsanalysis; and Laura Barnett's on boredom. Chapters 5 and 6 are informed by the experiential philosophy of Eugene Gendlin, himself influenced by Heidegger and Husserl: Professor Les Todres' chapter bridges the gap between Heidegger and Gendlin, and provides a brief case study; while Dr Greg Madison engages Professor Gendlin directly in interview. In Chapter 7, Professor Betty Cannon summarizes her own form of applied existential psychotherapy, grounded in the philosophy of Jean-Paul Sartre and integrating elements of Gestalt. There follow two chapters on critical psychiatry: Dr John Heaton and Dr M. Guy Thompson reflect on their personal experiences of R. D. Laing in relation to authenticity and the sceptic tradition; and in Chapter 9, Professor Keith Hoeller charts the development of Szasz's continuing battle against what he sees as the pseudomedicalization of therapy, and challenges us to rethink the foundations of our therapeutic practice. Professor Ernesto Spinelli and Professor Mick Cooper dialogue on dialogue in Chapter 10; while in the next two chapters, Dr Alfried Längle, a Logotherapist, and Professor Emmy van Deurzen look at the search for meaning in existential therapy and in life. Chapters 13 and 14 deal with existential therapy within contemporary society – the demands that are made of it, the role it may be expected to play: Dr Linda Finlay highlights the issues surrounding research, reminding us of our responsibilities, while Professor Kirk Schneider and Professor Simon du Plock discuss questions of contemporary relevance and look to the future. The book ends with a 'roundtable' chapter in which Professor Maurice Friedman, Dr Havi Carel, Judith Hassan OBE and Professor Donna Orange express their thoughts and feelings about death – that of others and their own. A brief conclusion draws out themes and impressions that have emerged from the book, and looks to the future.

References

Heidegger, M. (1962 [1927]) *Being and Time*, trans. J. R. Macquarrie and E. Robinson, Oxford: Blackwell.

May, R. (1961) *Existential Psychology*, New York: Random House.

May, R., Angel, E. and Ellenberger, H. F. (eds) (1994 [1958]) *Existence: A New Dimension in Psychiatry and Psychology*, Northvale, NJ: Jason Aronson.

Sartre, J.-P. (1996 [1943]) *L'Être et le néant: Essaie d'ontologie phénoménologique* [Being and Nothingness], Paris: Gallimard.

Chapter 1

Existential psychotherapy, discipline and démarche

Remembering essential horizons

Erik Craig

This chapter aims to provide a fresh overview of the historical circumstances and essential ideas that have contributed to the development of existential psychotherapy. One of the defining characteristics and strengths of the existential approach to psychology and psychotherapy is its concern with concrete lived-experience: more inclined to perception than abstraction, to sensation than conjecture, to description than theory, existential psychotherapists gravitate to ontology[1] rather than metaphysics. Whereas one might say the compelling human motive in classical psychoanalysis is to desire; in postmodern psychoanalysis to relate; or in Jungian analysis to individuate; in existential psychotherapy it is simply *to be*: our essence as human beings is grounded in our existence; we are ourselves only in our existing (Heidegger 1962: 153–154). Like psychotherapy, this is an heuristic not apodictic venture, an effort to discover, articulate and understand. A robust capacity for understanding, accepting and tolerating contingency, ambiguity, obscurity, and uncertainty is a hallmark of 'good enough' psychotherapy, not to mention a 'good enough' life.

Antonio, a bright, handsome Italian stockbroker from New York, twice divorced, spends 13 years after his second marriage looking for his ideal 'soulmate'. At 48 years of age, he watches his diet as carefully as the market, abstains from alcohol, paints, practises the guitar, religiously attends psychotherapy, and believes that if he lives well, he should be rewarded with good health, good loving, and a long, happy life. Why won't his life comply? In spite of his worldly success he is unhappy and often feels worthless. And this too: why doesn't one of the fine women whom he dates over the years stay with him or he with them? Impermanence, imperfection, and the haunting spectre of death mock his every effort to overcome them. He suffers as much from his own idea of the way things ought to be as he does from the way things actually are: if he cannot get his life to follow his vision for it, it will prove he, and perhaps even life itself, is worthless, nothing. Here he comes close to something: nothing. He is terrified that he is nothing at all, groundless.

He is not alone. We are born of vapours and to vapours return. And, indeed, what passes between, seen cosmically, amounts to very little more than vapour as well. Can I criticize Antonio for his wish to overcome his own human finitude, when I sit here defying my own mortality, chasing my own delusions just as tenaciously as Antonio? My delusions? Ah, for a few words on a shelf in the Library of Congress. What a bargain! My life for a few musty pages on some dusty old shelves, that will themselves one day also dissolve, like me, into dust! Yet, here, in this singular existential conundrum, our finitude and our flight from it, Antonio and I find ourselves together. Here, in the human condition, existential psychotherapy finds its most distinctive focus and conversation thrives.

Existential psychotherapy: a confluence of traditions

Existential psychotherapy owes its existence to two distinguished streams of human endeavour: first, to the scientific and healing tradition of psychoanalysis and, second, to continental philosophical traditions of hermeneutics, phenomenology and existential thought.

Existential psychotherapy is, first of all, a *discipline* practised by professionals who foster human understanding, authentic living, and reasonable well-being. The adjective 'existential' is a qualifier designating a *way* of thinking and practising psychotherapy, a *démarche*.

This chapter is an effort to explicate the nature and relation between *discipline* and *démarche* in existential psychotherapy. The discipline of psychotherapy (Latin *discere*: to learn) refers to the learning of a body of practical knowledge and knowledgeable practice. *Démarche* is a French word designating a manner of walking, the kind of intention and purpose one brings to a particular learning or practice. With respect to existential therapy, its *démarche*, drawn from continental philosophy, profoundly influences how the *discipline*, derived from depth psychotherapies beginning with psychoanalysis[2] is understood. What then, is the existential *démarche* in psychotherapy?

The existential démarche in psychotherapy

The continental philosophies which inform existential psychotherapy emphasize the historical and contextual embeddedness of human experience and dispute the notion that the natural sciences and mathematical logic have the final and most essential word about the question of what it is to be human. They are prime examples of what Dilthey (1989) called the human sciences (*Geisteswissenschaften*).

Existential thought and the human being

Existential thought, usually called *existentialism*,[3] is wholly concerned with the question of human existence. What is it to be human? What is it for human beings, distinctively *as human* beings, to enjoy health and suffer illness, to seek and lose, have and have not, to desire and despair, to think and feel, to understand and wonder, to see and fail to see, to apprehend possibility and fall short of it, to live and to die? What and who is this being, the human being, who is capable of all this, who *is* all this and more?

For existential thinkers and practitioners the only one place to look for the answers to these basic questions is in the everyday vicissitudes of human experience. Of course, you could say that the wonderment about the meaning of being human is not exclusive to existentialists and is the guiding motivation for all of psychoanalytic 'science' and that psychoanalysts, no less than existentialists, rely on the evidence of human experience for the development of its 'science'. Nevertheless, *how* existential thinkers go about discovering the human and *how* they then understand the human does distinguish them from other depth psychotherapists.

Phenomenology and the permission to be

Regarding the first of these hows, when it comes to epistemology and methodology, existential thinkers embrace *phenomenology*, an approach to philosophy and science that strives to avoid unexamined theories, assumptions, and presuppositions in order to allow things to 'speak for themselves'. Edmund Husserl (1859–1938) is generally recognized as the founder of phenomenology with his famous epistemological battle cry, return 'to the things themselves' (*zu den Sachen selbst*, Husserl 1970: 168). For the existential psychotherapist this means allowing the person's own words and experiences to speak for themselves without seeing them through some theoretical lens. To be phenomenological is to be open to the details of thought, feeling, imagination, and behaviour precisely as they occur and to understand them on the grounds of their 'self-showing'. To be phenomenological is to want whatever *is* to be and to be just what it is. Such 'permission to be' does not come easily, but requires significant and disciplined effort. If, for instance, clients describe emerging affectionate feelings toward a therapist, phenomenological therapists do their best to bracket out any theoretical considerations in order to let each person's perceptions and emotions show themselves and be understood in their own terms. In other words, phenomenologically oriented therapists do not assume that affectionate feelings are only, for example, disguised expressions of genital or childhood sexuality. Psychotherapy is understood as a unique here-and-now occurrence and affection can express any number of possibilities from a feeling of warmth, admiration or trust to an intense desire for some kind of sexual intimacy. Phenomenological inquiry in psychotherapy lingers sufficiently long with whatever appears so that its meaning can arise, not from theoretical considerations, but from the matrix of the unfolding dialogue between the two conversational partners.

Mitch, a fiftyish writer and political activist in his fourth marriage had come to psychotherapy in response to his wife's complaints about his 'insensitivity and dark emotions'. Although he acknowledged that his father abandoned him before birth and his mother was mercilessly depressed, he had considerable difficulty identifying with his wife's complaints and with any conception of himself as an unhappy person. A year into therapy he found himself quite unexpectedly talking about his mother, the constant heaviness of her depression, and the pervasive absence of human warmth and care in his childhood. He ended the session, rather typically for him, by claiming 'but that's the past and I've moved on'. However, the following week he reported a puzzling dream: he found himself in a home he shared with a woman who was just leaving as the dream began. As he looked around the house he realized there were places he knew nothing about. Opening one door, he found the furnace room but could not enter it because swirling dust and mist throughout the room made vision and movement impossible. He shut that door and opened another: there, in an attic-like room, he found dozens of tortoises crawling about the floor. Out of the ensuing detailed conversation, a rather plain-spoken account came forward: 'I hadn't realized the degree to which I had shut out the impact of having the mother I did. I could find no warmth in my childhood and lived as if among creatures who could barely move and existed within an impenetrable shell.'

According to the phenomenologically oriented existential analyst, Paul Stern, such a dream can be seen, when read straightforwardly, as in the above instance, as 'an artfully condensed biography' but only if 'we approach the dream gently, respecting its integrity, treating it courteously, as we might an honored visitor from abroad' (1972: 42–44). Such is the essential contribution of phenomenology to the spirit and practice of existential psychotherapy.

Hermeneutics and the circle of understanding

This brief example of a phenomenological dream 'interpretation' brings us to the third stream of continental philosophy that is critical for existential psychotherapists: *hermeneutics*. Generally thought of as the art and science of interpretation or understanding, hermeneutics can trace its heritage all the way back to Aristotle, though its more contemporary history began with the works of Schleiermacher (1768–1834) and Dilthey (1833–1911) and was continued by Heidegger (1889–1976) and Gadamer (1900–2002). Although each of these philosophers was responsible for significant developments in the modern history of hermeneutics, it was Martin Heidegger whose contribution was most radical and of particular concern for the thinking and practice of existential psychotherapy. Indeed, his influence enabled Ludwig Binswanger (1881–1966) and Medard Boss (1903–1990), the first two systematic practitioners of existential psychiatry and existential psychotherapy respectively, to move psychotherapy in a thoroughly human scientific direction (see Boss 1963).

Martin Heidegger made three major systematic contributions to hermeneutics that are particularly relevant for existential psychotherapy. First, following Husserl, he brought a phenomenological discipline and sensibility to the art and science of interpretation. Second, he used this phenomenological hermeneutic to analyze human existence and develop a fundamental, ontological understanding of the human (see below). Third, Heidegger instigated a major turn in the whole history of hermeneutics by showing the nature of human understanding as fundamentally circular. His revolutionary clarification of what Schleiermacher first called the 'hermeneutic circle'[4] disputed the possibility of pure or transcendental human understanding and, with it, the intellectual idealism of John Locke's tabula rasa and René Descartes' rational empiricism. For Heidegger, human beings do not perceive the world primarily through intellectual categories and logical reason but, rather, through being 'thrown' as a whole into an emotionally attuned worldly engagement. Human 'being-in-the-world' is shaped from the beginning both by mood (affect or emotion) and by cultural, historical, and biographical circumstances. This existential circumstantiality unavoidably fore-structures all human understanding. The hermeneutic circle of understanding is thus inescapable and always involves the co-arising of immediately given phenomena with an already existentially predisposed human understanding (Heidegger 1962: 188–195). This basic insight of Heidegger's led to the emergence of all postmodern 'philosophies of uncertainty'. It also established an ontological ground for the relational evocation of meaning within all psychotherapeutic conversation, a ground upon which contemporary intersubjective and relational psychoanalyses explicitly depend.

However crucial Heidegger's grasp of the fore-structure of human understanding, it was his second major contribution, noted above, namely his fundamental ontology of human existence that led Binswanger and Boss to found the first systematic approaches to existential psychiatry and psychotherapy respectively.

The ontological eye

Heidegger's (1962) fundamental or existential ontology was concerned with the being*ness* of human beings, that is, with explicating *those characteristics or conditions of human being that obtain for every moment of every human being's existence.* Thus, for example, he showed that in every moment of their being, human beings exist in time, in space, in a mood, embodied, in relation to others, as thrown into being-in-the-world, and as mortal. Heidegger referred to these and other fundamental or ontological characteristics of human beings as existentials (*Existenzialien*) or *existentialia* (1962: 70; 44). This differs significantly from what Irvin Yalom calls 'ultimate concerns', namely 'certain intrinsic properties that are . . . an inescapable part, of the human being's existence in the world' (1980: 8). For Yalom, these ultimate concerns are death, freedom, isolation, and meaninglessness. Although these are certainly issues with which many, if not all human beings may struggle from time to time, none of them are characteristic of all human beings in every moment of their existence. Death, for example, is a debt we must all pay for the gift of life. However, death is not an ontological or fundamental characteristic of human existence since, if it were, none of us would be here. What is an ontological characteristic is our *Being-towards-death*, always on our way to death, what Heidegger called *Sein-zum-Tode.*

Likewise, isolation is only possible because we are fundamentally social beings (even the hermit is with others in the manner of staying away from them) and meaninglessness only faces us as fundamentally meaning-seeking and -making beings. This does not at all negate the power of Yalom's four givens in our lives. Indeed, the world of existential psychotherapy is tremendously indebted to him for keeping the field alive, and popularizing it so successfully.

You may wonder, if psychotherapy must of necessity be an ontical enterprise – an everyday way of being – why it is at all necessary or useful to be concerned with ontology in the first place. I would reply that a phenomenological, hermeneutic understanding of human existence and how individuals live out their ontological structures can embolden and purify a therapist's understanding of an individual's situation. These ontological concerns, therefore, play a much more explicit role in existential psychotherapy than in other forms of psychotherapy. I shall illustrate the clinical significance of having 'an ontological eye' with respect to two ontological characteristics of human existence: its fundamental openness and unity.

The fundamental openness of human existence

Human beings exist as opening up to and for the world. Heidegger described this openness of human existence as a clearing (*Lichtung*) to highlight human existence as a disclosive realm within which beings and Being can appear and be understood. That we exist, most essentially, as a perceiving, understanding and responding realm of world openness or world disclosure is the ground for the most distinguishing focus of existential psychotherapy or analysis: namely, that *the overriding concern is not with the individual's psyche, soul, self, or personality alone but, rather, with the person's whole human existence, the person's whole being-in-the-world.* Human beings do not exist as epidermally entombed conscious entities but, to the contrary, as an opening up, presencing or clearing for being, a whole worlding. That human beings are ontologically open is what allows the world of beings, including one's own being, to appear and be understood. For existential therapists human beings *are* their openness, *are* their disclosedness, *are* their existence.[5]

This leads to what is a quite controversial subject among existential therapists: what do we make of the circumstance that, in spite of our fundamental openness as human beings, the world and we ourselves remain largely hidden to us? Readers will recognize that I am referring here to the phenomenon of what has been called 'the unconscious',[6] a realm of psychic reality that psychoanalysts generally take for granted but that many existential analysts vigorously criticize, if not outright deny.

Clearly, within the worlding as which we exist, things both show themselves and do not show themselves. The openness of human existence reveals closedness as well. If it were not for the fundamental concealment of being, phenomenology and science itself would be entirely unnecessary. This hiddenness of human existence is due, in part, to the concealment of being as such, the ontological circumstance that, as Heraclitus put it, 'Things keep their secrets' (2001: 9). However, the hiddenness of the world is also due to the circumstance that there are, as Freud once wrote, 'things that one would not care to admit *to oneself*: things that one likes to conceal from oneself' (1926: 188), the circumstance that led to Freud's invention of the concepts of repression and the unconscious. Although Freud's particular metapsychological ideas eventually required an almost ptolemaic system of structural and dynamic explanations, he was only trying to account for the simple fact that, like Mitch and Antonio, we find the painful realities of our lives hard to face and are inclined to close ourselves off from them by any means possible. Both Freud and Heidegger understood that anxiety about being oneself and being human was a central feature of human existence and that, as a matter of self-preservation, the human being is apt, as Heidegger put it, to flee in the face of itself (1962: 228–235). However, existential therapists, including some who appear in this volume, have pointed out that ontological and motivated hiddenness is no reason to presume the existence of any sort of thing as an 'unconscious consciousness' separate from and inaccessible to a conscious one. Even Freud himself, when thinking in descriptive terms, repeatedly rejected any such notion of a second consciousness: 'We have no right to extend the meaning of this word [conscious] so far as to make it include a consciousness of which its owner himself is not aware' (1912: 263).[7]

How can we understand the phenomenon of existential hiddenness phenomenologically and how might this phenomenological understanding inform existential therapeutic practice? Even as ontologically open realms of world disclosure, human beings constantly embody two different modes of relating to this openness: they relate in the manner of being conscious and in the manner of not being conscious. Both being conscious and not being conscious appear manifestly within the realm of world openness as which we exist. Naturally our potential for conscious access to both the world and ourselves is far outstripped by what actually exists. This remainder is silent, secret, concealed, hidden. Such is the human condition.

What might this mean for existential psychotherapy? First, it means the rejection of hubris. To pretend one knows what is hidden, on the grounds of theoretical assumptions and mythologies, is not only disrespectful of the secrecy of Being itself, but also of the integrity and autonomy of those who enter psychotherapy; to reject such hubris is the basis for wonder and awe. Second, it means that existential psychotherapy does not seek to throw theoretical flares into the territory of the *unknown*, but to walk quietly and gently at the very frontiers of *what is known*. Fortunately this uncanny limen between the known and unknown is often boldly illuminated by feelings of uncertainty, anxiety and ambivalence showing precisely where therapists must dare to dwell, forsaking arrogance and ambition, in order for the unseen to show itself in its own time and on its own terms.

With Mitch's dream, for example, I avoided clever symbolic interpretations, proffering, instead, the simplest of invitations: Tell me about a furnace room. And a tortoise? What was this furnace room like? And these tortoises? And can you say more about this woman who left you there alone in the house? Our conversation over his answers to these and other direct questions about the manifest dream just as he recalled it, gradually and gracefully illuminated those areas of existential darkness that had for so long obscured important features of his life as a child, and of his present manner of being in the world as a man. No assumptions or interpretations were made regarding that of which he was not yet conscious; yet, where he was once not conscious, he had begun to become so.

Existential psychotherapy has a great faith in the power of what appears of its own accord, without the 'help' of theoretical speculations, especially where genuine relationship and gentle readiness are found.

The fundamental unity of human existence

The Swiss psychiatrist Ludwig Binswanger called Cartesian dualism 'the fatal defect of all psychology' (1958: 193). For existential therapists the human individual exists as *Being-in-the-world*, as worlded, worlding, and not as a separate, isolated monad of consciousness wandering about in a body that, in turn, wanders about in a world of other entities and beings. The meaning and practice of existential therapy rests on the premise that individuals and their worlds, that self and other, are ontologically indivisible. The world and all the people we encounter there constitute our existence, just as we do theirs. Even as I write and you read, we constitute one another. The individual constitutes world, just as world constitutes self. We are all, in a very real sense, constantly 'one-ing'. Hence existential psychotherapy's focus: not on the personality alone but, rather, on the whole world of relational events and possibilities that constitute each and every human being.

> Whenever I met with Antonio or Mitch, I found my own way of being radically influenced by the very different kind of men each of them were. However, I was no chameleon either. I was entirely myself with each of them, yet my distinctive 'own-most' existence was also existentially constituted by theirs. For me, there was never any loss of 'my-own-most-self', rather only a gain, an existential modification of my very own 'being-a-whole', by 'being-with' this inimitable other. Nor could I ever have related to Antonio the way I did with Mitch and vice versa. Hence, the conversation that opened up between Mitch and me in relation to his dream could never have occurred with anyone else: the dream was not so much interpreted, as relationally understood.

Causal, reductionist, dualistic concepts like transference, countertransference, objectify and reify the existential experience of being-with-one-another. Existentially, we are with-one-another from the beginning, not just interactionally or intersubjectively, but ontologically. Although the terms transference and countertransference refer to our existential historicality – namely the phenomenon that we 'carry across' time certain historical ways of relating that were first developed in earlier contexts – they do so in a manner that is disruptive and disrespectful of our lived experience of temporal continuity. The challenge for existential therapists is to remain faithful to the unitary phenomenon of historically informed human relatedness as it occurs in each living moment of being-with-one-another.

The discipline of psychotherapy: a deep, long listening

I would like to think that history will say that the turn of the nineteenth and twentieth centuries marked the appearance of a new kind of human activity: a deep, long, wholesome listening to human unhappiness. This unique kind of disciplined listening was actually instigated by a few intelligent but troubled women who told their doctors to be quiet and listen, as the famous Anna O put it, to their 'talking cure'. In addition to developing the parameters of the therapeutic situation based on these early therapeutic encounters (Freud 1911–1915), the work of Sigmund Freud and his followers raised profound questions regarding human nature, relatedness, and suffering that lie at the heart of the discipline of psychotherapy. The fundamental hiddenness of human existence (found in what Freud called the unconscious and repression), the fundamental meaningfulness of human existence and human suffering (e.g. found in the meaning of dreams, parapraxes, symptoms, and human behaviour in general), the fundamental historicality of human existence (e.g. found in transference, countertransference, and the aetiology of neurosis) are all phenomenologically given realities with which existential therapists must contend, each in their own way, whether or not they agree with psychoanalytic interpretations of these ontological characteristics.

Since early in the last century, the discipline of psychoanalysis and depth psychotherapy has, in general, moved in an increasingly humanistic direction, challenging old deterministic and reductionist assumptions to embrace more adaptive, cultural, interpersonal, conative, experiential, and, especially, relational perspectives for understanding human beings, human suffering and the therapeutic alliance. Old stereotypes of silent, uninvolved, medically minded analysts have long since disappeared, so that Roger Frie (this volume, p. 21) can claim quite correctly that a century's worth of developments in psychoanalysis has yielded 'ways of thinking and practising analytically that have much in common with existential therapy today'. Today, empowered by its own phenomenological hermeneutic understanding of human and clinical phenomena, existential psychotherapists no longer need to reject what their depth psychological colleagues bring to the discipline of psychotherapy. Indeed, our analytical forebears were serious and devoted servants of the human, however they defined it, and we existentialists too follow in this great tradition of human service. We are both indebted to and belong among these depth psychological others, can call them colleagues, comrades, friends, and be proud to do so. As testimony to the importance to humanity of the discipline of psychotherapy, I offer no compendium of fashionable evidence-based studies, but rather this: even today, in London, one can see strewn about the floor beneath the Grecian urn containing Sigmund Freud's ashes, flowers and notes of gratitude from those who have found liberty from their suffering as a consequence of the simple conviction that one who is broken can be made whole again through the patient presence of a single attentive listener, a listener who practises the discipline of psychotherapy.

The distinctive démarche of existential psychotherapy

I shall close with five fundamental ways in which existential psychotherapy differs from other psychotherapeutic approaches. First, existential psychotherapy has sought to ground its thinking about human nature and human suffering in an understanding of the human *qua* human, rather than man as an object like all other natural objects, fit for calculative, natural scientific investigation. Second, this philosophically grounded understanding of the human led directly to the recognition that human beings do not exist apart from their world, but as fundamentally being-in-the-world, as worlded and worlding. This radical eschewal of Cartesian dualism means that existential psychotherapy focuses not on understanding an isolated human personality but, rather, on *the whole human existence*. Third, whereas, psychoanalysis is particularly impressed by the power and impact of what is unconscious, existential psychotherapists are impressed by the potency of *being conscious*. The existential psychotherapist realizes that beyond any so-called abnormal condition, we suffer from our very awareness of our all too contingent human existence. Fourth, the capacity to perceive, understand and reply to one's world, including oneself as the orienting feature of that world, allows for a critical margin of reflexivity, choice, and action that fundamentally alters old deterministic, cause and effect models of human behaviour. The reality and ambiguity of our *situated freedom* is something with which we are both faced and blessed in every moment of our lives. Finally, all forms of psychotherapy understand that human beings are historical beings, that they are *always on their way*, in every moment of their lives carrying forth both their whence and their whither. However, for existential psychotherapy it is *the future* and human possibility that opens the way for destiny: though our past is certainly given, it is primarily our future possibility that shapes our present purpose and direction.

I realize that others would characterize the discipline, the démarche, and distinctiveness of existential psychotherapy in quite different terms and in a different light than I have attempted above. Clearly I have been influenced by my own life history, my existential teachers, supervisors and friends, and especially my own experience with those whom I have been fortunate to have served as therapist. I hope where there is disagreement it will be seen as grounds for deeper thought and, hopefully, dialogue.

Notes

1 Ontology refers to the study of being and is concerned not just with *particular beings*, like the particular book you are holding or you yourself the particular (human) being you are, as you sit there reading – but with their *beingness*, the *form or function* of any being that makes it the *kind* of being it is, for example, your book's book*ness*, or your own human*ness*. Of course the kind of beingness that concerns existential psychotherapists most of all is humanness.

2 By depth psychology (Bleuler 1910) I mean simply all those therapies, originating with Freud but including Rogers and the existentialists that eschewed a strictly rational natural scientific approach to psychotherapy and embrace a respect for the mysteriousness of human existence.

3 I have tended, throughout this chapter, to avoid the term existentialism as the ism implies a relatively unified school, if not, dogma. No such 'school' exists and, indeed, the very concept is contrary to the whole intent of existential thinking.

4 Friedrich Schleiermacher (1998), a crucial figure in history of hermeneutics, was not only the first to define it as a science independent of any distinct regional discipline (e.g. law, theology, philosophy, etc.) but also the first to suggest that adequate understanding must incorporate the author's psychology. In coining the term 'the hermeneutic circle' Schleiermacher pointed to the circumstance that understanding involves a dialectic between the part and the whole: i.e. one needs to grasp the sentence to grasp the paragraph, the paragraph to grasp the sentence.

5 It is important to clarify that the ontological distinction applies here as well: whereas ontically speaking, in this everyday moment, you may be open or not open to what you are reading, ontologically speaking you can in no way escape *being* open, by virtue of your very existence as human. Such ontological openness may manifest itself ontically by interest or disinterest, agreement or disagreement. To clarify further, the ontic or ontical refers to our everyday world of particular being. The ontologic or ontological refers to being*ness*, the universal characteristics of a class of particular beings that make each member of that 'class' the very *kind* of being it is, e.g. the *catness* of all particular cats, the *humanness* of all particular human beings.

6 In seeking to approach 'the unconscious' phenomenologically, I have emphasized as Freud did when thinking descriptively, the adjective 'unconscious' to mean simply what is hidden, that is, invisible, secret, unthought, etc. (Craig 2007, 2008). Nevertheless, one should be clear that there is no standard existential position regarding the problem of 'the unconscious'. Thus, whereas Rollo May (1967) was manifestly comfortable with a psychoanalytic view, Medard Boss (1963) rejected it entirely. There are countless variations between.

7 Ironically, existential criticisms of Freud's view of the unconscious are often grounded in unexamined assumptions about Freud rather than Freud's own understanding, especially his descriptive understanding of being conscious or not – terms that he understood primarily as adjectives describing the quality of experience. Although Freud posited a dynamic unconscious, an organized structure of mental activities unavailable to consciousness, he also recognized this was a hypothetical construct, one that lay outside the realm of verification and falsification.

References

Binswanger, L. (1958) 'The existential analysis school of thought', trans. E. Angel, in R. May, E. Angel, and H. F. Ellenberger (eds) *Existence: A New Dimension in Psychiatry and Psychology*, New York: Basic Books.

Bleuler, E. (1910) 'Die Psychanalyse Freud's: Verteidigung und kritische Bemerkungen', *Jahrbuch fur Psychoanalytische und Psychopathologische Forschungen, II Band* (II Hälfte): 623–730.

Boss, M. (1963) *Psychoanalysis and Daseinsanalysis*, trans. L. B. Lefebre, New York: Basic Books.

Craig, E. (2007) 'Hermeneutic inquiry in depth psychology: a practical and philosophical reflection', *The Humanistic Psychologist*, 35 (4): 307–320.

Craig, E. (2008) 'The human and the hidden: existential wonderings about depth, soul, and the unconscious', *The Humanistic Psychologist*, 36 (3–4): 227–282.

Dilthey, W. (1989) *Introduction to the Human Sciences*, R. A. Makkreel and F. Rodi (eds), Princeton, NJ: Princeton University Press.

Freud, S. (1911–1915) 'Papers on technique', *Standard Edition*, 12: 83–173, London: Hogarth Press.

Freud, S. (1912) 'A note on the unconscious in psychoanalysis', *Standard Edition*, 12: 255–266, London: Hogarth Press.

Freud, S. (1926) 'The question of lay analysis', *Standard Edition*, 12: 177–258, London: Hogarth Press.

Heidegger, M. (1962 [1927]) *Being and Time*, trans. J. R. Macquarrie and E. Robinson, Oxford: Blackwell.

Heraclitus (2001) *Fragments*, trans. B. Haxton, New York: Viking.

Husserl, E. (1970) *Logical Investigations: Volume 1*, trans. J. N. Findlay, New York: Harper and Row.

May, R. (1967) *Psychology and the Human Dilemma*, Princeton, NJ: Van Nostrand.

Schleiermacher, F. (1998) *Hermeneutics and Criticism*, trans. A. Bowie (ed.), Cambridge: Cambridge University Press.

Stern, P. (1972) *In Praise of Madness*, New York: Norton.

Yalom, I. (1980) *Existential Psychotherapy*, New York: Basic Books.

Chapter 2

Existential psychotherapy and post-Cartesian psychoanalysis

Historical perspectives and confluence

Roger Frie

The relationship between existential therapy and psychoanalysis is often characterized by outmoded stereotypes. As a result, existential therapy and psychoanalysis tend to be seen as separate and opposed. When discussing psychoanalysis, contemporary existential therapists usually refer to the classical model developed by Freud and his followers. Most psychoanalysts, at the same time, know little about the work carried out by existential therapists. To be sure, existential therapy and psychoanalysis developed out of different intellectual contexts. Whereas existential therapy is grounded in the precepts of existential–phenomenological philosophy, classical psychoanalysis traces its roots to late nineteenth century scientific determinism. Yet much psychoanalysis today bears little resemblance to its historical roots: contemporary psychoanalysis, particularly the post-Cartesian interpersonal and intersubjective perspectives, has more in common with existential therapy than with Freud. In contrast to classical psychoanalysis, these schools have intellectual roots and therapeutic objectives that are surprisingly similar to existential therapy. Indeed, observers often overlook the degree to which existential therapy and post-Cartesian psychoanalysis are inherently intertwined.

Using a historical perspective, this chapter seeks to show how existential therapy evolved out of the early critique of Freud by pioneering existential psychoanalysts. Whereas some of these pioneering existential thinkers and clinicians left psychoanalysis altogether, others remained within the psychoanalytic tradition and helped develop new, often radical ways of thinking and practising analytically that have much in common with existential therapy today. In so doing, this chapter aims to challenge the stereotypes that continue to characterize the relationship between existential therapy and psychoanalysis, and to examine the confluence of contemporary post-Cartesian psychoanalysis and existential therapy. This chapter is also a call for therapists of these respective modalities, who wish to further their understanding of theory and practice within their own discipline, to each develop a greater awareness of what has been happening in the other modality since those pioneering days. It is as a result of these shared heritage and objectives that existential therapists and contemporary post-Cartesian psychoanalysts are in a privileged position to mutually enrich one another. Indeed, by engaging in dialogue, it may become possible to recognize the similarities that exist between their respective philosophies and therapeutic outlooks. In a book that celebrates existential therapy, its legacy, vibrancy and dialogue, this chapter highlights the legacy that existential therapy has drawn upon, as well as the importance of opening itself up further to dialogue with closely related disciplines.

The existential–phenomenological critique of Freud

The proximity of existential therapy and contemporary psychoanalysis has its basis in the rejection of the dualism of mind and body, and self and other, which pervades Cartesian philosophy and classical psychoanalysis alike. Within the clinical setting, Cartesian dualism is perhaps most evident in the artificial separation of human affect from the embodied and social contexts in which it emerges. Human affect and action always unfold within a lifeworld that defies simple or straightforward reduction to its constituent parts.

The move beyond reductionism and dualism is central to the existential–phenomenological and hermeneutic traditions of philosophy. The philosophers associated with these traditions, from Dilthey through Heidegger and Gadamer, seek to account for human experience not from the 'inside-out', but from the perspective of the lived world. While a discussion of their individual differences is beyond the scope of this chapter (see Burston and Frie 2006), they formulated a post-Cartesian philosophy, paying particular attention to prereflective, somatic and relational experience and the ways in which we are always and already embedded in social and linguistic contexts.

As the direct result of work undertaken by a group of early psychoanalysts who identified with the existential–phenomenological tradition, this post-Cartesian philosophical perspective was introduced to the clinical setting. Like such existential–phenomenological philosophers as Heidegger, Buber, Sartre, or Merleau-Ponty, these clinicians were not wholly united in background or outlook.[1] They tended to be European psychiatrists, trained in psychoanalysis, who turned to existential–phenomenological philosophy in an attempt to overcome the reductionism and dualism inherent in Freudian theory and practice.

Early psychoanalysts such as Binswanger, Boss, Fromm, Fromm-Reichmann, Laing, and May fundamentally challenged and revised traditional Freudian psychoanalytic theory and technique. They did so, not as naïve outsiders, but rather as trained psychoanalysts who founded revisionist institutes and schools of thought. The extent to which these clinicians were indebted to and allied with Freud and psychoanalysis is frequently overlooked, if not altogether forgotten. Indeed, the close relationship of these pioneering existential–phenomenological clinicians to psychoanalysis is crucial to the theoretical and clinical efficacy of the existential tradition today. Binswanger was the earliest and in some ways, the most important of these pioneers and I will pay particular attention to the development of his ideas vis-à-vis Freud and psychoanalysis.

As an early supporter and long-term colleague and critic of Freud, Ludwig Binswanger (1881–1966) holds a unique place in the history of existential therapy and psychoanalysis. Binswanger's relationship with Freud began in 1907 and lasted until Freud's death in 1939. While Binswanger published some early psychoanalytic case studies, he opposed the determinism of the psychoanalytic theory of mind and all but rejected the causality of drive theory and the concept of the unconscious. Yet Binswanger was one of the very few serious critics of psychoanalysis with whom Freud remained on friendly terms (Fichtner 1992). Following Dilthey, Binswanger believed that the natural science approach was, on its own, unable to account for the nature of lived experience. As Binswanger put it:

> In every psychology that makes the person, as such, into an object – particularly those psychologies founded by natural scientists such as Freud . . . – we find a rift, a gap through which it is clear that what is being scientifically studied is not the whole person, not human-being as a whole. Everywhere we find something that overflows and bursts the bounds of such a psychology.
>
> (Binswanger, in Needleman 1963: 169)

Binswanger's critique of Freud's naturalism also extended to psycho-analytic technique. In contrast to Freud, who argued that psychoanalysis was appropriate only for neurotic patients, Binswanger worked extensively with patients in the psychotic, schizophrenic, and manic-depressive spec-trums and revised the methods of classical psychoanalytic technique accordingly. Binswanger developed an interpersonal style of interaction, more appropriate to the needs of his patients, and more akin to his own growing philosophical interests, which would later draw heavily from the work of Buber and the philosophy of dialogue. In describing Freud's clinical approach, which emphasized the anonymity and authority of the analyst, and was characterized by the analyst's interpretation of the patient's unconscious behaviour, Binswanger remarks: 'In place of a reciprocal, "personal" communication within a we-relationship, we find a one-sided, i.e. irreversible, relationship between doctor and patient, and an even more impersonal relationship between researcher and the object of research' (Binswanger 1942: 62). For Binswanger, the impersonal nature of the classical psychoanalytic relationship could have disastrous results. When the person 'is objectified, isolated and theorized into an ego, or into an Id, Ego and Superego, [he or she] is thereby driven out of [his or her] authentic sphere of being, namely existence, and ontologically and anthropologically suffocated' (Binswanger, in Needleman 1963: 170–171). Indeed, it was precisely Binswanger's interest in the broader contexts of human existence that led him to search for new ways of conceptualizing human development and experience.

Binswanger sought above all to develop an account of human experience that was not reductionist. This approach culminated in his first book, *Introduction to the Problems of General Psychology*, published in 1922. Although the book was dedicated to his teachers, 'Bleuler and Freud', it marked Binswanger's turn toward phenomenology. Drawing on Husserl, Binswanger argued that the object of investigation must always be seen in its full phenomenal reality. Binswanger's purpose was to understand and explain human beings in the totality of their existence, not simply as natural objects constructed from various parts. Binswanger developed his phenomenological perspective in an attempt to describe how the person is concretely experienced, an approach he would later refer to as 'phenomenological anthropology'.

While Husserl's project of phenomenology provided Binswanger with a method to account for the lived experience of the person, it was Heidegger's fundamental ontology (1962), particularly the notion of being-in-the-world, that enabled him to develop a philosophically oriented approach to understanding human experience which sought to account for the human being's 'total existence'. Binswanger asserted that the analyst must seek to understand the lived world of the patient as it is experienced by the patient. In contrast to the past-focused approach of psychoanalysis, Binswanger sought to understand experience as it is lived in the present and thus to uncover the structures of phenomena interpreted by a patient's context of meaning.

Binswanger's reception of Heidegger was not uncritical, however. Just as Binswanger was unable to accept Freud's account of interpersonal interaction, in his chief and still untranslated work, *Basic Forms and Knowledge of Human Existence* (1942), Binswanger argues that Heidegger's treatment of the social dimension is unsatisfactory.[2] Binswanger turns instead to the philosophy of dialogue, from Feuerbach through Buber, to develop a theory of intersubjectivity, aspects of which are later reiterated in the works of Theunissen (1977) and Habermas (1985). Binswanger was especially interested in a phenomenology of interpersonal love that emphasizes the role of the other person in the creation of self-understanding. As a clinician, Binswanger believed that psychoanalysis was dependent upon the emergence of a type of loving I–Thou relationship between therapist and patient. As such, Binswanger's view of clinical work, like his account of human experience in general, is thoroughly relational in nature.

By drawing variously on the ideas of Husserl, Heidegger and Buber, Binswanger developed a new therapeutic perspective known as 'Daseinsanalysis'. Today, however, this term is associated with Binswanger's younger Swiss colleague, Medard Boss (1903–1990). Like Binswanger, Boss worked as an assistant to Eugen Bleuler at the Burghoelzli Hospital. Boss began his career as a classical psychoanalyst. In fact, Boss had 26 analytic sessions with Freud in Vienna in 1925, before completing his analytic training with Karen Horney and Kurt Goldstein in Berlin, where he graduated from the Berlin Institute. Beginning in 1938, he became associated with Carl Jung, who revealed to Boss the possibility of a psychoanalysis not bound up in Freudian interpretations. Over time, Boss read the works of Ludwig Binswanger and Martin Heidegger. But it was his first personal meeting in 1947 with Heidegger that led to a lifelong friendship with the philosopher and had a decisive impact on his philosophical thinking and therapeutic practice.

Heidegger (1987) and Boss together developed the Daseinsanalytic approach to therapy. At Boss's behest, Heidegger visited Zollikon over a series of many years to discuss his philosophy with a group of psychiatrists and thus laid the groundwork for Daseinsanalysis. From the very start, Boss sought to create a radical post-Cartesian approach to medicine and psychology, grounded in Heidegger's philosophy. Whereas Binswanger was interested chiefly in creating a philosophical approach to understanding human experience and considering its relevance for therapeutic practice, Boss developed a specific approach to working therapeutically. Together with his colleague, Gion Condrau, he founded a teaching institute in Zurich in 1971, known as the Daseinsanalytic Institute of Psychotherapy and Psychosomatics. It is interesting to note, however, that despite the radicality of Boss's Daseinsanalytic approach, in his private practice he worked in the tradition of the classical analyst, maintaining an analytic distance and anonymity within the therapeutic setting (private communications, Gerald Izenberg and William J. Richardson).

By contrast Erich Fromm (1900–1980), like Binswanger, developed a more interpersonal approach to therapeutic practice, which was mirrored in his emphasis on the social nature of human experience. Erich Fromm's academic background was in sociology and he trained as a psychoanalyst under Hans Sachs and Theodor Reik in Berlin. He was introduced to psychoanalysis by Frieda Fromm-Reichmann (1889–1957), a psychiatrist who also completed her training with Sachs in Berlin. Although Fromm and Fromm-Reichmann are not always linked with existential phenomenology, they were instrumental in communicating and translating the ideas of this tradition, which is why I include them with this group. Both bridged the disciplines of continental philosophy and psychoanalytic practice and emphasized the impact of politics and economics on the development of human psychology.

In 1927 Fromm became a founding analyst of the Frankfurt Psychoanalytic Institute. Later that year, at Max Horkheimer's invitation, Fromm joined the Frankfurt Institute for Social Research, becoming its director for Social Psychology. During this time, Fromm and Fromm-Reichmann established a relationship with Martin Buber, a connection they maintained throughout their careers. When the National Socialists came to power in 1933, they immigrated to the United States.

While Fromm trained as a classical psychoanalyst, his studies in sociology and psychology led him to take issue with Freud's emphasis on the individual nature of the psyche. Fromm powerfully states his opposition to Freud and classical psychoanalysis:

> The fundamental approach to human personality is the understanding of man's relation to the world, to others, to nature, and to himself. We believe that man is primarily a social being, and not, as Freud assumes, primarily self-sufficient and only secondarily in need of others in order to satisfy his instinctual needs. In this sense we believe that individual psychology is fundamentally social psychology, or in Sullivan's terms, the psychology of interpersonal relationships.
>
> (Fromm 1941: 247)

By emphasizing the inherently relational nature of human experience, Fromm essentially rejects the basis of psychoanalytic drive theory. The end of his association with Freudian psychoanalysis also marked the end of his tenure with the Frankfurt School and his colleagues, Adorno and Horkheimer. This led first to a professional association with Karen Horney and then with the interpersonal analysts, Harry Stack Sullivan and Clara Thompson.

In 1946, Fromm, Fromm-Reichmann, Sullivan and Thompson founded the William Alanson White Institute of Psychiatry, Psychoanalysis and Psychology. With its focus on understanding the social and cultural contexts of human experience, the White Institute became the home of interpersonal theory and practice. The White Institute, and its sister organization, the Washington School of Psychiatry in Washington DC (also founded by Sullivan and Fromm-Reichmann) fostered the emergence of existential therapy in North America. Indeed, over the years, such key existential–phenomenological thinkers and clinicians as Martin Buber, R. D. Laing and Maurice Friedman, taught at these institutes.

Perhaps most importantly, one of the leading early psychoanalysts at the White Institute and a founder of existential therapy was Rollo May (1909–1994). May underwent his training analysis at the White Institute with Erich Fromm and became training and supervising analyst, as well as a leading author. Together with Ernst Angel and Henri Ellenberger, May published the path-breaking book *Existence: A New Dimension in Psychiatry and Psychology* in 1958. This book introduced the existential–phenomenological tradition to a professional and public audience and demonstrated a new, non-reductionist therapeutic understanding. It also introduced Binswanger to an English-speaking audience for the first time. May eventually left New York and the White Institute for San Francisco, a burgeoning centre for existential–humanistic psychology, where he helped to establish the Saybrook Institute. While May would become better known as a leader of humanistic psychology, his thinking and practice were inalterably grounded in the interpersonal psychoanalytic tradition.

Although R. D. Laing's name is not often identified with mainstream psychoanalysis, he completed his psychoanalytic candidacy at the British Institute of Psychoanalysis during the 1950s. A psychiatrist by training, Laing (1927–1989) began to develop his individual perspective early on and was aligned with the so-called Middle Group, between Anna Freud on the one side and Melanie Klein on the other. He was analyzed by Charles Rycroft and supervised by D. W. Winnicott, among others. As his thinking grew more independent, he moved away from the psychoanalytic establishment and in 1965 became a founder of the Philadelphia Association in London, where he taught and began to develop his radical theories and techniques. In elaborating his early approach to the self and other, Laing drew on the ideas of Husserl, Heidegger, Sartre and Merleau-Ponty, and identified his work as phenomenological. The connection to Sartre was particularly important and Laing remains one of the few psychoanalysts to acknowledge a significant debt to the French philosopher.

In discussing the impact of existential–phenomenological thought on psychoanalytic revisionism, it would be remiss not to include the work of Jacques Lacan (1900–1981). Because Lacan is generally seen as a representative of the philosophical transition from French structuralism to post-structuralism, he is not commonly grouped with such clinicians as Binswanger, Fromm, or Laing. While there are many obvious and important differences, there are also noteworthy parallels. Lacan allied himself early on with Binswanger's phenomenological approach (Frie 1997) and was similarly critical of Freud's protobiological theory of mind. He turned first to the writings of Hegel, Heidegger, and Sartre, and eventually to structural linguistics in order to rewrite Freud's project from the perspective of language. With time, Lacan made fewer and fewer outright references to existential–phenomenological thought, though the imprint of the early Heidegger and Sartre continues to be evident in his writings.

The proximity of the early Lacan (1977) to the existential–phenomenological tradition is nowhere more apparent than in his trenchant critique of American mainstream psychoanalysis of the mid-twentieth century, known as 'ego psychology'. Lacan believed that the central focus on the ego and its defences was a return to the very Cartesian thinking that Freud had sought to overcome. Lacan questioned the notion of the ego's autonomy because he conceptualized the human subject as embedded in the symbolic realm of language and tradition. The existential–phenomenological tradition similarly rejects the reification of the mind and the Cartesian distinction between internal and external realms of experience that is carried over into classical psychoanalysis because it views the person as inherently embedded in interpersonal contexts.

All these early existential–phenomenological critics of psychoanalysis used their psychoanalytic training to develop post-Cartesian ways of thinking about and engaging with the Other. Together, they helped set the groundwork for the introduction of a two-person, context-sensitive psychology. They abandoned Freud's exclusive emphasis on the intrapsychic model of the mind and revised or rejected his theory of drives to include the role of social factors on human development and experience. They challenged the notion of analytic neutrality in order to demonstrate the importance of reciprocal interaction between therapist and patient, based on the notions of mutuality and equality. They emphasized the relevance of the here and now over past experience and rejected the determinism implicit in the psychoanalytic view of symptom formation and human development.

Post-Cartesian psychoanalysis

Many contemporary post-Cartesian psychoanalysts embrace the same perspectives. Where once there was a focus only on internalized objects and object choices, these psychoanalysts conceptualize human development and experience in terms of interactions between embodied, contextualized persons, not isolated minds. The role of bodily or somatic experience has become central to the study of dyadic interaction, and has particularly influenced investigations of gender. In contrast to the Cartesian split between internal and external experience that underlies the traditional Freudian theory of the unconscious, current interest in implicit or unformulated experience sheds new light on dissociative states of mind – for example, somatic experiences that may not be open to reflective awareness. Most importantly, perhaps, the emphasis on social contexts of experience has provided the means to address therapeutic issues within wider social and political spheres. Of the many and varied approaches in psychoanalysis today, there are two which I identify as being particularly relevant in their proximity to existential therapy, both historically and in the novel ways they have built on their intellectual roots: interpersonal psychoanalysis and intersubjective systems theory. I will outline the salient aspects of each briefly here.

The interpersonal tradition was founded by Erich Fromm and Harry Stack Sullivan. In addition to its early association with existential–phenomenological thinkers and clinicians, interpersonal psychoanalysis is indebted to the philosophy of American Pragmatism, particularly the work of George Herbert Mead. Drawing on Mead (1934), Sullivan presents human experience as an unfolding interaction between interpersonal, environmental influences and a personal meaning system that shapes our perception and responses. Thus, in addition to being interested in a patient's history and pattern of interpersonal experiences, Sullivan wanted to know what a particular experience meant to a person. He believed that the way in which a person experienced an event was influenced by the ways the person comes to know the world, through the formulation of a set of personal ideas, assumptions, and imaginations, based on developmental experience, which he called 'personifications'. In other words, Sullivan argued that therapists must be attentive to the particular way in which the person experiences his or her world and the way in which this world-view develops. Though Sullivan used a different set of terms from Binswanger's, he was in fact making a very similar point. In contrast to Freud, Sullivan, like Fromm, radically delimits biological drives or instincts, and emphasizes instead the importance of interpersonal relations. This is 'the antithesis of any document of human instincts' (Sullivan 1950: 302). Thus, for Sullivan as for Fromm, the aim of psychoanalysis is not to make the unconscious conscious in the traditional Freudian sense, but to help patients develop new ways of relating to others and the world around them.

In contrast to the classical psychoanalytic emphasis on neutrality and objectivity, interpersonal psychoanalysis sees mutuality as crucial to the therapeutic process. Psychotherapy, on this view, can only be undertaken by persons who are prepared to be exposed to the myriad, subtle and overt reactions that occur between two human beings in dialogue with one another. What is therapeutic, as Harry Guntrip suggests, is '"the moment of real meeting" of two persons as a new transforming experience' (1969: 353). The contemporary interpersonal psychoanalyst, Darlene Ehrenberg, refers to such moments as 'the intimate edge' of therapy. She says that psychoanalytic

> work does not stop . . . when each is truly touched in some profound way by the other and by their interaction; rather, it takes on new dimensions as the affective complexity of what gets activated in the moments of meeting can be clarified and explored in an endless progression.
>
> (Ehrenberg 1992: 40)

These moments of face-to-face meeting require the active involvement of both participants. By allowing for an ongoing interaction between the analyst and patient, the interpersonal approach allows for the generation and understanding of new experiences of mutuality and self-awareness.

From a post-Cartesian perspective, clinical phenomena, like human experience generally, can only be understood within their contexts. The analyst and patient form an indissoluble dyad, and it is the unfolding, context-bound nature of this relationship that becomes the focus of therapeutic inquiry. Human experience is not the product of an isolated, intrapsychic mind but is seen as evolving within interpersonal, embodied contexts of existence. This approach is akin to Heidegger's notion of being-in-the-world, according to which the person is inseparable from his or her world. The role of psychotherapy, on this view, is to reach an understanding and appreciation of human experience as it emerges in interaction between the analyst and patient, and in social contexts more generally. In this way of practising, there is no talk of a patient's intrapsychic world, of internalization, projections, or even of projective identification.

It is precisely the focus on unfolding contexts of experience that most connects interpersonal psychoanalysis with intersubjective systems theory, developed in the work of Robert Stolorow, George Atwood, and Donna Orange. Their appreciation of the importance of continental philosophy, especially the works of Heidegger and Gadamer, has provided the basis for a post-Cartesian perspective that combines contextualism with a hermeneutic sensibility to therapeutic dialogue. Given the turn to contextualism, the continued use of the term 'intersubjectivity', (which was first applied to psychoanalysis by Binswanger and Lacan), is somewhat unfortunate. Despite the recognized Cartesian trappings of this term, however, intersubjectivity continues to be used because it has become so widely equated with the post-Cartesian 'intersubjective' orientation in psychoanalysis.

In the main, intersubjectivity theory seeks to comprehend psychological phenomena as forming at the interface of reciprocally interacting persons and worlds, not as products of isolated intrapsychic mechanisms or interpsychic processes. Intersubjectivity theory rejects the notion of the isolated mind and asserts that all selfhood develops and is maintained within the interplay between worlds (Orange et al. 1997). The therapist, or analyst, on this view, is not simply treating 'the patient', or imposing structure and theory on to human experience, but sharing in the unfolding existence of another person, thus expanding the scope and possibility of being, while 'holding one's theories lightly'. It follows that the therapist does not proffer interpretations from an 'expert' or power-imbued position, but is engaged in an unfolding hermeneutic dialogue with the other. Indeed, intersubjectivity theory, like interpersonal psychoanalysis, denies the validity of analytic neutrality and suggests an 'empathic–introspective' approach to analytic work, while emphasizing the importance of mutually interacting worlds of experience within the clinical setting (Orange, 2009). Therapeutic change and personal growth consist of the achievement of increased intimacy and relatedness to oneself and others, and consequent recognition of new ways of being in the world. As Stolorow suggests:

> Forming and evolving within a nexus of living systems, horizons of experiencing are grasped as fluid and ever-shifting, products of both the person's unique intersubjective history and of what is or is not

allowed to be felt within the intersubjective fields that constitute his or her current living.

(Stolorow 2002: 683)

The rejection of the objectivist epistemology of classical psychoanalysis thus renders a 'one person psychology' obsolete. But post-Cartesian psychoanalysts go further, rejecting the so-called 'two person psychology', which they see as perpetuating the notion of isolated and separate minds. Instead, many post-Cartesian psychoanalysts (Frie and Coburn 2010) seek to develop a 'contextual psychology', which can account for the constitutive role of relatedness and contexts in the making of all experience. In their turn to a thoroughgoing contextualism, post-Cartesian psychoanalysts suggest that the historical and social matrix in which persons are embedded provides the ground for all understanding (Frie and Orange 2009), thus evoking Charles Taylor's (1989) notion of 'self-interpreting beings'.

On this view, the therapeutic dialogue can increase understanding and unsettle previously held convictions or beliefs. When Gadamer speaks of 'horizons of understanding' he is concerned with the way in which understanding is emergent in ongoing dialogue, thus leading to the possibility for expanding horizons and even a fusion of horizons that can serve as the basis for further dialogue. The hermeneutic stance of the post-Cartesian analyst, and the attempt to hold one's theories lightly, helps to create a willingness to listen, to be responsive to the face of the Other, and to be open to new affective experiences.

What distinguishes our humanity is not any rational capacity that would catapult us into a divine world of pure ideas, but rather only the ability to go beyond our particularity to take into account the heritage that can help us grow above our limited selves.

(Gadamer and Hahn 1997: 164)

Conclusion

Just as there is no single definition of existential therapy, there are myriad ways of thinking and practising psychoanalytically today. My objective has been to deconstruct the traditional oppositional relationship by demonstrating the extensive historical and contemporary links between existential therapy and post-Cartesian psychoanalysis. Given my own background in both existential and post-Cartesian psychoanalytic perspectives, I have been struck by the parallels, but also saddened by the astounding lack of constructive dialogue between them: to my mind, they are mutually supportive endeavours.

Notes

1 Much scholarship, beginning with Rollo May *et al.* (1958), presents existential psychiatry and psychoanalysis as a chiefly Heideggerian enterprise. This overlooks the work of other, equally important philosophers and influences, particularly the dialogical tradition and the work of Buber (Frie 1997; Burston and Frie 2006). The original focus on Heidegger also conflated very different social and political perspectives. Whereas Sartre was engaged in many left-wing causes throughout his life, and Buber's work had a lasting impact on education and theology, Heidegger's reputation was inalterably tarnished by his personal and political involvement with National Socialism in Germany. Indeed, no discussion that examines the clinical application of Heidegger's ideas is complete without also addressing his political past (a problem that is particularly challenging for the Daseinsanalytic school of Medard Boss). The facts speak for themselves: Heidegger was a vocal member of the Nazi Party and never publically repudiated anything he said or did at that time. His politics or his actions cannot be ignored, yet his thinking remains profound and has direct bearing for psychotherapy and psychoanalysis (see Frie and Hoffmann 2002).
2 For a full discussion of the Binswanger–Heidegger relationship and its ramifications for the development of Daseinsanalysis, see Frie 1999.

References

Binswanger, L. (1922) *Einfuhrung in die Probleme der Allgemeinen Psychologie* [*Introduction to the Problems of General Psychology*], Basel: Franke.

Binswanger, L. (1993 [1942]) *Ausgewählte Werke Band 2: Grundformen und Erkenntnis menschlichen Daseins*, M. Herzog and H. J. Braun (eds), Heidelberg: Asanger.

Burston, D. and Frie, R. (2006) *Psychotherapy as a Human Science*, Pittsburgh: Duquesne University Press.

Ehrenberg, D. (1992) *The Intimate Edge*, New York: Norton.

Fichtner, G. (ed.) (1992) *Sigmund Freud—Ludwig Binswanger. Briefwechsel, 1908–1938*, Frankfurt: Fischer.

Frie, R. (1997) *Subjectivity and Intersubjectivity in Philosophy and Psychoanalysis*, Lanham, MD: Rowman and Littlefield.

Frie, R. (1999) 'Interpreting a misinterpretation: Ludwig Binswanger and Martin Heidegger', *Journal of the British Society for Phenomenology*, 29: 244–258.

Frie, R. and Coburn, W. (eds) (2010) *Persons in Context: The Challenge of Individuality in Theory and Practice*, New York: Routledge.

Frie, R. and Hoffmann, K. (2002) 'Bridging psychiatry, philosophy and politics: Binswanger, Heidegger, and antisemitism', *Journal of the British Society for Phenomenology*, 32: 231–240.

Frie, R. and Orange, D. (eds) (2009) *Beyond Postmodernism: New Dimensions in Clinical Theory and Practice*, London: Routledge.

Fromm, E. (1941) *Escape from Freedom*, New York: Basic Books.

Gadamer, H.-G. and Hahn, L. E. (1997) *The Philosophy of Hans-Georg Gadamer*, Chicago: Open Court.

Guntrip, H. (1969) *Schizoid Phenomena, Object Relations and the Self*, New York: Basic Books.

Habermas, J. (1985) *The Philosophical Discourse of Modernity*, Cambridge: MIT Press.

Heidegger, M. (1962 [1927]) *Being and Time*, trans. J. R. Macquarrie and E. Robinson, Oxford: Blackwell.

Heidegger, M. (1987) *Zollikoner Seminare*, M. Boss (ed.), Frankfurt: Vittorio Klosterman.

Lacan, J. (1977) *Ecrits, A Selection*, New York: Norton.

May, R., Angel, E. and Ellenberger, H. (1958) *Existence: A New Dimension in Psychiatry and Psychology*, New York: Basic Books.

Mead, G. H. (1934) *Mind, Self, and Society*, Chicago: University of Chicago Press.

Needleman, J. (1963) *Being-in-the-World. The Selected Papers of Ludwig Binswanger*, New York: Basic Books.

Orange, D. (2009) *Thinking for Clinicians*, London: Routledge.

Orange, D., Atwood, G. and Stolorow, R. (1997) *Working Intersubjectively: Contextualism in Psychoanalytic Practice*, Hillsdale, NJ: Analytic Press.

Stolorow, R. D. (2002) 'From drive to affectivity: Contextualizing psychological life', *Psychoanalytic Inquiry*, 22: 678–685.

Stolorow, R. (2005) 'The contextuality of emotional experience', *Psychoanalytic Psychology*, 22: 101–106.

Sullivan, H. S. (1950) 'Tensions interpersonal and international', in H. Cantril (ed.), *Tensions that Cause War*, Urbana, IL: University of Illinois Press.

Taylor, C. (1989) *Sources of the Self*, Cambridge, MA: Harvard University Press.

Theunissen, M. (1977) *Der Andere*, Berlin: de Gruyter.

Chapter 3

Daseinsanalysis

A dialogue

Alice Holzhey-Kunz and Tamás Fazekas

DASEINSANALYSIS: THREE ALTERNATIVE APPROACHES TO PSYCHIC SUFFERING[1]

Alice Holzhey-Kunz

The reader may be surprised that I am restricting my article about Daseinsanalysis to the question of how psychic suffering is conceptualized within it. I offer two reasons for my choice. First, I consider the topic of psychopathology to be the most relevant for psychotherapy, whatever the modality. All special forms of therapeutic strategies are consequences of how psychic suffering is understood. Therefore, it reveals much more of the essence of a psychotherapeutic movement than the mere description of the techniques it employs and the humanistic ideals which inform it. Second, Daseinsanalysis is, to an important degree, not a psychotherapeutic modality but a specific mode of psychiatric investigation. This applies to Ludwig Binswanger, one of the two founding fathers: he developed Daseinsanalysis as a specific method for exploring psychosis. Only through Medard Boss, the other founding father of Daseinsanalysis, did it become a form of psychotherapy. One therefore has to focus on psychopathology to understand Daseinsanalysis as a whole. This is most interesting, as I hope to show, because not only do Ludwig Binswanger and Medard Boss differ totally in their conceptualization of 'mental illness', but I myself have added a third Daseinsanalytic approach to this topic, which is neither in the tradition of Binswanger nor of Boss, although, like them, I refer to phenomenological thinking and to the philosophical anthropology of Martin Heidegger.

Let us understand why I think the essence of any psychotherapeutic movement expresses itself in the underlying conceptualization of psychic suffering. My argument goes back to Sigmund Freud, the founding father of modern psychotherapy. Today, psychoanalysis is usually considered a specific treatment for neurosis, which was then unique and is now one of many. In his famous *Introductory Lectures on Psycho-Analysis*, Freud stresses the point that psychoanalytic treatment has its roots in the discovery that seemingly meaningless neurotic symptoms have a hidden meaning (1916–17: 83). Therefore, when you apply the Freudian technique without agreeing with the psychoanalytic concept of neurosis, this technique changes its character altogether.

The discovery of a hidden meaning in neurotic symptoms contradicts the medical–psychiatric understanding of psychic symptoms as manifestations of mental illness – not that Freud ever considered psychic suffering to be 'normal' or healthy. The crucial point is to stop thinking in terms of medical categories of normality versus abnormality or health versus illness: whenever we think in medical terms, we always ask what, in neurosis, is wrong, and therefore 'defective'. Freud looked instead for the hidden meaning of seemingly odd or bizarre thoughts, feelings, or behaviours. Thus, since the beginning of modern psychotherapy, there have been these fundamentally opposing ways of conceptualizing psychic suffering: either as a negative deviation from psychic 'health' or 'normality', or as a cryptic manifestation of meaningful, but unconscious purposes.

Since Freud, every concept of psychic suffering is either a medical one based on the categories of health and illness, or a hermeneutic one, guided by the category of hidden (unconscious) meanings. This difference is crucial, and to emphasize it is all the more important today, when medical thinking is gaining ever greater control over psychotherapy. And the greater that control, the more psychotherapy changes into a mere technical treatment of so-called 'disorders', or technical instructions for developing social skills – independent of all humanistic ideals. Only when you understand psychic suffering as expressing a hidden meaning will you practise psychotherapy as the hermeneutic task of looking for your client's hidden problems, conflicts, anxieties and wishes.

As I have mentioned, Daseinsanalysis was divided, almost from its beginning, into two theories which have very little in common besides their name and some other terms borrowed from Heidegger. Let me explain first the two quite different Daseinsanalytic concepts of psychic suffering developed by Binswanger and Boss, and then add my own concept, which combines Freud's discovery concerning psychic suffering with philosophical discoveries concerning the human condition made by Kierkegaard, Heidegger, and Sartre.

Ludwig Binswanger: an exploration of the world underlying 'mental illness'

In 1909, through Jung, Ludwig Binswanger (1881–1966) discovered Freud's psychoanalysis, to which he initially adhered. However, Binswanger's theoretical interests soon developed beyond his initial ties to psychoanalysis.[2] His prime concern was to establish psychiatry as a science and to overcome its bleak condition as a mere conglomeration of disconnected subdisciplines. He felt that this task could be accomplished only if psychiatry was geared to the 'whole human being' rather than the brain or the mind. He thus took as his basis Heidegger's existential concept of human being as 'Dasein' or 'Being-in-the-world'.

What Binswanger calls 'Daseinsanalysis' is a contribution to psychiatry, a new scientific method of psychiatric investigation which does not follow the usual course of using the two guiding medical categories of health and illness, but works from the notion of the 'world-project'.[3] We may say that the introduction, in the investigation of psychiatric illnesses, of the term 'world-project', drawn from Heidegger's lecture 'The Essence of Reason', is Binswanger's original and highly productive contribution to psychiatry.[4] The term 'world' used in it does not mean the universe of things or the external world, but rather a whole in the sense of the all-embracing 'horizon' of meaning in which all human experiencing, thinking, and acting takes place. For Binswanger, each individual person moves in a world of his or her own, which is unmistakable and unique, even though the different social and cultural worlds to which the person belongs overlap within it. Everything that happens to him, everything he undertakes, all his experiences and behaviour have a meaning in his own world-project, be they normal or pathological.

To avoid any misunderstanding of the 'world-project' as the conscious world view or *Weltanschauung* of a person, Binswanger describes it, following Kant, as a 'transcendental *a priori*' (Binswanger 1958: 205). With this, he wants to emphasize that the world-project is an 'ultimate given', which cannot be derived from anything else – not even genetically from childhood experiences; rather, it is the precondition for all psychological manifestations. It even precedes the dynamic unconscious discovered by Freud and shapes human existence from the beginning.

Everything a person feels, thinks or does has a meaning in his own individual world-project; this also applies to experiences and behaviour diagnosed as absurd or abnormal. The introduction of the term 'world-project' in psychiatry leads to a hermeneutic approach to pathological symptoms: these become understandable when seen within the specific world-project by which they are determined. With this hermeneutic postulate of a hidden meaning to seemingly meaningless symptoms, Binswanger's Daseinsanalysis sides with Freud's psychoanalysis.

Binswanger's investigation of the 'mentally ill' person combines Freud and Heidegger in a highly original way: from Freud he takes the insight that symptoms have a hidden meaning, from Heidegger he learns that the ultimate ground of how the individual thinks, feels and behaves is not unconscious wishes and anxieties from early childhood, but the world-project as the basic individual horizon of meaning.

Although I think Binswanger's concept of psychic suffering is highly original and fertile, I see two problems in it which derive from the supposed a priori character of the world-project. First, it puts a premature end to the hermeneutic approach – since the ultimate ground of all experiences and behaviour, and the hermeneutic horizon for their interpretation, is itself no longer hermeneutically explicable. If the world-project is an a priori given, we cannot ask of it: 'Where from, why, and what for?' Instead, the question now relates to the specific structure of a particular world-project; and the structural analysis is guided by the norm of a 'structural whole'. Such a norm then allows one to look for 'abnormal deviations' from the natural structural wholeness of human Being-in-the-world. Although Binswanger criticizes the use of the term 'illness' as applied to psychiatry, he comes to an analogous evaluation, by describing the psychotic world-project as deficient in character.

The other problem of which Binswanger appears unaware is his peculiar, deterministic view of human existence. He himself declares of Daseinsanalysis, with its concept of the world-project: 'But I dare say that we can throw some more light on it [the problem of predisposition] when we view it from an anthropological angle' (1958: 203). In fact, the ground of potentiality of all psychological phenomena can only be innate, constitutional conditions. It is therefore no surprise that Binswanger only makes a few references to the relationship between Daseinsanalysis and psychotherapy. (His highly regarded lecture 'On Psychotherapy' from 1935, published in France with an introduction by Michel Foucault, certainly shows the influence of Heideggerian thinking, but does not deploy the Daseinsanalytic concept of the world-project that was only developed later.) When abnormal deviations from the norm of structural wholeness are not the result of an individual history, but determine this history from the beginning, it is difficult to explain how psychotherapy could alter the world-project.

Medard Boss: a 'Dasein-appropriate' description of 'being ill'

Unlike Binswanger, Medard Boss (1903–1990), from the outset, understood Daseinsanalysis as a psychotherapeutic practice. It was therefore only logical that in 1970 he created a training centre in Zurich for 'Daseinsanalytic psychotherapy and psychosomatics'.

Boss was initially a committed supporter of Freud's and remained a member of the Swiss Psychoanalytical Society throughout his life. In the early 1940s he turned to Ludwig Binswanger's theories, and his book on *The Meaning and Content of Sexual Perversions*, first published in 1947, was entirely indebted to Binswanger's concept of the world-project. But the second edition of it four years later was based on a completely different conception of 'Being-in-the-world'. This reorientation resulted from Boss's encounter in the interval with Martin Heidegger, which led to a lifelong friendship and collaboration.

Heidegger's participation in the development of Daseinsanalysis was not restricted to philosophical guidance. In conjunction with Boss, he conducted the Zollikon seminars at Boss's home in Zollikon between 1959 and 1969; these were attended mainly by psychiatrists-in-training. Heidegger's interest, however, did not lie specifically in psychiatry and psychotherapy, but in medicine in general and indeed in its modern form as an applied natural science. He believed that he could exert an influence as a philosopher by highlighting to the doctors the philosophy that underpinned their activities – a scientific paradigm informed by Descartes' 'dictatorship of mind' still in force to this day. This paradigm devalues everything that exists – even the human being – to the rank of mere objects measurable and calculable by a human being conceptualized as a subject. The whole of medicine also bows to this, which is why its key concepts of 'health' and 'illness' are now only understood in technical terms. Against the backdrop of this critique, Heidegger undertook to inform the doctors present about a 'Dasein-appropriate' concept of health and illness. The goal was therefore not a new understanding of psychopathological phenomena, but the overthrow of the scientific paradigm pervading medicine and psychology (including psychoanalysis) in favour of a new approach.

The scientific paradigm is rooted in the modern philosophy of the subject. What has to be overcome, therefore, is all thinking proceeding from subject and subjectivity, because, according to the late Heidegger and consequently for Boss, this is identical with reducing the world to the sum of exploitable objects. Overcoming the so-called 'possessive subjectivism' in medicine and psychology is therefore the main goal of Boss's Daseinsanalysis; the specifically Daseinsanalytic psychotherapy forms a field of application for the new conception. For Boss and his school, this gives Daseinsanalysis a unique significance and distinguishes it from all other medical–psychological and psychotherapeutic approaches, which, according to Boss, are all united and remain rooted in Cartesian philosophy despite all their differences.

For Heidegger and Boss, the task is thus to implement a 'Dasein-appropriate pathology'. What counts is the implementation of a desubjectivized definition of health and illness. This implies that Freud's discovery, which leads to a hermeneutic approach to psychic suffering, is not even discussed. In his major work *Existential Foundations of Medicine and Psychology*, Boss puts forward 'a general Daseinsanalytic phenomenology of being ill'. While he speaks, intentionally, of 'being ill' rather than of 'illness', his pathology, unlike that of Binswanger, is clearly a medical one. Following Heidegger's explanations in the *Zollikon Seminars* (2001: 46f), 'being ill' is interpreted privatively as 'a lack of health' (1994: 197ff). Because Descartes is blamed for the body–mind dualism, Boss avoids any distinction between purely somatic and psychic or psychosomatic illnesses. What is new in this pathology consists precisely in eliminating this distinction and regarding every form of being ill as a 'constraint' on human openness and freedom. So the basic term of this pathology is 'constraint', and the basic question is always in which way and how strongly someone's openness and freedom towards the world is constrained.

The direction of Daseinsanalytic psychotherapy emerges from its definition of the essence of human being as 'openness and freedom' on the one hand, and from the understanding of psychic suffering as: a falling behind in one's own possibilities of openness and freedom towards the world. The goal of a Daseinsanalytic psychotherapy thus consists fundamentally in giving patients space to make up for what, until now, had been missing or constrained in their own psychic development. For this, the psychoanalytic setting and the practical advice given by Freud are maintained. Boss even claims that there could be no better recommendations than those Freud gave in his 'Recommendations to Physicians Practising Psycho-analysis' (1912). Boss therefore calls Daseinsanalysis a psychoanalytic practice purged of Freud's theoretical errors. But in fact it is not only purged of psychoanalytic 'metapsychology', but also of Freud's discovery of a hidden meaning to psychic suffering. And if there is no hidden meaning, there is no place for a hermeneutic approach; thus Boss's practice can be called Daseinsanalytic, but not Daseinsanalytic–hermeneutic.

An existential interpretation of the hidden meaning in psychic suffering

As a trainee at the newly founded Daseinsanalytic Institute in 1971–75, I gained a very close understanding of Medard Boss's thinking because I was already familiar with the philosophy of Husserl and Heidegger. But soon I began to doubt the usefulness of introducing the late Heideggerian thinking on Being into the field of psychic suffering. I missed what I found in Freud: the search for a hidden meaning in seemingly bizarre experiences and behaviours, rather than the mere description of how these were falling short of an ideal of openness and freedom towards the world. Already in 1975, I wrote a long article about Boss's main work, *Existential Foundations of Medicine and Psychology*, where I expounded the problems that arise when one deprives human existence of its basic element: by the time of the Zollikon seminars in 1959, Dasein had become the mere sum of 'intangible capacities for receiving–perceiving [*Vernehmen*] what it encounters and what addresses it' (Heidegger 2001: 4). There was no longer any place for 'self-relatedness' – for openness to oneself as a *fundamental* aspect of the human being. I still think that, by removing self-relatedness from the concept of Dasein, Boss's Daseinsanalysis descends into mere medical–psychiatric thinking; this, I believe, represents a retrograde step in relation to Freud's discovery. Thanks to my good acquaintance with *Being and Time* (Heidegger 1996), I knew that I did not have to leave the philosophy of Heidegger altogether, but just go back to his fundamental early work to correct this basic flaw and gain the possibility of a Daseinsanalytic–hermeneutic approach to psychic suffering. For in *Being and Time*, Heidegger had not yet intended to overcome the concept of subjectivity, but sought to think it in an existential way; and to avoid confusions, he termed it 'Dasein' (being-there). It has been my passionate interest ever since to elaborate an existential–hermeneutic theory of psychic suffering.

According to the fundamental rule of all hermeneutics, you can only find a hidden meaning of something when you discover its context. For Freud, for instance, the neurotic symptoms belong to the unconscious (repressed) individual history of early childhood with its fears, wishes and conflicts. For Binswanger, they belong to an even deeper context he calls the individual world-project. *Being and Time* offers us, I believe, yet another possible context of meaning: namely the existential relationship that all human beings have to their own being.

Let me give a short explanation of what I mean by this. Since Descartes, to be a subject implies relating to oneself. When Heidegger speaks of 'Dasein' as having 'a relationship towards' its own being, he introduces a distinction not made before him: between relating ontically to oneself as this individual person, and relating ontologically to oneself as being human and therefore thrown into the incontrovertible givens of existence. Thanks to this distinction it is possible to realize that self-relatedness has a twofold ontic–ontological meaning. This means that in being a subject, I not only live in the constant awareness of myself as this individual person, but also in constant awareness of what it means to be human as such. For Heidegger, the essence of the human being lies exactly in this: in being disclosed for the ontological truth of one's own being. But if this is true, then all human beings exist as reluctant philosophers, because they are always already unintentionally disclosed for what is the explicit topic of philosophy: ontology. Three examples of everyday life may elucidate what sounds at first rather enigmatic.

- When I feel hungry, this awareness of myself as being hungry has both an ontic and an ontological meaning. The ontic meaning is mostly the one I focus on and consists in all the thoughts and actions directed at satisfying my hunger; the ontological meaning is mostly screened out and consists in the sheer fact that this need pursues me as long as I live, that it demands satisfaction regardless of whatever I myself would like to be doing and whether I am in any position to satisfy it. This ontological meaning faces everybody with the pure facticity of their embodiment and the demands this entails. Similarly with the onto-logical meaning of feeling tired or having a headache. Such common feelings of tiredness or bodily pain always point to the sheer fact of our embodiment and therefore of being determined by laws of nature we cannot overcome. All these bodily sensations refer to our being constantly threatened by physical weakness, physical illness, and death.

- When I look at my watch because I want to know the time, this look does not only give me the concrete information I am looking for, but it confronts me unintentionally with the ontological fact that time is passing, that I am subjected to the laws of time, that my life will come to an end. So every look at my watch also refers to my being mortal.
- When I have to make a decision in whatever realm of daily life, this pending decision points to the ontological fact that, as a human being, I cannot avoid choosing and being responsible for my choice. This responsibility is all the heavier to bear because, at the moment of decision, one can never be sure whether it is the right decision, or whether it will have bad consequences for myself or for others. This is even true when I am forced by someone else to take a certain decision or when I avoid taking any decision: I am then responsible either for having surrendered to the will of another, or for my avoidance or non-decisiveness. So every decision, even the most unimportant one, refers to our having to lead our own life and be constantly threatened by possible failure and guilt.

My proposal for an ontological interpretation of psychic suffering, based on Heidegger's discovery of a (pre-)ontological awareness of one's own being, refers to what is an issue for everybody. That explains why Freud is right in saying that even the healthy person who is clearly not suffering from any manifest psychic symptoms is virtually neurotic. But what is the difference between potential and actual psychic suffering? It is useless to look for an answer in *Being and Time* (1996), as Heidegger is only interested in the distinction between inauthentic and authentic ways of relating to one's own being. But this distinction cannot explain psychic suffering. According to *Being and Time*, we all live 'proximally and for the most part' inauthentically, and the authentic confrontation with the anxiety-inducing truth of one's own being is rare and never lasting. Heidegger stresses the point that living inauthentically is by no means pathological, but on the contrary average and therefore normal. Therefore there must be a third way of relating to one's own being, that is neither inauthentic nor authentic and brings psychic suffering. I call it an oversensitivity to the ontological meaning of ontic happenings and actions. Whoever is oversensitive in this way is constantly exposed to anxiety-loaded ontological experiences of the human condition in everyday life. Some examples: many people cannot find a 'normal' way of handling feelings of hunger, tiredness or physical pain because they are too absorbed by the ontological dimension and implications of their embodied condition; other people have enormous difficulty handling everyday issues of time because these confront them incessantly with the fact that they are temporal and cannot avoid getting old and going towards death; and others cannot come to any decision because they are all too aware of the unpredictable risks of even the most well-pondered decision. Because of this special sensitivity, their daily life is overloaded with ontological meaning which makes it difficult, if not impossible, for them to appropriately assess and handle concrete ontic matters. Of course, everybody has their 'thin-skinned' spot and tends to overreact when this area of life is touched upon. That is why everybody is, as Freud says, 'virtually neurotic'. But the more frequently and intensely a person experiences the ontological dimension of ontic matters, the more he or she may become overly preoccupied by it.

We can now offer an initial summary of a Daseinsanalytic–hermeneutic approach to psychic suffering. It is based on the distinction between ontic and ontological meaning, and guided by Freud's discovery that apparently meaningless, psychopathological acts or thoughts, far from merely manifesting mental inadequacy, can have a hidden meaning which has to be unveiled and interpreted; that meaning, I believe, is ontological.

When I use the term 'suffering', I allude to Freud who was the first to conceptualize suffering in a non-medical way, defining neurosis as a 'suffering from reminiscences'. That is quite unusual, because one usually speaks of suffering from an illness. When neurotic persons suffer from reminiscences, they suffer from important personal issues in which they are secretly engaged. When I define psychic suffering as a suffering 'from one's own being', I interpret these personal issues even more fundamentally: not just as repressed infantile issues from early childhood, but as ontological ones – issues which do not lie merely in the individual past, but in our human condition. But although I propose an ontological interpretation of psychic suffering, I attribute high relevance to the past, and especially early childhood, because obviously childhood emerges as the period of primary and basic experiences of one's own being. Thus Freud's understanding of neurotic suffering remains true from a Daseinsanalytic perspective, but requires ontological deepening.

The hidden meaning of psychic suffering is, however, only half understood when we discover what the neurotic person is suffering from. It is equally important to find out what he is suffering *for*. A person who is hypersensitive to the hidden ontological dimension of ontic issues, and therefore exposed to anxiety-loaded, ontological experiences, tries to seek refuge from it. This purpose constantly insinuates itself into his or her life. Therefore psychic suffering always contains not only a special awareness of a basic ontological truth concerning the human condition that most people usually screen out in everyday life, but also an ardent wrestling with this life-threatening truth. This wrestling with one's own being can only have one purpose: to free oneself from what one experiences as too heavy a burden. Of course, this purpose is illusory. The secret wrestling of all psychic suffering is therefore always directed at a fundamental impossibility.

Let us return to some examples for clarification. It is highly probable that people with a so-called eating disorder are not simply oversensitive to the ontological dimension of their basic bodily need to be fed: they are rebelling against being incontrovertibly dependent on the fulfilment of this need and act out their revolt through special techniques of not eating 'normally'. One can therefore guess that someone with a depressive disorder is not only oversensitive to the ontological truth that nobody can lead an active life without risking failure and be responsible for it, but rebels against this unbearable truth of unavoidable guilt and acts it out by refusing to lead an active life altogether. There are many forms of wrestling with ontological givens; different forms of psychic suffering can thus be interpreted as different forms of 'acting out' the illusory desire of overcoming the insurmountable givens of human existence and the suffering that comes of one's oversensitivity to them.

Since its beginning with Binswanger and Boss, Daseinsanalysis has gone hand in hand with a phenomenological method of investigation; this applies to a hermeneutic approach to psychic suffering as well. Thus in a Daseinsanalytic therapy, any interpretation of the hidden ontological meaning of psychic suffering can only be gained working together with the suffering patient.

THE FUTURE OF 'BEING-ONESELF': MODERN DASEINSANALYSIS AND ITS CHALLENGES
Tamás Fazekas

Daseinsanalysis is grounded in Heidegger's philosophical thought; this has given it its originality, value and strength, yet it has also been the source of a continuing debate. This is partly due to the richness of Heidegger's philosophy – how do we translate into therapeutic practice concepts such as Dasein, being-in-the-world, authenticity, 'letting be'? It is also due to the way that Heidegger's philosophy evolved over the decades, from *Being and Time* (1996) to his collaboration with Medard Boss in the *Zollikon Seminars* (Heidegger 2001) and the *Existential Foundations of Medicine and Psychology* (Boss 1994). While these may hark back to *Being and Time*, they have also been marked by the thought of the so-called 'late Heidegger' as exemplified in, for instance, the *Discourse on Thinking* (1969). Without entering the debate of whether there was a 'turn' in Heidegger's thought, the difference in emphasis that characterizes these two periods in his philosophy can be seen reflected within the Daseinsanalytic movement and its two founders, Ludwig Binswanger and Medard Boss. These differences continued to have an impact on Alice Holzhey-Kunz and Gion Condrau, the leading philosophers and therapists who further developed the tradition, and Alice's paper has summarized very clearly the way this discussion still shapes modern Daseinsanalysis today. As a young physician and Daseins-analytic therapist, I have chosen to follow Hansjörg Reck in his search for a united Daseinsanalytic school. Although Reck has put enormous effort into his constructive work towards a cohesive Daseinsanalytic movement, such a united tradition has yet to be fully established; still, to my mind, it is the only valid future for Daseinsanalysis.

It follows from the above that I do not believe the distinctions which Alice draws between Binswanger, Boss and their respective legacies to be quite as clear-cut as she suggests. This should not surprise us, for the philosophy that grounds them is not as divergent as is sometimes claimed and can arguably be viewed as a difference of emphasis. Thus already in *Being and Time*, *Dasein* as being-in-the-world had replaced the Cartesian subject; and the concept of *Dasein* as a 'clearing' – as openness and dis-closedness to itself and the world (and the world to it) – was already crucial to Heidegger's thought at the time. And while Boss's main focus is indeed the client's openness to the world, yet it does not preclude all self-relation: for openness includes openness to oneself. Furthermore, there is room for a hermeneutic approach within a Bossian perspective: to help uncover the hidden meaning of the obstacles that get in the way of openness and freedom, and help understand what is preventing a deficient mode of being-in-the-world from developing into being-oneself in the fullest possible sense.

Alice has put forward convincingly her own way of integrating different psychotherapeutic traditions: she has challenged classical Daseinsanalysis, and has thereby demonstrated its tremendous potential for diversification without losing its uniqueness. I simply could not add anything essential to her statement (p. 43) that:

> When I define psychic suffering as a suffering 'from one's own being', I interpret these personal issues even more fundamentally: not just as repressed infantile issues from early childhood, but as ontological ones – issues which do not lie merely in the individual past, but in our human condition.

What I would like to do, is simply add a few footnotes to this crucial topic. More still than a specific mode of psychotherapeutic and psychiatric investigation, Daseinsanalysis, in its various interpretations, aims to be a practical, applied philosophy and phenomenology; its unique commitment is to help human beings by letting them become aware of their ontological human essence. Dasein must be translated into therapeutic terms, because it speaks to us directly in our everyday life; and without a philosophical basis, we would only treat symptoms, not dis-eases. However, I would like to stress that in relation to psychopathology any proposed universal human condition can become a pitfall if it gets interpreted in a dogmatic way: just as there is a danger for our clients of being 'oversensitive' to the ontological dimension of their existence, so there is a danger of reductionism for us, as therapists, through attaching overarching importance to that ontological dimension. If we agree that questioning human Being as such implies questioning the human condition with all the plenitude of its various horizons, then we realize from our experience in daily life that, neither ontologically nor in ontic matters, can life ever be reduced to a single existential condition. Ontological meaning is identical with our being-in-the-world in its fundamental wholeness, in other words: I *am* my onto-logical meaning. And while it may be helpful to get back to our Freudian roots and to its concept of neurosis as having a hidden meaning, we have to agree that, as Daseinsanalytic psychotherapists, we do not apply any technique, whether Freudian or Bossian.

Second, I would like to emphasize the pre-eminence of the relationship between therapist and client in bringing about therapeutic change, above and beyond the various theories of psychopathology. Daseinsanalytic psychotherapy focuses on human relationships in their richness and with all their limitations, and the therapeutic relationship is a paradigmatic example of openness and freedom. An open and serene relationship, free from constructed technique or dogmatic theory, is the 'drug' of any psycho-therapist. Every human being is born open for the world, open for others and otherness, open for his very own possibilities. The drug called relationship works by letting the patient feel this openness (again). It opens the patient for being-himself/herself, for new possibilities of Being and it equally opens the therapist on his way of infinite learning from the richness of life.

Third, I too would like to challenge Heidegger's stark dichotomy between authenticity and inauthenticity and, more controversially still, his view that we live mainly inauthentically, with only rare moments of authenticity. There is, I believe, a wide spectrum of possibilities between authentic and inauthentic living: one that can be expressed in terms of our openness to and engagement with the possibilities before us. Knowing that we are always attuned, always having emotions even if we are in a 'pallid' mood, we have to ask ourselves whether our feelings are appropriate for us or not. When, in my suffering, I connect with the ontological dimension of my life and feel overloaded by it, that is not the cause, but the result of my inauthentic life. (In that sense the distinction between authenticity and inauthenticity can indeed explain some psychic suffering.) When, on the other hand, I live my life in openness to the possibilities within my reach and do not seek what is beyond them, there can come no suffering from such an adequate being-in-the-world – adequate in its original sense of equal-to. This adequacy is, I would argue, like 'oversensitivity', another such way of being-in-the-world that lies on a continuum between authen-ticity and inauthenticity. We all see clients who fulfil many of the criteria of authenticity and resoluteness, yet have a very inadequate relationship to their possibilities. Such a view of an (in)authenticity spectrum, existing from birth onwards, would have important therapeutic implications.

My fourth footnote takes the form of a question: I would be interested to know what place Alice gives to Kierkegaard and Sartre in her understanding of psychopathology and how she integrates their views with her focus on oversensitivity.

Finally, I would like to consider future challenges for Daseinsanalysis. To live their existential being-open to the full, Daseinsanalysts need to take their social and political responsibilities seriously within their country's national healthcare system and face the challenges of growing migration and globalization. We need a phenomenological and hermeneutic approach to the topic of interculturality, for neocolonialism is probably the most dangerous side effect of psychotherapy. By colonizing the other with our own (cultural) assumptions or dogmatic theory of psychopathology, we ignore the otherness of the other, fostering assimilation instead of being-oneself. Neo-colonization and power go hand-in-hand with aggression. The global increase of aggression and violence also reminds us to take our social responsibility as psychotherapists seriously. We need to understand the phenomenon of aggression as a deficient mode of being-with, a dis-ease comparable with racism, and see the fear which the otherness of the other seems to cause in some people and the defensive behaviour it engenders. Daseinsanalytic theory and practice have to include prevention and management of destructive aggression. And if we are about to review any theory of culture, we will have to reassess the Daseinsanalytic theory of human childhood development (including the development of aggression). From the very beginning of life, the human being is a free and open, perceiving being. Being-for-another and inter-human relationships start in the womb, including presumably the potential to 'fall' in with the 'They'. The human being perceives concrete others from the beginning of his life. We are learning to respect the infant with all his or her competences, openness and freedom. Future challenges in child psychotherapy will include novel approaches to children's dreams and nurturing their ability for philosophical thinking. In my opinion, the 'active serenity' of the Daseinsanalytic therapeutic relationship opens the way towards therapy with young children, toddlers even. Training that is being-open and being-free for the other and his possibilities, a training that is being-oneself could also include Daseinsanalytic group therapy and art therapy.

I have outlined some of the challenges which, I believe, lie ahead for Daseinsanalysis if it is to continue to translate Heidegger's philosophical reflections on Da-sein into effective therapeutic practice for the twenty-first century. I have sought to express, in response to Alice's paper, my vision for the future in terms of a broadly united Daseinsanalysis, comprising a variety of approaches which will enable us better to face new issues of daily life and the challenges they present. Future Daseinsanalytic psychotherapists will have to work with novel therapeutic strategies, fostering the development of modern Daseinsanalysis by appreciating the rich potential of the original return to the question of Being and the original idea of healing by being-oneself in the fullness of our possibilities.

HOW TO GIVE DASEINSANALYSIS A 'VALID FUTURE'
Alice Holzhey-Kunz

I am grateful to Tamás's reply for two reasons: first, because he suggests that other challenges are awaiting Daseinsanalysis in the future, besides simply looking for a hermeneutic approach to psychic suffering – to which I agree; second, because he makes several statements worthy of discussion. Tamás's reply starts with the admission that he has chosen to follow Hansjörg Reck in his search for a 'united Daseinsanalytic school'. His 'footnotes' to my paper are evidently guided by this objective and refer to statements which seem opposed to it. Let me start with his first objection: he does 'not believe the distinctions which I draw between Binswanger, Boss and their legacies to be quite as clear-cut as I suggest'. This is not a matter of 'belief' or 'non-belief': the distinctions made in this article are far from being only 'suggestions', they are the result of a long-term, in-depth study of the work of both authors and just a summary of what I explain in much more detail in other publications of mine (Holzhey-Kunz 1988, 1997).

Tamás pleads for a 'modern Daseinsanalysis'. But what should it be like? Towards the end of his first footnote he states that '*we have to agree that as Daseinsanalytical psychotherapists, we do not apply any technique, whether Freudian nor Bossian*'. If this sentence, instead of aiming at Freud and Boss, were related to the constantly growing demand for manualized treatments based on quantitative research, I would have no objections. But Tamás seems to believe that the only alternative to such treatments, which mistake the soul for a machine, is to abandon all technical thinking and completely and solely trust in the therapeutic relationship. He even calls the therapeutic relationship a 'drug'; I certainly do not think that it ought to work as a drug, because transference and countertransference are inevitable parts of it. As I mention in my paper, Boss claims that Daseinsanalytic psycho-therapy is a psychoanalytic practice guided by the three Freudian rules of 'abstinence', 'free association' and 'evenly suspended attention'. Boss never doubted that the therapeutic relationship needs to be counterbalanced by rules which the Daseinsanalytic therapist must obey to avoid surreptitious abuse, whether one-sided or mutual. He adopted the Freudian rules because he was very well aware that they differ completely from technical methods in the usual sense. The philosopher Paul Ricoeur highlights the key differ-ence when he calls the psychoanalytic technique a 'non-technique' because it 'remains within the dimension of veracity and not of mastery' (Ricoeur 1974). As long as Daseinsanalytic psychotherapy understands itself as an *existential–analytical process within the dimension of veracity*, it has to obey these rules. In my understanding of Daseinsanalysis, there is another Freudian rule to adopt, which Boss rejects (at least in theory) as non-phenomenological: *the rule of interpreting*. Because Boss reduces psychic suffering to a form of impairment, he has no need for interpretation. But as soon as you accept the Freudian discovery of a hidden meaning in neurotic symptoms, then interpreting this meaning must represent a significant psychotherapeutic intervention. Therefore I plead for the rehabilitation of interpreting in Daseinsanalytic psychotherapy and I discuss the various respects in which Daseinsanalytic interpretations differ from psychoanalytic ones: for instance, phenomenological dwelling on the symptoms, acknowledging the true core in psychic suffering, and introducing the ontic–ontological distinction which is denied by the patient's acting out. Needless to say, any interpretation is part of what happens in the relationship between the analysand and the analyst, and therefore always has a fundamentally relational aspect which has to be considered. Similarly, interpretations should only be used when they can fulfill the function of encouraging the patient's ability and readiness for a more truthful self-perception.

The third footnote, which refers to Heidegger's concept of authenticity and inauthenticity, reveals a similar attitude. Tamás 'challenges' Heidegger's 'view that we live mainly inauthentically with only rare moments of authenticity', because he "believes that there is a 'wide spectrum of possibilities between'". Although I agree that this distinction should be discussed in favour of a hermeneutic understanding of psychic suffering, I cannot follow this challenge because it takes the terms authenticity and inauthenticity in their usual psychological meaning and not in the strict ontological sense Heidegger has given them. Will this kind of contradicting of Heidegger be a sign of 'modern' Daseinsanalysis? Will the united school of Daseinsanalysis not only be freed of any technical guidance, but also of any philosophical guidance based on a real acquaintance with *Being and Time* as well? I hope not.

The fourth footnote is formulated as a question. It asks what place I give to Kierkegaard and Sartre in my understanding of psychopathology. I gladly confess that the longer I read them the more space I give them. Of course not in the sense of gradually replacing the importance of Heidegger, but in broadening the ontological guidelines which allow an existential–hermeneutic approach to psychic suffering. While Heidegger's analysis of anxiety (*Angst*) opens the way to this specific kind of approach in general, Kierkegaard's more detailed description of the various forms of anxiety and its relations to despair on the one hand, and Sartre's analysis of shame on the other hand are of great help in discovering and interpreting the specific ontological meaning of the different forms of psychic suffering. Similarly,

Sartre's analysis of bad faith for an existential concept of the unconscious is of vital importance for Daseinsanalysis, as soon as it accepts the Freudian discovery of a hidden meaning of so-called mental disorders and looks for an existential interpretation of it. I am also glad to say that I got the idea of studying their work from Binswanger, who has always underlined their importance for a better understanding of psychopathological phenomena. Referring to them has a long tradition in Daseinsanalysis, which I now carry on.

Notes

1 We finally opted for 'psychic' to translate *'seelisches' Leiden*, literally 'soul suffering'. *'Seelisch'* is commonly translated as 'mental' with all the misunderstandings, misinterpretations and baggage that this involves.
2 For an overview of the three stages of Binswanger's thought, see my chapter 'Ludwig Binswanger: Psychiatry Based on the Foundation of Philosophical Anthropology' (Holzhey-Kunz 2006).
3 Following a long discussion with my friend Anna Binswanger in Toronto in 2006, I have decided to translate Weltentwurf as 'world-project' (translated in *Existence* as 'world-design').
4 For the first time in his essay of 1947, 'Über die daseinanalytische Forschungsrichtung in der Psychiatrie', published in English as 'The Existential Analysis School of Thought', in May *et al.* (1994: 191–213).

References

Binswanger, L. (1958) 'The existential analysis school of thought', trans. E. Angel in R. May, E. Angel and H. F. Ellenberger (eds) *Existence. A New Dimension in Psychiatry and Psychology*, New York: Basic Books.

Boss, M. (1994 [1979]) *Existential Foundations of Medicine and Psychology*, trans. S. Conway and A. Cleaves, New York: Jason Aronson.

Freud, S. (1912) 'Recommendations to physicans practising psychoanalysis', *Standard Edition*, 12: 109–120, London: Hogarth Press.

Freud, S. (1916–17) 'Introductory lectures on psycho-analysis', *Standard Edition*, 16 and 17, London: Hogarth Press.

Heidegger, M. (1969) *Discourse on Thinking*, New York: Harper Perennial.

Heidegger, M. (1996 [1927]) *Being and Time*, trans. J. Stambaugh, Albany, NY: State University of New York Press.

Heidegger, M. (2001) *Zollikon Seminars. Protocols, Conversations, Letters*, M. Boss (ed.), trans. F. Mayr and R. Askay, Evanston, IL: Northwestern University Press.

Holzhey-Kunz, A. (1988) 'Emancipation and narcissism: on the meaning of desire, *Humanistic Psychologist*, 16: 186–202.

Holzhey-Kunz, A. (1997) 'What defines the Daseinsanalytic process?', *Existential Analysis*, 8 (1): 93–104.

Holzhey-Kunz, A. (2006) 'Ludwig Binswanger: psychiatry based on the foundation of philosophical anthropology', in E. Wolpert, K. Maurer, A. Rifai, E. Vorbach and M. Hambrecht (eds) *Images in Psychiatry. German Speaking Countries*, Heidelberg: Universitätsverlag.

May, R., Angel, E. and Ellenberger, H. F. (eds) (1994 [1958]) *Existence: A New Dimension in Psychiatry and Psychology*, New York: Jason Aronson.

Ricoeur, P. (1974) 'Technique and nontechnique in interpretation', trans. W. Domingo, in D. Ihde (ed.) *The Conflict of Interpretations*, Evanston, IL: Northwestern University Press.

Chapter 4

Tedium, ennui, and atonement
Existential perspectives on boredom

Laura Barnett

LXXVIII
Spleen

When, like a lid, the low, heavy sky weighs down
Upon my spirit, groaning in the grips of boredom,
. . . .
A long procession of hearses without drums or music
Slowly files through my soul; vanquished, Hope
Weeps, and intolerable, tyrannical Anxiety
Plants its black standard upon my downcast skull.

(Baudelaire, 1959)[1]

Profound boredom is, I believe, a central issue both for our clients and for present-day western society.[2] It can be experienced as an intolerable state in which despair and anxiety meet, or it may lurk concealed behind 'being busy', 'having fun', 'leisure', 'unemployed', 'stress', 'depression', etc. It can be found embodied in our relationship to others and to the world – to television, the computer, toxic substances, fashion and the creation of 'celebrities', etc. Yet it tends to be trivialized and underestimated. This chapter begins with Heidegger's concept of being-in-the-world and moves on to consider various synonyms, antonyms and translations of 'boredom'. In so doing, it looks at how the different nuances that emerge can contribute to our understanding of boredom, as we encounter it in the counselling room.

Being-in-the-world

For Heidegger, the 'in' of being-in-the-world is not the 'in' of containment: it refers to the way we 'dwell' within a network of meanings – he sees it as cognate with English 'inn' (1962: 80; 54). The 'in' of 'being *in* fashion' evokes clearly such an embodied, psychological, social, cultural, economic network of meanings; similarly, being *in* limbo, also describes a particular way of *dwelling in* and relating to the world, where our usual network of meanings has been temporarily suspended.

'Attunement' and time are two important aspects of being-in-the-world. For Heidegger, human existence (*Dasein*) is 'thrown', not simply at birth into a particular era, culture, family, set of genes etc., but in every situation which we encounter: for we always *already* find ourselves encountering it from a particular perspective and in a particular mood. Our mood is a way of tuning in to the world, Heidegger calls it *Stimmung* (mood, literally: tuning); it colours the way we understand the world and the meaning-ful ways in which we relate to it. Heidegger regards some forms of attunement as being more 'disclosive' than others – as more conducive to opening human existence to itself and the world, and the world to it. These he calls *Grundstimmungen* (fundamental attunements); they include anxiety, boredom, joy and despair.

Boredom

Boredom 1852: '1. = *Boreism* . . . 2. the state of being bored, tedium, ennui' (*OED*).
Bore: 'arose after 1750; etymology unknown. 1. The malady of *ennui*, supposed to be specifically "French", as "the spleen" was supposed to be English' (*OED*).

In *Fundamental Concepts of Metaphysics: World, Finitude, Solitude* (1995), Heidegger devotes over one hundred pages to boredom. (All page references in this chapter are to this Heidegger text, unless otherwise specified.) While we are often aware of something being boring (e.g. a lecture, waiting for a train), Heidegger argues that there is a deeper, more essential form of boredom that usually eludes us. He distinguishes between three forms of boredom, all of which involve a 'confrontation with time'. He calls the first form (pp. 78–106), 'becoming bored by' (*gelangweiltwerden von*), as when we are waiting for a train: as we try to pass the time, we experience a 'paralysing', 'fluttering unease . . . that does not allow us to find anything that could grip us, satisfy us or let us be patient'. We try to 'fill time', to occupy ourselves, since 'being occupied gives our dealings with things a certain manifoldness, direction, fullness'. However, when we 'become bored', things around us 'refuse us' what we 'expect of' them, they have nothing to offer us, they 'abandon us to ourselves' and we feel 'left empty'. This resonates with my therapeutic experience of patients in hospital: they may have books, crossword puzzles, a television set, yet feel 'oppressed', '*held in limbo by time as it drags*'. According to Heidegger, boredom is characterized by two 'structural moments' – '*being left empty*' and '*being held in limbo*'. These, however, take on a different significance in each of the three forms of boredom.

In the second form of boredom ((pp. 106–132) *sich langweilen mit/bei*, lit. to bore oneself with), Heidegger argues, it is not so much the situation as such that bores us. He gives the example of deciding to go out for dinner with friends. Time here is not dragging and we may feel that we are enjoying ourselves, yet, on occasion, underlying our sense of 'casualness', there is an 'I know not what that weighs upon us', a 'peculiar dissatis-faction' that leaves us empty.

I am often reminded of Heidegger's second form of boredom when some clients talk of going to the pub for 'a laugh' and 'a few pints' with their mates: 'this casualness is a being left empty that is *becoming more profound*' and '*grows from the depths*'. They do not express any feeling of boredom and yet, with some clients (especially those in hospital with alcohol-related diseases), I sense that at the pub it is not only pints that they empty and lose count of, but also themselves: entirely in the present, with no thought of past or future, bringing 'time to a stand', they 'slip away from' themselves. Unlike the first form of boredom that comes from an external situation, the second form '*arises from out of Dasein itself*'.

In what Heidegger calls the third form of boredom (pp. 132–160) or 'profound boredom' (*es ist einem langweilig*, lit. it is boring for one), we are very much aware of being bored (unlike the second form), yet we do not try to 'kill time' (as in the first form):

> How dreadful boredom is . . . I lie prostrate, inert; the only thing I see is emptiness, the only thing I live on is emptiness, the only thing I move in is emptiness. I do not even suffer pain . . . I am dying death . . . My soul is like the Dead Sea, over which no bird is able to fly.
>
> (Kierkegaard 1987: 37)

Or as Warhol put it: 'I'm sure I'm going to look into the mirror and see nothing. . . . Everything is nothing' (cited in Svendsen 2005: 102). The '*indifference* enveloping beings *as a whole*' characterizes the 'emptiness' of profound boredom for Heidegger. Throughout the '*unifying horizon of time*' beings 'refuse themselves', 'simultaneously withdraw'.

Heidegger argues that in profound boredom as, literally, 'the while becomes long' ('boredom' in German is *Langeweile*) and '*expands itself into the entire expanse of the temporality of Dasein*', we become aware of our time as finite. We also become conscious of the importance of engaging with our life and its possibilities, which in our boredom we are leaving 'unexploited'. For Heidegger, at the other end of the continuum from *Langeweile* lies *Augenblick* (German for 'moment', literally eye-glance): 'The moment of vision ruptures the entrancement of time, and is able to rupture it, insofar as it is a specific possibility of time itself' (p. 151), for in it present, past and future are held simultaneously in sight. Such 'moments of vision' are decisive as they are times when human existence shoulders its freedom and responsibility: when Dasein allows itself to be aware of both its finitude and its possibilities, makes choices according to what is properly meaningful to it, owns these decisions and puts them into action. These are moments of 'authenticity' when, in its freedom, 'Dasein *resolutely discloses* itself *to itself*', not as a ' rigidly erected' ideal, but 'as that which must first precisely wrest its own possibility from itself again and take itself as itself in such a possibility'. Boredom and the moment of vision, as two opposite ways of living time are thus, Heidegger argues, intimately connected. In that sense, the 'telling refusal' of beings in boredom is also a 'telling announcement' of Dasein's possibilities and its freedom; they form '*the one* unitary phenomenon in which we, or rather the Dasein in us oscillates'. In summary:

> Whereas in the first case of boredom we are concerned to shout down the boredom by passing the time so that we *do not need to listen to it*; and whereas in the second case what is distinctive is a *not wanting to listen*, we now have a *being compelled to listen*, being compelled in the sense of that kind of compelling force which everything *properly authentic* about Dasein possesses, and which accordingly is related to Dasein's *innermost freedom*.
>
> (p. 136)

In all three, it is '*the finitude of Dasein that resonates . . . and attunes us through and through*' (p. 170). Thus even the unease of the first form of boredom echoes that of profound boredom and can be disclosive of our freedom.

Heidegger also views boredom within the context of our age: contemporary Dasein is 'attuned through and through' by 'emptiness as lack, deprivation and *need*' (p. 162). While we may confront various needs in our society, our communal, 'bustling self-defense' conceals our fundamental need from ourselves. This historical contextualization of boredom fore-shadows his later interest in the contextualization of anxiety and technology within the history of the concealment and unconcealment of being.[3] I would suggest that the technological stance, anxiety and boredom are inter-connected. In this technological age, Heidegger argues, we seek to discover every one of earth's treasures and resources, to control and master the world as 'standing reserve', and, through this excessive 'uncovering' of being, we lose sight of its truth and mystery; this arouses our anxiety (Heidegger 2003; for therapeutic implications see Barnett 2009: 17f). Similarly, in our attempts to combat boredom, we may try every new gadget and thrill-producing adventure that technology now offers us, from the most innocuous pastime to acts of extreme violence – the world of

technology is boredom's oyster. Yet, rather than discovering the satisfaction that comes from engaging meaningfully with the world, while
respecting its mystery, this brings with it the anxiety attached to evading
our essential need and losing ourselves.

Heidegger speaks of the mutual affinity of certain moods for one
another: boredom, *Langeweile*, is a homesickness, a sense of not feeling at-
home-in-the-world (p. 80) – *lange Zeit haben* in Heidegger's South German
dialect is 'to be homesick'.[4] Here it meets anxiety as 'unheimlich'
('uncanny', literally not-at-home-like). As a mood that holds us in a limbo
of indifference and meaninglessness, 'boredom rests upon the nothing that
interlaces existence; its dizziness is infinite, like that which comes from
looking down into a bottomless abyss' (Kierkegaard 1987: 291). These
words echo Kierkegaard and Heidegger's famous descriptions of anxiety.

If we think of boredom as springing 'from a quite determinate way and
manner in which our own temporality temporalizes itself' (p. 127) we are
better placed to observe in our clients the relationship and differences
between boredom and despair. Clients may describe a present that stretches
out interminably, beyond which they cannot see (the future has, as it were,
dropped out).[5] It is a feeling of wading through treacle with no way out:
wading without any sense of agency, ad infinitum, in a world that is finite.
Despair, on the other hand is future oriented: it is a view of the future as
bleak and unendurable. Yet, paradoxically, in the moment, despair can be
alleviated by a sense of agency and the possibility of a way out, albeit
through defiance or the thought of suicide (Heaton 2009); boredom, however, 'takes everything from one, even the desire to take own's own life'
(Stendhal, cited in Svendsen 2005: 26).

How do we detect our clients' boredom if, as Heidegger claims, it lies
concealed? As with anxiety, we may see it in the activities with which they
busy themselves: 'That the eccentric diversion is based upon boredom is
seen also in the fact that the diversion sounds without resonance, simply
because in nothing there is not even enough to make an echo possible'
(Kierkegaard 1987: 291). Hours spent polishing, shopping, or in front of
the television or computer, remarks such as 'I'm so busy, I have no time to
get bored' can all be tell-tale signs. In hospital, it may lie dormant while
patients sleep the time away, reluctant to reflect upon the recent threat to
their health and possibly confront their ageing and mortality. Time,
Heidegger reminds us, is 'time for' and, as such, lies at the heart of our
freedom: it is embodied in the choices we make – and there are countless
ways to fill time if we choose to 'counteract' our boredom. Heidegger's
second form of boredom emphasizes the distinction between occupations
that feel essentially *worthwhile* (i.e. worth my while – an apposite expression that German does not have) and a more 'inauthentic' or 'fallen' way of
spending time. Boredom may lurk behind other moods; it may also be
masked by diagnostic terms such as 'depression'. The diagnosis medicalizes

the problem and places it outside the client, and the antidepressants dampen the client's ability to feel his or her mood with acuity. The client thus misses an opportunity to 'shoulder[s] once more his very Dasein' (p. 171) and question his being-in-the-world.

Tedium

Whereas 'boredom' is of recent history and unknown etymology, 'tedium' has barely changed from Latin *taedium* 'disgust, weariness'. Heidegger's phenomenology of boredom focuses primarily on 'time' and 'emptiness' and their intrinsic relationship. This may be due in part to his speaking a Germanic language of boredom (*Langeweile*), in which the 'while becomes long'. Metaphors of satiety and disgust underlie a parallel language of boredom, illuminating another aspect of that mood: thus, besides '*taedium/ tedium*', Ancient Greek *proskores* (satiating, tedious), and slang expressions such as English 'fed up' and French 'ras le bol'. Interestingly the *Oxford English Dictionary* suggests French 'bourrer' (stuff, satiate) as a possible etymology for 'bore', but dismisses it for want of any semantic link.

Phenomenologically, these words highlight aspects of the physicality of the experience of boredom: I am 'sated' and any more is 'nauseating'; disgust, *dégoût*, – *je n'ai goût à rien*, literally 'I have no taste for anything'. In tedium, I am 'sick and weary of' life, *taedium vitae*. In Roquentin's 'nausea', the world is bland, *fade*; the '*dégout d'exister*' imbues his whole being-in-the-world (Sartre 1972: 145; 1976: 378). In *À Rebours*, the wealthy, bored aesthete Des Esseintes wastes away, so nauseated is he with food and life (Huysmans 1947).

In what relation do these metaphors stand, phenomenologically, to Heidegger's sense of 'being held in limbo' and 'emptiness'? They could be seen to offer, as it were, the 'gut reaction' to 'being held in limbo'; yet how can 'satiety' and 'emptiness' both be used to characterize boredom?[6] In 'satiety', with what am I 'fed up'? It may be with what I am doing right now, like listening to a boring lecture; or wasting time that could be spent in a more satisfying way; or I may be fed up with what I am doing with my life (Heidegger's three forms of boredom). In all three examples our time is filled, yet unfulfilled: it is filled, 'fed up' with nothingness, and faces us with nothingness. The satiety metaphors embedded in 'tedium' also stress the fact that I can tolerate that sense of emptiness no longer, nor bear the thought of spending another moment in this limbo: 'in this [indifference] . . . Dasein becomes satiated with itself. Being has become manifest as a burden' (Heidegger 1962: 173, 134).

These metaphors can also express an underlying disillusion with my lack of certain qualities or capacities, with the world at large, with God even. Here, it rejoins Kierkegaard's distinction between 'despair over' [my situation] and 'despair of' [my felt resourcelessness] (Heaton 2009: 127). An implied disapproval of God's creation is also what made *acedia* (literally 'care-lessness, indifference') a deadly, capital sin (*caput*, font of all sins) for the 'desert father' hermits in fourth century Egypt and monks in the Middle Ages, as the 'noonday Demon' visited torpor and disgust upon them. (That *acedia*, care-lessness, should have been a deadly sin is interesting in relation to Heidegger's description of Dasein's ontological structure as 'care'.)

Thus 'satiety' and 'emptiness' paradoxically meet in describing a 'peculiar dissatisfaction' (p. 118), from the most trivial (waiting for a delayed train) to the most essential – not attending to my need to make choices about my life and take responsibility for myself. Heidegger touches only briefly upon the concepts of satisfaction and 'dissatisfaction' in his exposition of boredom and yet, to my mind, they have a central place in the phenomenology of that mood – as the various translations and synonyms of 'boredom' attest. Indeed, 'profound satisfaction' could be seen as a polar opposite of 'profound boredom' – where Heidegger places 'the moment of vision' and authenticity.

If disgust and satiety can be seen to characterize boredom, it is no surprise that attempts to overcome the emptiness of boredom by filling one's time with ever more distractions are doomed to failure: so that 'demonically possessed by boredom in an attempt to escape it, one works one's way into it' as 'one indulges in the fanatical hope of an endless journey from star to star' (Kierkegaard 1987: 291). Satiety turns to surfeit, yet emptiness survives, as witnessed in countless journals (Samuel Johnson, Marquis de Sade, etc.), novels and plays. Similarly, we see clients unsuccessfully turning to 'workaholism' and diversions of all kinds – from partying and substance misuse to sex and acts of violence, in an attempt to conquer boredom. The crucial factor is that of essential satisfaction, of seeking to fulfil our 'need', so that it 'properly satisfy us' (p. 121), rather than simply to fill the emptiness.

Ennui

> Accidie maketh hym hevy . . . he doeth alle thing with anoy, . . . ydelnesse, and unlust . . . Thanne comth the synne of worldly sorwe, swich as is cleped tristitia . . . Therof comth that a man is annoyed of his owne lyf.
>
> (Chaucer, *The Parson's Tale*, cited in Healy 1984: 17–18)

'Ennui', the common word for 'boredom' in eighteenth- and nineteenth-century England, comes from the Late Latin *inodiare* (as does Chaucer's 'anoy'), itself derived from the phrase *mihi est in odio* (literally 'to me [it] is in hate'), I hate; both French 'ennui' and English 'annoy' long retained that strong sense of 'odium'. Interestingly, the translations which Cotgrave's bilingual *Dictionarie* (1611) gives for French 'ennui' include almost all the aspects of boredom highlighted so far: 'annoy, anguish; wearisomeness; tediousness; loathing; satietie; discontentment' (cited in Healy 1984: 19).

S'ennuyer, 'to be bored', is a reflexive verb in French (*ennuyer* means 'to bore [others]'); this highlights the element of strong dissatisfaction with oneself, even self-loathing, that often accompanies profound boredom, '*ennui . . .* where the "I" is chained to, and stifled in the "Myself"'' (Lévinas 1996: 198). Sartre, in *Being and Nothingness* (1976: 112–113) uses the example of this reflexive verb to illustrate how the self of the for-itself (i.e. human existence/consciousness) never quite coincides with itself.[7] There is always a gap between 'I' and 'myself' (an equivalent example in English would be 'I am enjoying myself'). That gap, the 'nothingness' between I and myself, is, he argues, where my freedom lies. So while the reflexive form '*je m'ennuie*' suggests dissatisfaction with oneself, it also puts the freedom to change that mood, and the responsibility to do so, firmly within oneself, rather than seeing the remedy as being out there in the world. Ennui for Sartre and Camus also goes hand in hand with meaninglessness and alienation: 'The term "absurdity" now springs from under my pen . . . I realised that I had found the key to Existence, the key to my nauseas, to my own life' (Sartre 1972: 183–184), a feeling echoed by Camus' character Meursault (1942).

By looking at boredom from the perspectives of '*Langweile*', 'tedium' and 'ennui' and the metaphors inherent in those words, we are now in a position to offer a fuller description of the experience of profound boredom. In boredom, we are 'held in limbo'; we survey the world with indifference, weariness and apathy, without any zest for life, rejecting any possibility before us; the world around us, existence even, has become meaningless; we experience alienation and an essential dissatisfaction (loathing even) with ourselves, the world, maybe God; this leaves us feeling empty and at the same time 'fed up' – we cannot bear any more, we feel sick of it and of ourselves, and resourceless to change it. Yet the remedy lies within our grasp. The problem is that, on the whole, we do not understand what lies at the root of our boredom, or, in Heidegger's words, we do not want to listen (p. 136) to our essential need.

Finding a way out of boredom

I asked 20 non-therapists and 20 therapists what, to them, was the opposite of boredom. The non-therapists' list consisted of the following nouns and adjectives: excitement, amusing, manic, hyper, engagement, stimulated, busy, enjoying, enthusiastic, motivated, scintillated, interest, enjoyment; interestingly, one teenager replied 'contentment', another 'happiness'. If amusement, excitement, busy-ness, etc. are what most people see as the opposite of boredom and seek as an antidote to it, it is not surprising that their attempts at conquering boredom so often prove vain: listlessness is replaced by restlessness, emptiness by 'fill-ment' not fulfilment. The therapists' list had overlaps (interest, engagement, enthusiasm), but also pointed to a sense that, in boredom, something more essential was not being attended to – e.g. 'engaging with, as opposed to disconnected from, one's feelings' (Julien 2008). Thus distractions and diversions would only disconnect us further. My own 'forethought' in writing this chapter was: 'a capacity to be alone with oneself in a satisfying manner'. On further reflection, I would speak not of opposites, but of moods with which boredom cannot coexist – these would include satisfaction, openness to the world and a sense of *thauma*, 'wonderment and awe'. And this may indicate their therapeutic value.

But how do we go from the indifference and dissatisfaction of profound boredom to engagement and contentment? How do we open ourselves to the world, rediscover meaning in things and reconnect with our zest for life? Heidegger claims that 'the temporal character of being held in limbo' comes from being 'impelled through the entrancement of time toward the moment of vision' (p. 148) and that the 'moment of vision' alone can rupture that entrancement (p. 148). It is not clear, however, how much control we have in bringing that moment about. Kierkegaard suggests that:

> Just as an experienced sailor always scans the sea and detects a squall far in advance, so one should always detect a mood a little in advance. Before entering into a mood, one should know its effect on oneself and its probable effect on others.
>
> (1987: 299)

We saw above that, for Sartre, *je m'ennuie* manifests in the non-coincidence of the pronouns (je/me) the freedom that lies at the heart of the for-itself – and Heidegger's second form of boredom, *sich langweilen* (*ich langweile mich*, literally *I* bore *myself*) mirrors French *s'ennuyer* exactly. As an experienced sailor we may then scan the sea and seek to discover (or, in therapy, we may jointly seek to discover) what lurks beneath and ahead – for, as Heidegger points out, this second form of boredom often lies concealed. But how do we emerge from profound boredom? What if we have gone in too far? Could it be that 'the best way out is the way through'? That as we wade around in it, interminably it seems, a shift eventually occurs, something might catch our attention and lift the veil of indifference that enveloped our world. Meaning reenters our world: 'one enjoys something totally accidental' (Kierkegaard 1987: 299), and this may enable us to reach a 'standpoint' from which to review our situation, to change 'the eye with which one sees actuality' (ibid. 300), or to reach Heidegger's moment of vision, which is also a moment of action.

As the metaphors present in tedium and ennui indicate, there are a number of moods that constellate boredom; there is also, we saw, a constellation of moods which cannot coexist with boredom. Far removed from boredom, there is a place of openness to the world, where things no longer 'refuse themselves': it is a particular way of being with myself-in-the-world, where I can be alone without experiencing meaninglessness, dissatisfaction, indifference or emptiness; where I am at one with myself, without either listlessness or restlessness, without self-loathing and self-berating, and also at one with the world – I do not seek to change the givens of my existence, yet accept my responsibility for the things that I can change. It is a place of peace and reconciliation with myself and the world in the face of the mystery of existence. There was a beautiful expression in the English language which meant just that until its meaning gradually shifted away from 'reconciliation and concord' towards 'reparation and expiation'. That expression is the fourteenth century 'at onement', now 'atonement'. Many routes lead to that state, for the Greeks it was *harmoniè*, *yoga* for the Indians. Interestingly, these two words are grounded in roots that hark back to joining synergetically: *harmoniè* evokes the metaphors of joining the tonalities of our life harmoniously, like the strings of a lyre and harnessing our energies, like horses to a chariot; *yoga* (cognate with Latin *jugum* and English 'yoke') that of sub*jug*ating the diversions and passions that disperse us.

This way of being-in-the-world which is beyond activity and passivity (p. 161), yet free from the indifference and lethargy of boredom, where time leaves us at peace (p. 98), where we become open to what lies ahead on the other side of the horizon is what, in his later works, Heidegger called *Gelassenheit*, 'letting be'. 'Boredom is the root of evil[8] . . . Idleness is not the evil; indeed it may be said that everyone who lacks a sense for it thereby shows that he has not raised himself to the human level' (Kierkegaard 1987: 289). Nietzsche speaks of a 'tranquil movement; . . . the artists' and philosophers' vision of happiness' (cited in Svendsen 2005: 59), a 'delight [that] is superhuman whereas boredom is human all too human' (Svendsen 2005: 59).

Conclusion

> [Boredom] is your window on time's infinity. . . . Don't try to shut it; on the contrary throw it wide open. . . . For boredom . . . puts your existence into perspective.
>
> (Brodsky 1997: 109)

> He who completely entrenches himself against boredom also entrenches himself against himself.
>
> (Nietzsche 1996: 359)

Kierkegaard saw boredom as 'the root of evil' and many, from Samuel Johnson to Bertrand Russell, have recognized it as a major existential challenge or plague of existence; yet it is often trivialized, or else medicalized. The clinical model is not new; and there may come a time when diagnosing 'depression' in instances of boredom, and imputing it to a chemical imbalance in the brain, will appear just as misguided as diagnosing 'melancholia' due to black humours in the spleen.

Heidegger has drawn attention to the existential dimension of boredom, its frequent concealment and our need to guard it from falling asleep (1995: 79). The therapeutic relationship is a privileged place in which to awaken, name and own the mood of boredom, to allow this destabilizing 'homesickness' in which existential questioning, reflection and freedom can develop. Lévinas, we saw, viewed boredom as being 'where the "I" is chained to and stifled in the "Myself"' (1996: 198). I believe the experience of non-judgemental acceptance by a therapist can in itself help break the stiflement of boredom and its associated moods: that it may become for clients an apprenticeship in reconciliation, leaving alienation, meaninglessness and dissatisfaction behind, so as to be able to be at one with, and open to, themselves and the world.

Focusing on the language of boredom, in both English and related languages has helped uncover and develop different facets of that mood, in particular the central phenomenon of dis-satisfaction. This chapter is thus also, incidentally, a plea against the standardization of training in psychotherapy and a mandatory first degree in psychology. I believe that my background in Indo-European comparative philology has left me with a particular interest in and feel for the semantics of my clients' linguistic world – the way they use language to express their lived meanings and experience. On a personal note, writing this chapter has also helped me to question my own life, by distinguishing those diversions that emerge out of boredom from those that arise out of my wish and need to relax. By uncovering areas of boredom in my life, seeking to listen to and act upon them, I hope I am being more truthful with myself, in the Heideggerian sense of truth as aletheia – bringing out of concealment.

The final word goes to Heidegger:

> We can only ask whether contemporary man . . . does not suppress that profound boredom . . . whether he does not conceal his Dasein as such from himself – in spite of all his psychology and psychoanalysis, and indeed precisely *through* his psychology . . . Yet to question this fundamental attunement . . . [means] to liberate the humanity in man . . . *to let the Dasein in him become essential.*
>
> (1995: 166)

Notes

1 In this paper, translations from the French are my own.
2 However, boredom is no modern mal: Donne in 1622 already bemoaned the spread of 'spleen' (letter cited Healy 1984: 20). Each century, and individual countries, have since claimed it as their particular disease, ascribing its rise to various causes – including a post-WWII tendency to potty-train children at an earlier age! (Bernstein cited Healy 1984: 56).
3 I do not use a capital B to mark the ontological difference between *Sein* and *das Seiende* (being and beings), as I believe that 'Being' introduces religious connotations.
4 I am indebted to Salome Hangartner for this information.
5 Healy calls 'hyperboredom' a 'psychic black hole'.
6 Phillips calls the paradox of that double-felt sense – 'there is something I desire and nothing I desire' – the 'curious paralysis of boredom' (Phillips 1994: 80).
7 Unlike the in-itself (e.g. a stone) which is through and through itself.
8 Kierkegaard here takes a view that harks back to the Christian sin of *acedia*.

References

Barnett, L. (ed.) (2009) *When Death Enters the Therapeutic Space: Existential Perspectives in Psychotherapy and Counselling*, London: Routledge.
Baudelaire, C. (1959 [1857]) *Les Fleurs du Mal*, Paris: Librairie Larousse.
Brodsky, J. (1997) *On Grief and Reason Essays*, New York, Farrar, Straus and Giroux.
Camus, A. (1942) *L'Étranger*, Paris: Gallimard.
Healy, S. D. (1984) *Boredom, Self and Culture*, Madison, NJ: Fairleigh Dickinson University Press
Heaton, J. (2009) 'Reflections on suicide and despair', in L. Barnett (ed.) *When Death Enters the Therapeutic Space: Existential Perspectives in Psychotherapy and Counselling*, London: Routledge.
Heidegger, M. (1962 [1927]) *Being and Time*, trans. J. R. Macquarrie and E. Robinson, Oxford: Blackwell.
Heidegger, M. (1995 [1983]) *The Fundamental Concepts of Metaphysics: World, Finitude, Solitude* (lecture delivered 1929–30), trans. W. McNeill, and N. Walker, Bloomington, IN: Indiana University Press.
Heidegger, M. (2003 [1949]) 'The question concerning technology', trans. W. Lovitt, in M. Stassen (ed.) *Martin Heidegger, Philosophical and Political Writings*, New York: Continuum.
Huysmans, J.-K. (1947 [1884]) *Á Rebours*, Paris: Bibliothèque Charpentier.
Julien, C. (2008) Personal communication.
Kierkegaard, S. (1987 [1843]) *Either/Or, Part I*, ed. and trans. H. V. Hong and E. H. Hong, Princeton, NJ: Princeton University Press.
Lévinas, E. (1996 [1974]) *Autrement qu'être et au-delà de l'essence*, Paris: Livre de Poche.
Murray, J. A. H., Bradley, H., Craighie, W. A. and Onions, C. T. (eds) (1888–1933), *The Oxford English Dictionary*, Oxford: Clarendon Press.

Nietzsche, F. (1996 [1878]) *Human, All Too Human: A Book for Free Spirits*, trans. R. J. Hollingdale, Cambridge: Cambridge University Press.

Phillips, A. (1994) *On Kissing, Tickling and Being Bored*, London: Faber and Faber.

Sartre, J.-P. (1972 [1938]) *La Nausée*, Paris: Gallimard.

Sartre, J.-P. (1976 [1943]) *L'Être et le néant, essai d'ontologie phénoménologique* [*Being and Nothingness*], Paris: Gallimard.

Svendsen, L. (2005 [1999]) *A Philosophy of Boredom*, trans. J. Irons, London: Reaktion Books.

Chapter 5

Experiential–existential therapy

Embodying freedom and vulnerability

Les Todres

Since the early 1970s I have been interested in the relationship between phenomenology, existentialism and hermeneutics. My enquiry into the possibility of conceiving academic psychology as a human science, as distinct from that of the natural sciences, led me to the work of Amedeo Giorgi (e.g. 1970, 1985). Giorgi was engaged in considering how the phenomenological philosophy of Edmund Husserl could provide both a philosophical underpinning for psychology, as well as a practical direction for qualitative research. In a certain sense, Husserl came to sit on one of my shoulders and, in spite of the critique of his so-called 'essentialism' by a number of philosophers and practitioners, he continues to beckon me in helpful ways. At the same time, I was also engaged in psychotherapeutic training, and through this was introduced to the Daseinsanalytic approach of Medard Boss (1963, 1979) and thus to Martin Heidegger. Heidegger, in a similar sense, came to sit on my other shoulder, and in spite of my Jewish heritage and some real questions about his involvement with the Nazi Party, he remains a source of productive philosophical and personally dramatic beckoning that I have far from exhausted. I have also greatly benefited from other philosophers who have taken the broad traditions of phenomenology and existentialism forward in interesting and different ways such as Lévinas, Merleau-Ponty, Buber, Gadamer and Gendlin. Then there was some interesting work which linked Heidegger with Asian thought (Parkes 1987; May 1996). I saw this link as an important dimension which helped to suggest some radical spiritual implications for Heidegger's philosophy as well as for the transpersonal potentials of existentially oriented psychotherapy. And who can forget Freud? This brief and overly simplistic personal–historical fragment may serve to begin to open up a path towards expressing a personal view of an experiential–existential therapy of a particular kind: where phenomenological–embodied process (the epistemological concern) and existential themes of actualities and possibilities (the ontological concern) come together.

The epistemological concern: phenomenological–embodied process

The rich implications of Husserl's thought for psychotherapy have still to be systematically articulated, but I would like to highlight three emphases that I have found very fruitful: languaging experience, horizon, and the lived body.

Languaging experience

Husserl (1970a, 1970b) pointed again and again to the challenge of what it takes to be attentive to what occurs in experience. For him, this was not just a project of self-knowledge but a philosophical project: how what appears in consciousness is the credible starting point for knowing what can be known and even more, for saying something about the relationship between the known and the unknown. He was thus interested in 'subjectivity' *how* we know, as well 'objectivity' *what* there is to know, even if this 'what' differs from the traditional western way of enframing 'reality'. His 'method' was to reflect on experience in a particular way: to attend to experience before it is categorized as 'inner' as opposed to 'outer', 'mental' as opposed to 'physical', 'intellectual' as opposed to 'emotional'. Within such a spirit, we were called upon to attend to experience before the so-called 'objects' of experience are abstracted out from their flowing context; to suspend 'handed down' generalizations that may prevent us from looking again at what presents itself to consciousness. Such 'looking again' may be an important foundation for learning something new; and learning something new about oneself and the world may be a particularly important component for an authentic psychotherapy. It is thus no surprise that emerging and novel approaches to psychotherapy are concentrating less on the traditional emphases on 'cognition' and 'emotion' and more on 'attention' – 'how' and 'to what' to attend. And for Husserl, 'experience', in the way that he understood it, was the philosophically reliable 'place' to begin to attend. So, because the notion of 'experience' is so central to his path, Husserl needed to clarify what is meant by experience. Husserl (1970a) does this early on in his writings on 'consciousness', but I believe that the depth of the implications of 'experience' reached a more mature stage in his later writings on the 'lifeworld' (Husserl 1970b). I cannot do justice to the complex trajectory of his thought that threads through a number of years and writings, but there are a few things that are of particular import for the definition and practice of experiential–existential therapy as I see it.

Experience needs experiencing; to have experienced is to have 'gone through' an experience – a living ground of happenings that are concrete and specific: 'I was at home when I had this thought; the phone rang and it startled me.' One can be deluded or misinterpret one's experience but such delusion or misinterpretation always occurs with reference to a world of experience: the three-eyed monster shows its body, the unseen ghost enters my world. This is why Husserl was so interested in description: to attend to what happens in concrete experiencing as closely as possible and then to describe 'that' as it comes to one in everyday terms. This is not to say that his phenomenological 'method' did not proceed to reflect on what this meant for philosophical purposes, but he wanted such reflections about meaning to be grounded in 'that' and other experiences. There is one last thing I would like to draw out at this stage before thematizing the notions of '*horizon*' and '*the lived body*'. What is most originally announced in experiencing is the 'lifeworld', a holistic stream of happenings that are relational rather than exclusively 'inside' us or 'outside' us. Although my lifeworld is unique in some sense in the way that it is gathered for me, it is also shared with other persons, beings and things. Who knows where my lifeworld begins and yours ends? It is a realm of ambiguity whose meanings are forever negotiated. In a sense, even 'I' am not what I was and I carry this otherness as part of me. And this is where phenomenologically oriented reflection is needed. Language of some kind (even art or dance) is deeply implicated in phenomenologically oriented reflection, in that language provides the distance or space required to reveal something as 'that which stands out' and thus the possibility of relationality with things. The horizons of the lifeworld have multiple meaningful potentials depending on our mode of interaction, and language is an important mode of interaction. To live both actively and meaningfully one may need both the intimacy-making closeness of phenomenological attentiveness to experience, as well as the space-making distance of phenomenologically oriented reflection. Phenomenological process thus means a creative tension of closeness and distance, experience and reflection, never fully rupturing either.

Horizon

Clearly, parts of the unknown exist and live in our lives, even though we often do not know what they are in a thematized sense. Consistent with Husserl, I believe that there is another way that we can conceptualize what has been called the 'unconscious' in a phenomenological way. When Husserl attended phenomenologically to the lifeworld, he noticed that what is given to us in any moment of experiencing is never given to us completely or all at once (Husserl 1970a). Let us start perceptually: spatially, I do not see all parts of the tree even though it gives itself to me as a whole tree – I could not see the branches that I do without the 'more' of the tree that I cannot now see. Similarly, I do not see the tree now in all its temporal moments even though it has a history without which it would now not be what it is. Although not presently known in consciousness, some of these dimensions can become known – by walking around the tree or by visiting the tree at other times. But there are things about the tree which I may never be able to know: the appearance of the tree is connected to a disappearing horizon of spatial and temporal relationships as its background, out of which it is precisely so, now. We can do this thought experiment not just on a per-ceptual phenomenon, but on an emotional experience or on a behavioural phenomenon as well. This logic may have important implications for the phenomena that arise in psychotherapy. The point is that, in relation to a personal life, our experiences and behaviours disappear into an inter-dependent horizon of happenings that may never be able to be fully understood, even if they are the background without which the present moment would not be happening. This raises some strange questions: What is part of 'me' and not part of 'me'? How far do 'I' go out? How far do I go 'back'? The psychoanalytic tradition approached similar questions in different ways: this tradition saw how the effects of earlier times in one's life and one's involvement with intimate others could all live impactfully in one's present emotional, cognitive and behavioural life, even though what it was about these earlier times and involvements may be unknown. But the notion of the phenomenological horizon is more radical than this and asks: what are the ontological boundaries of the breadth and depth of the 'unconscious', if the 'unconscious' is conceived of as *experiencing disappearing into its multiple background horizons*? How far does such an 'unconscious' extend through personal history, others, culture, ecological connections, and even deep down and far out to 'who knows where'? The so-called 'unconscious' is not then 'inside' me: it is continuous with, and in relationship with, the depth, breadth and history of the 'world' – whatever 'worlding' is altogether, beyond our objectifying reductions (Brooke 1991). Within this perspective, there is a large limit to what we can know about 'what is in the dark'. Instead of the quest to make the 'unconscious' conscious, a phenomenological acknowledgement of disappearing horizons would ask a different question: what about the unknown do I need to *encounter* to help me live forward, and what can I trustingly leave and thank as the unknown? Note that I do not even presume here the '*knowing*' of the 'unconscious' as necessary, but rather a certain kind of encounter with the unknown in our lives, the kind of relationship that we have with such 'otherness'. The question of 'what kind of encounter' with 'what kind of unknowns' may be productive for experiential–existential therapy. This question may be partially answered when I consider the next theme of the lived body, and further, when I consider the existential themes that Heidegger encounters in his phenom-enological enquiries into human being and being-in-general.

Lived body

The body grounds our experiencing. It gives us a position in the world from where we see, think, feel and act. But phenomenologically it is often in the background, as the 'from where we live'. In a sense we are engaged 'out there' with things and situations in the world; we are not self-enclosed, but experientially 'there' with all the happenings of the lifeworld. So much so, that we are often lost 'there' or 'then', pre-reflectively caught up in 'the situation with Michael', 'my impending graduation', 'the gentleness of the rain'. And this is often fine. As a Japanese text says: 'not knowing is most intimate'. But in all this, we are countless times called back from 'what we are experiencing' to 'how we are experiencing' – every time we notice a feeling or sensation in a more focal way or even when we are looking for the right words to say. But I go too fast.

Husserl (1989) introduced the idea of the lived body and Merleau-Ponty (1962) took this emphasis forward in interesting ways through his notion of body–subject and body–object. However, in my view, it is the philosopher and psychotherapist Eugene Gendlin (1981, 1991, 1992, 1996, 1997a, 1997b) who has most fruitfully laid out the therapeutic implications of focusing on the felt body as a 'royal road' for encountering the 'kinds of unknowns' that may be productive for experiential–existential therapy. Although Gendlin is sometimes appropriated as belonging to the humanistic and person-centred therapy tradition (he contributed to the development of non-directive therapy in the mid-1950s), and sometimes categorized as enacting a dualistic ontology by some existential thinkers, I do not believe that Gendlin's contributions are best understood within either a humanistic or a dualistic context. How so?

For Gendlin, what the felt body opens up for attention and interaction is not a self-enclosed 'inner world' of experiencing. Rather, it opens up the continuum between what is closest to self (the 'ownness' of having one's experience even before it is reflectively patterned by language) and what I have called the disappearing horizons of lifeworld contexts (even as far as to what can never be known). In his philosophy of 'entry into the implicit' (Gendlin 1991, 1992), Gendlin develops his own experience-near terms for what I believe I am referring to as 'horizon'. He refers to the 'more' of experiencing, 'unseparated multiplicity', the 'implicit', 'how interaction is first' and how bodily felt experience is not first revealed as already formed 'units' but is before the 'patterns' which come to organize them. I understand these terms as indicating an ontological non-separation between 'inner' and 'outer' where what Heidegger called Being is exceedingly presencing to this particular person in 'thrown' and 'gathered' ways that are more than a known pattern. To attempt to make all of such 'unconscious contents' conscious would be like pissing in the wind. So does this mean that our encounter with 'what is not known' is futile and has no therapeutic potential when engaging in the phenomenological rhythm of attention and languaging? No, because one of the gifts of the felt body, as Gendlin articulates it, is that the changing and holistic felt sense that the lived body carries from moment to moment is a highly productive 'messenger', a messenger of what needs to be attended to in one's relationship with 'what is there'. 'What is there' in one's living situation as given by the bodily felt sense contains relevant aspects of one's horizon for living forward in meaningful ways. So the lived body announces what needs to be attended to in the unknown horizon carried in more-than-conceptual ways. It is these more-than-conceptual presences carried in the body that can prefigure our perception, emotion and behaviour. The past is important, in this sense, as it is still living in some way as an inchoate presence; similarly with all the spatialities and othernesses into which I disappear, they are important as they are living inchoately in some way. The next question is: what is it about all this that is therapeutically important? Recall the earlier question: what is it about the unknown that I need to *encounter* in order to help me live forward, and what can I trustingly leave and thank as the unknown? The short answer within this perspective is that the body can tell me what does not feel right, what it is that requires interaction with, even if it cannot immediately tell me how to live forward from that. This is not to say that the lived body is not deeply complicit in helping one to know if the next steps feel credible. But 'how to live forward from that' is a much more complex question, and I believe that this is where we need help from an ontological interpretive framework as we engage with the questions of existence: what it means to be, death, the future, others, ethical claims and a heart that comes from vast mysterious callings.

The ontological concern: existential themes of actualities and possibilities

I would now like to concentrate on the interpretive phase of phenomenological–embodied process. Different interpretive frameworks move phenomenological–embodied process forward in different ways, meaningfully addressing what one is 'in' and providing some meaningful paths forward that speak to one's dilemmas and conflicts about how to live. But 'any narrative' won't do. Many of the interpretive frameworks that have arisen can be seen to be helpful. Thus from the psychoanalytic tradition, one could say, for example, that amongst other things Freud's interpretive framework is centrally guided by the quest to find liveable ways for passion and sexuality to be expressed within society and 'civilization'; that Jung points out the possibility of experiencing one's personal identity as continuous with historical resources far greater than is given in one's personal history – and therefore the possibility of living forward with a sense of belonging to 'energized' resources that one learns to draw on in creative ways. As to Heidegger's (1962) interpretive framework for Being and beings, its value lies in providing an ontology that emphasizes a certain *directionality* for living that is highly compatible with the human realm, between earth and sky. And I also want to briefly indicate why an understanding of such an ontology can assist experiential–existential therapists in offering a 'meeting-with' clients that is ontologically invitational, and why such *ontological invitation* is relevant to psychotherapy.

On his way to being claimed by the thinking of Being, Heidegger attended to the phenomenon of what is given to human beings as human beings. In *Being and Time*, Heidegger (1962) began to articulate a number of fundamental themes which characterize human existence in an ontological way. He focused on the meaning of being human and how this cannot be understood without understanding the relationship between human beings and being-as-a-whole, with and beyond human beings. His characterization of the human condition was refined over the years and took on a particular emphasis in his later works. Mugerauer (2008), for example, is able to read Heidegger with the benefit of hindsight and, as such, gathers together the complexity of his thought with reference to a meditation on the themes of homelessness and homecoming in both ontological and ontic contexts. This interpretation is exciting as I believe that it can provide healthcare disciplines with a much needed understanding of the possibility of well-being as a distinctive phenomenon and one that is not just defined as the absence of illness (Dahlberg *et al.* 2009; Todres and Galvin 2010). However, with reference to Heidegger's relation to psychotherapy, I would like to gather together what I see as two central themes from *Being and Time* that underpin his view of human existence: *the stretching–carrying of both freedom and vulnerability*.

Vulnerability[1]

> Dasein is that being whose being itself is at issue.
>
> (Heidegger 2001: 124)

> That Being which is an *issue* for this entity in its very Being, is in each case mine.
>
> (Heidegger 1962: 67; 42)

The vulnerability that accompanies this existential task is encountered in the finitude which death imposes, the fragilities and needs of the human body, the insecurities of belonging, of being 'thrown' into this circumstance, culture and time. Beyond its specific circumstances, existential vulnerability can speak like a great wound of homelessness. For Heidegger, there is something unavoidable about such existential vulnerability and homelessness if I am to take on a life that is 'mine' to live. It is, however, within the gift of human beings to engage with or flee in many different ways from the existential vulnerabilities that are given with the human realm. We can even walk a path of great refusal, one that attempts to prop up the pretence or the hope of a kind of invulnerability that would deny the existential limits that are given. In my book *Embodied Enquiry: Phenomenological Touchstones for Research, Psychotherapy and Spirituality* (Todres 2007) I consider, through the figure of Narcissus, the many ways that we can become self-enclosed, cutting ourselves off from the relational openness that would reintroduce the vicissitudes of existential vulnerability. But implicit in this story of choice, of encountering or refusing the givens of existential limits, there is something else of ontological depth: a certain kind of freedom.

Freedom

The freedom that is given to human beings is not just the freedom to choose, giving one some meaningful level of personal agency. It is more radical than this. Rather it is a freedom that participates in an *ontological openness* in which self, other and world cannot simply be objectified as 'something' that is settled. Narcissus hoped to possess and grasp himself in a fixated and irrevocable way, thus possessing and grasping others. He refused the ambiguity of the freedom that was offered. However, the freedom of openness is not an absolute freedom, but rather a relational and situated one, a freedom *for* the beings and things of the world, rather than a freedom that is 'above it all': 'Freedom is to be free and open for being claimed by something' (Heidegger 2001: 217). There is a certain soberness in Heidegger and a certain madness in Narcissus, even though both are passionately interested in freedom. However, whereas for Narcissus, it is freedom *from* the wound, for Heidegger, it is freedom *for* the wound: 'Now how is it with consciousness? To stand in the clearing, yet not standing like a pole, but rather sojourn in the clearing and be occupied with things' (Heidegger 2001: 225).

In his sobriety about the truth of suffering and the responsibility to exercise a situated freedom, is Heidegger's analysis suggesting a merely stoical therapeutic implication to us as existential therapists? Does this mean that what we can hope for is to help facilitate our clients to become resolute in authentically facing the vulnerabilities of what has been existentially given, and to facilitate the independent courage to exercise personal freedom and agency in spite of all this? So far so Sartre. No, I believe, with Medard Boss (Boss 1963, 1979), and from encountering the full trajectory of Heidegger's (1971) thought, that the facing of finitude and existential vulnerability does not just leave us with becoming preoccupied with finitude and vulnerability as 'objects' or figural phenomena. Rather, such encounter potentially carries a more foundational gift: the capacity for greater *intimacy* with what appears, in actuality and possibility, with self, others, and world – the human realm, between earth and sky. This willingness to feel and take on an existential level of human vulnerability does not mean that one resigns oneself to specific vulnerabilities in life that can be avoided – it does not mean becoming passive. Rather it means that one is more pointed towards dealing with the kinds of vulnerabilities that are possible to deal with within the existential limits that surround them. Giving ourselves to the existential vulnerabilities of life constitutes a path of embodied intimacy. This can lead to a greater sense of being-at-home in one's body and world, and a greater sense of empathy for others as fellow carriers of existential vulnerability.

So far I have indicated the potential gift of encountering existential vulnerability. But I would also like to indicate something of the gift of encountering existential freedom. The gift of taking on the freedom that is ontologically given constitutes a greater *creativity*, to see the world and situations with a certain freshness and novelty; a freedom for a non-repetitious future, a freedom for possibility. Such freedom is often scary because it is in tension with our need for a certain sense of security. Heidegger's (1962) meditations on *das Man*, the 'They', and authenticity focus on the different ways in which greater freedom of thought, interaction and self-identity are avoided or embraced. He indicates the great cost of avoiding one's 'ownness' and the responsibility for one's life, but also the cost of leaving the 'familiar' in order to take on a life that is uniquely one's own: for this journey of taking on existential freedom confronts us with many ethical and moral issues. Through his articulation of 'care' as an ontological structure, Heidegger points out that human beings are called to be the 'there' of being, to *care* for Being and beings. So this kind of care goes hand in hand with concern about one's own existence as well as that of others, and even about all phenomena in the manner of their appearing. This kind of freedom is thus a 'letting be' kind of love. So the gift of encountering this kind of existential freedom is a kind of freshness of welcome where others and things are not just imprisoned 'as they were' but can become the 'what next' of what they are becoming: the creative welcome of the future. This is not just a gift to others but a gift to myself as the giver of freedom: I myself experience a certain freshness and novelty in my perception and thought.

Coming back to the issue of a client in psychotherapy, these gifts circle towards the heart of the everyday present, and towards the heart of the everyday future. I would thus like to revisit the earlier question about the value of Heidegger's ontology as an interpretive framework that may give a powerful *directional emphasis* to the carrying forward of embodied–phenomenological process.

The action of ontological invitation: a specific kind of directional–interpretive framework

Being the kind of experiential–existential therapist that is informed by the issues pointed to so far, I attend to my client, Sarah, in a way that implicitly includes both an epistemological concern and an ontological concern. The epistemological concern comports me towards the facilitation of the carrying forward of Sarah's phenomenological–embodied process. A focusing-oriented therapist in the tradition of Gendlin (1996) would in many ways recognize what Sarah and I were doing. I help Sarah to come into contact with her bodily felt sense of her situation, 'how things are', 'there', and the quality of the felt senses that may benefit from attention. I provide a space in which Sarah can often pause so that she can bodily sense into something fresh or complex in her present experiencing, something that may want more room or some kind of expression, or even some privacy of being 'let-be'. And I accompany Sarah in her quest to find words that best describe the moment to moment nuances of what she is experiencing now. As the process unfolds, there is an intensifying sense of inclusive welcome from both Sarah and myself to the presencing phenomena that come from 'somewhere' into Sarah's lived body, to a form of language that feels right for it, and by that, into the space between us, even palpably presencing in some way as if 'in the room' or even interacted within my own body. The experiencing changes and the languaging moves forward in unanticipated ways that do not necessarily have a logical or narratively coherent trajectory. Sometimes Sarah sighs with relief as something unknown carried by her in her lived body, in some kind of 'close-to-it' way, differentiates–distances itself into languaged meanings that say something of what it was, and is now carried forward into the meaningful company of her conscious life and projects. She does not necessarily solve 'it' but can now begin to 'care for it' as part of the phenomena and 'beings' for which she is called to be responsible. Informed by my epistemological concern I attempt to be very respectful and facilitative of all the ways she is herself practising phenomenological–embodied process, the rhythm of concrete experiencing and languaging, where implicit horizons of her lifeworld gather in just 'this way', for now, towards the task of living forward.

But what of my ontological concern, my ontological invitation to Sarah? Do I speak to her of death, responsibility, existential guilt, freedom? I very seldom do this unless it comes up thematically as an issue from Sarah herself. So how am I directionally focused? In what sense do I embody an ontological invitation to Sarah that speaks of the potential gifts of existential vulnerability and freedom?

A Heideggerian interpretive framework acts indirectly rather than directly as part of an 'otherness' that is difficult to specify. (We need studies of how different ontological frameworks inform the implicit invitational presence of the therapist, and how such implicit invitational presence acts in the concrete situation of therapeutic interaction.) But there is something that I can say about the shape of my ontological invitation to Sarah. Both Heidegger (1962) and Boss (1963) have written of an 'anticipatory care' that is different from an 'intervening care'. It involves caring for people in their possibilities. So when Sarah speaks about different levels of struggle with intimacy, in addition to just meeting her specifically in those details of her life, I also see 'in' those details their connection to the ontological shape of human possibility as a whole, as briefly indicated in this chapter. As such, any experiential presence or phenomenon is understood as something not to be 'got rid of' but something that is already calling towards greater intimacy and freedom, even if in very frustrated or misunderstood ways. My ontological invitation is a process one: to facilitate ways to be in a relationship of 'welcome curiosity' with whatever experiential phenomenon arises and where it may be calling to (and from). So, in my ontological invitation, I stand specifically in this 'process way' of inviting – of helping to show that any experiencing is connected to a larger movement towards intimacy and freedom. In his writings on psychopathology, Boss (e.g. Boss 1963) demonstrates, through a number of case studies, how so-called 'psychopathological phenomena' can be understood as a truncated attempt to achieve more healthy existential possibilities (for example, the need to 'devour' another can be seen as a truncated attempt to become lovingly at-one-with). Thus, within this hermeneutic framework of an 'ontological invitation', I stand as an 'otherness' that offers not just an interpersonal relationship of potential shared humanity, but also represents, for now, the 'ethical' calling of Being. My presence and care are directed towards this specific experiential phenomenon as it presents itself (without looking suspiciously for anything else there); it helps Sarah notice how the intentionality 'in' the experiential phenomenon can find a place in her personal, embodied and social world, and open up possibilities for her. Together, we are engaged with the 'no simple answer' of how Sarah's emerging 'possibility face' can live in the world. Concretely, in my ontological invitation, I may then often frame my reflections in terms of the 'towards' of the experiencing (for example, the 'something missing' that the sadness reveals). This reveals more of her human world – between sky and earth – the limitations and the possibilities there. Sarah tastes more of the 'freedom–wound' quality of living a human life (Todres 2007); as such, she is released more into the *intimacy* of 'wearing' the we-wound-vulnerability, the anxieties, insecurities and mixed feelings associated with intimacy and finitude. She is also released more into the *novelty* of the freedom–creativity of not trying to reduce being-self or being-other to a certainty or a thing. The horizon of Being can begin to be left as 'horizon' – to be 'let-be' as a mysterious, but supportively beckoning other. At its outer boundaries, a Heideggerian ontological framework thus melds with what has been called 'spiritual' possibilities of a particular kind – the possibility of a non-objectifying experiencing that disappears into a great supportive mystery. This kind of 'unconscious' actively calls not just to 'homeless' lands but to homecomings within the homeless.

Introduction to Gendlin's response

Eugene Gendlin responded to this chapter in the personal style by which he has become well known, where philosophy and reflection emerge freshly in the uniqueness of this embodied moment even as they implicitly carry 'ontological' themes and contexts. This sets the scene for understanding how the 'ontological invitation' spoken of in the above section can only be offered in process ways that are alive between therapist and client, in forms that are not necessarily best captured by 'handed down' philosophical categories, even those as penetrating as Heidegger's.

Gendlin unfolds his response by focusing particularly on the meaning of 'coming home' as a felt experience, how this can occur in the immediacy of a therapeutic relational encounter, and how questions of 'ontology' may most meaningfully be dealt with in therapy in 'process terms' (Gendlin 1997b) rather than in 'philosophical content' terms.

The process and sequence of Gendlin's response

I read your paper when it came, and pondered . . . and took the ponder with me . . . I'll comment in the form of asking you. That way the potential of the ponder won't get lost.

In the last part of the paper you reassert the usual homeless questions. I felt a big gap. No, you can't tack those back on unchanged, after all that. I thought, 'But what *actually does* go there?' Then I took that question with me. But now I'll ask you.

The 1940s and 1950s were still before most people got in touch with their feelings. Young people found their feelings, then their mothers also did. You're not old enough to remember the time. Since about the 1980s people don't think finding their feelings is remarkable anymore.

Before that, people in this culture were inwardly homeless, concretely so every day and especially at night. Questions had not only no thinking– answer but also no felt referent either. Intellectual thinking (philosophy, theory) hasn't caught up with this, but the spirit is different today. Not so haplessly lost.

And now, with the focusing stuff we come actually home, grounded inside, in the body, and the body on the earth and in the big unknown that we're part of and sitting in. But the larger home we don't know although we feel ourselves in it.

So all those ontology questions need to re-emerge different. We're between life and death, with immense pain all around us and some in us, and the beauty of it all – every little leaf and dot of light and shadow shape on the wall, just as before, but? I loved the description (on page 76) and more and more every line. What I mean by 'home' is thick all through here. How different this is in your body from 'clinical distance', from the arguments about 'not gratifying the patient', about restitutional symptoms, or the old type of existential analyst who would argue with her about death, responsibility, existential guilt and freedom, no different from the other kind of analyst arguing with her over being more feminine – no lived felt line into her body from either one. Here, these issues do not now come up in the old homeless general terms; they come up in specific ways in seemingly small but real versions, not even recognizably the same issues.

From Heidegger you pick the one spot in all of *Being and Time*, where he has a human concern along three lines. Made me smile.

You seem to say as therapist you might tack on some ontological question but I feel sure you wouldn't really, or only to ask into her sadness for whatever would come back out of that and lead to those topics. So, I have to ask you how Heidegger's earth and sky stuff and your 'freedom wound' changes when it is 'released into' the real two people process you practise and described up to this spot, rather than into the generalities you have in this last half of this last paragraph. It poses a real ponder: in what new shape are these dimensions unavoidable now?

Note

1 In my interpretation of the notion of freedom–wound where I refer to terms such as anxiety and ownness, I have been inspired by Heidegger's exposition of '*unheimlich*' [etymologically: not-at-home-like, *editors' note*] and '*eigentlich*' [etymologically: own-like, *editors' note*] respectively, though take full responsibility for taking these forward in my own ways.

References

Boss, M. (1963) *Psychoanalysis and Daseinsanalysis*, trans. L. B. Lefebre, New York: Basic Books.

Boss, M. (1979) *Existential Foundations of Medicine and Psychology*, trans. S. Conway and A. Cleaves, New York: Jason Aronson.

Brooke, R. (1991) *Jung and Phenomenology*, London and New York: Routledge.

Dahlberg, K., Todres, L. and Galvin, K. (2009) 'Lifeworld-led healthcare is more than patient-led care: the need for an existential theory of well-being', *Medicine, Health Care and Philosophy*, 12 (3): 265–271.

Gendlin, E. T. (1981) *Focusing*, New York: Bantam.

Gendlin, E. T. (1991) 'Thinking beyond patterns: body, language and situations', in B. Den Ouden and M. Moen (eds) *The Presence of Feeling in Thought*, New York: Peter Lang.

Gendlin, E. T. (1992) 'The primacy of the body, not the primacy of perception', *Man and World*, 25 (3–4): 341–353.

Gendlin, E. T. (1996) *Focusing-Oriented Psychotherapy: A Manual of the Experiential Method*, New York: Guilford Press.

Gendlin, E. T. (1997a) *Experiencing and the Creation of Meaning*, Evanston, IL: Northwestern University Press.

Gendlin, E. T. (1997b) *A Process Model*, New York: The Focusing Institute. This revision of a 1981 version is also available since 1998 at http://www.focusing.org/process.html, in a version with several typographical corrections.

Giorgi, A. (1970) *Psychology as a Human Science: A Phenomenologically Based Approach*, New York: Harper and Row.

Giorgi, A. (ed.) (1985) *Phenomenology and Psychological Research*, Pittsburgh, PA: Duquesne University Press.

Heidegger, M. (1962 [1927]) *Being and Time*, trans. J. Maquarrie and E. Robinson, Oxford: Blackwell.

Heidegger, M. (1971) *Poetry, Language, Thought*, trans. A. Hofstadter, New York: Harper and Row.

Heidegger, M. (2001) *Zollikon Seminars*, M. Boss (ed.), trans. F. Mayr and R. Askay, Evanston, IL: Northwestern University Press.

Husserl, E. (1970a) *Logical Investigations*, 2 vols, trans. J. N. Findlay, New York: Humanities Press.

Husserl, E. (1970b) *The Crisis of European Sciences and Transcendental Phenomenology: An Introduction to Phenomenological Philosophy*, trans. D. Carr, Evanston, IL: North Western University Press.

Husserl, E. (1989) *Ideas Pertaining to a Pure Phenomenology and to a Phenomenological Philosophy. Second Book*, trans. R. Rojcewicz and A. Schuwer, Dordrecht: Kluwer.

May, R. (1996) *Heidegger's Hidden Sources*, trans. G. Parkes, London: Routledge.

Merleau-Ponty, M. (1962) *The Phenomenology of Perception*, trans. C. Smith, London: Routledge.

Mugerauer, R. (2008) *Heidegger and Homecoming: The Leitmotif in the Later Writings*, Toronto: University of Toronto Press.

Parkes, G. (ed.) (1987) *Heidegger and Asian Thought*, Honolulu: University of Hawaii Press.

Todres, L. (2007) *Embodied Enquiry: Phenomenological Touchstones for Research, Psychotherapy and Spirituality*, Basingstoke: Palgrave Macmillan.

Todres, L. and Galvin, K. T. (2010) '"Dwelling-mobility": an existential theory of well-being', *International Journal of Qualitative Studies on Health and Well-being*, 5: 3. (Online.)

Chapter 6

Palpable existentialism

An interview with Eugene Gendlin

Greg Madison and Eugene Gendlin

Introduction

My interview with Eugene Gendlin forms the centrepiece of this chapter. To frame the dialogue, I offer my own introduction to Gendlin's thought, with special emphasis on the experiential concept of *carrying forward*, followed by my concluding remarks about an experiential form of existential therapy. Although Gendlin agrees with much of the introduction and conclusion, he would want to derive it all philosophically, highlighting for the reader the actual process of concept formation and other specific aspects of his philosophy.

Gendlin's way from philosophy to psychotherapy

Gendlin's orientation to philosophy, and to life, seems to me to involve a mingling of the constantly inquisitive with the ubiquitously sceptical. At university he found that he could take up the vocabulary of any philosophical system and from within that worldview he could translate his own concerns into that language. His philosophical ideas could be expressed across many systems without losing what he wanted to say; his points were more than the language of any particular discourse. This is because he found a way to remain grounded in his own experience, allowing him to generate new concepts while also checking alternative theories and ideas with what he knows from his own living.

Gendlin realized that he was doing a kind of phenomenology, but a phenomenology that came *back to* experience after it formulated something *from* experience. He was discovering that there is a kind of unformulated experience that can be pointed to – *an experience that is not itself* just another formulation but implicitly includes everything that we have previously formulated and lived. There is *something* coming freshly that is more than set content and symbols (something that is not itself a 'thing'). Gendlin was beginning to formulate the concretely felt *relation* between experience and concepts.

Gendlin imagined that psychotherapy would be a unique place to investigate how symbols such as words, images, phrases, or concepts arise freshly from unformulated implicit experience. He joined Carl Rogers's counselling centre in Chicago, but there he found that therapists did not understand his philosophical inquiry. Gendlin was interested in 'pre-conceptual feelings', not just talk or defined emotions. He did not deny that the content of what a client says can be meaningful and revealing, but he insisted that words alone are never the sole avenue to the meaning that each person actually lives. Gendlin found that the extent to which clients refer directly to their bodily-felt experience during sessions correlates with 'successful' therapy outcomes as defined by various measures including the client's own evaluation (Gendlin *et al.* 1968). Clients who can pause and 'check' their words and ideas with the body sense of their issue remain grounded in their actual experience – they sense a bodily-felt response when they express how they really live a particular situation. Gendlin developed the Focusing (1981) instructions in an attempt to assist more people to gain direct access to their lived meanings in this bodily-felt way.

Gendlin's Focusing is a special kind of thinking that brings to awareness the ongoing *process of symbolizing*. He emphasizes the ground of thinking as much as the explicit fruit that it bears: 'The process of forming and thinking is never limited by the possibilities we formulate. Those are only products from it' (Gendlin, personal communication). In my view Gendlin's writing allows words to acquire novel meanings in order to point the reader to this process level where new concepts can be formulated from experience.

Gendlin's emerging philosophy

The comments that I offer here can only present some results from the philosophy Gendlin has worked out in two long texts (Gendlin 1997a, 1997b) and many articles. Gendlin's philosophy continues the existential tradition of phenomenological attention to concrete human living with his fundamental reconsideration and direct employment of the body. Human embodiment was crucial in the philosophy of Merleau-Ponty (1962). Already for Sartre (1956) and Heidegger (1962) *the body* is not just the object that appears in the mirror. It is not just a fragile machine that medicine repairs, an inert lump for the sculptor to mould, a computer that needs upgrading.

In addition, for Gendlin the body is not a passive derivative of culture – Gendlin's conception of the body is always *more than* these models of the body: the living body *is interaction*. We *feel* our life events because our bodies are a *continuous experiencing of* the whole situation that we are living. We are not only taking in information through five senses and then computing that information in the mainframe of the brain. The whole body *is* interaction with its environment in an intricate way. This back and forth being–world interaction is so radically characteristic of 'body' that *to talk of a separate 'body' and 'environment' leads us into familiar but mistaken assumptions about living.*

For Gendlin 'environment' does not mean just what is 'out there', 'external'. Gendlin says that we *are* body–environment interaction, a vastly larger system than the body of medical science. This echoes Merleau-Ponty and others in the existential tradition: 'We are both subject and object, where the subject *is* his body, his world, and his situation, by a sort of exchange' (Merleau-Ponty 1964: 72).

I see Gendlin's practice of Focusing as offering phenomenological access to the sentience of the world, living right now *as* unique bodies. Attending to this sentience can generate a murky, difficult to describe *felt sense*, usually in the middle area of the body. Such a felt sense gives us information about our living in actual situations because life is not formed out of isolated internal objects or bits of perception: 'We humans live from bodies that are self-conscious of situations. . . . "Conscious", "self", and "situations" are not three objects with separate logical definitions' (Gendlin 1999: 233). Situations *are* body–environment process, and direct access to this is therapeutically vital for the client, because it offers a tangible *sense* that can *unfold* step by step into novel less restrictive ways of living these situations. It is this process of new bodily *unfolding* that we will explore further in the interview below.

As existential psychotherapists we also stress the importance of embodiment, yet often without an awareness of *how* to pay attention to the body. We struggle to translate philosophical insights into moment-by-moment sensitivities in our sessions with clients (Madison 2001). A felt sense typically forms in the trunk area, as an unclear but tangible sensation. *If attended to directly where it forms in the body, a felt sense can respond with new meanings confirmed with shifts in the bodily feeling.*

Carrying forward

I would say that the practice of Focusing allows each of us to explore the function of experiential *symbolizing* that inspired Gendlin's research into psychotherapy. Through attention to the felt sense we witness how implicit feeling generates explicit content, and how experience *carries itself* further. This movement is referred to as a felt shift. The feeling in the body changes physically when a symbol touches the meaning that's implied: for example, a tight chest loosens and becomes warm. We may feel the desire to insist on an explicit truth that is forever pinned down, but this seems at odds with the nature of felt experiencing that grounds human truth. The fact that human knowledge is not final, but always leads to further steps that can change it, is to be expected and welcomed. The contemporary western tendency to concretize is a ubiquitous obstacle to remaining open to phenomenological *process*.

We can of course read theory or logic into process post hoc and this can be helpful in highlighting aspects of the phenomenon that might have been overlooked. But this must now be employed with a metaphoric pointing towards what is, fundamentally, a process interacting with its own situations of people, places, culture and the whole environment. In 'process' there is no 'entity–self' separate from environmental interaction; but there is a personal *responsiveness* that is a unique opening upon the world of experience.

Carrying forward can help us think and act creatively, so it is obviously not just adaptation to the existing environment: 'Living bodies have a holistic life-forward direction that is usually called "adaptive" as if they only fit themselves to external requirements. But in fact the living systems create new and more intricate meanings and actions' (Gendlin 2003: 113). Gendlin was eventually convinced that 'the ongoing bodily experiencing has its own inherent life-forwarding implying. The little steps that arise at the edge are creative, imaginative, and always in some positive direction' (p. 113). Clearly the definitions of 'life-forward' and 'positive' cannot be reduced to cultural specifics. In his discussion paper, 'Planks', Gendlin writes:

> Postmodernism and existentialism rightly questioned all concepts, codes, and orthodoxies, but found nothing else. There seemed to be no human nature because only explicit human forms were considered, and of course these vary among the cultures. . . . There is a human nature but it does not consist of these or those conceptual or cultural forms. It is not originated by culture nor by arbitrary self-making. These greatly elaborate but do not create it.
>
> (Gendlin 2008: 6)

Carrying forward, then, 'is the characteristic continuity we experience when new sentences and then new concepts articulate and explain what we had understood only implicitly' (Gendlin 2008: 4). Words that arise from a felt sense already *imply* all the thinking up to that point, as well as the whole situation that the felt sense is about. When direct experience arises as a 'datum', it brings the whole experience with it, bodily. When a confusing formulation in a theory finally clarifies, the verbal expressions that facilitate the *becoming clear* happen simultaneously with the 'tight-confused' feeling in the stomach releasing into a new space in the body. In that space the person can now explicate many strands of the theory that have not yet been formulated explicitly. The person is no longer standing on top of the theory simply reiterating its tenets, but is now standing on the ground from which the theory was developed. I am convinced that this conception of human process has implications for how we actually practise existential therapy and how we *understand* that practice.

Through the evocative impact of this existential sensing, the *experiential–existential* stance (Madison 2010) offers a tangible touchstone that may be missing from more conceptual forms of existential therapy. Sensitive attending to what shifts the body-sense and what doesn't can result in making language work *for us* rather than the reverse, at times evoking quite poetic expressions in order to carry implicit experience into a saying that is 'true' in the new sense of carrying forward.

My view of Gendlin's contribution, sketched out above, sets the stage for the edited interview below. The interview took place in Gendlin's home outside Spring Valley, New York, over three hours on Thursday afternoon 20 August 2009.

Interview with Eugene Gendlin

Gendlin: I want to say two things about the body. We start with the ordinary body that's sitting here in the chair and then sense that body from the inside. So it's not like there are two different bodies. In German they have this convenient distinction between *Körper* and *Leib*, and by *Leib* they go on abstractly without letting you know it's the same body as *Körper*. So in German I always use *Körper* because it helps me emphasize that this body right here is the one that we feel from the inside. It's not some other phenomenological invention. And I show how and where in the body to sense. The second point I want to make about the body is that we can also *think* from the body as we sense it from inside and this is a superior and different kind of thinking, both logical concepts and experience. The concepts in my philosophy come from this new kind of thinking but most words are still imbued with the old meanings. So the words end up saying the opposite of what you really want to mean because the vocabulary of the concepts is so traditionally within that model of separate cognitive units, each one is itself and they relate only by external relations.

Madison: So instead of being restricted to only the explicit existing meanings, there is a subtler body process. It moves in an organized, not arbitrary way, and this process can have practical outcomes.

Gendlin: Yes. When you pay attention to your bodily-felt sense there is movement there. In fact the very coming of a felt sense is already a carrying forward. A felt sense has to be distinguished from emotions; a body sense of a situation is not an emotion. A felt sense has a life forward direction. This is mysterious when you think in the old way, in terms of 'what is', which assumes entities, unit contents. In my philosophy there is no just 'is', there is always process. When you think in terms of process it's perfectly obvious that *all* living, even a single cell, has an organized *forward*. It implies its next step. When you contact some sense in the body that doesn't feel good, for example, present difficulties that come from childhood, they are not *only* stuck. They have a *forward movement* also. When you find that old experience in the body, you understand it from its viewpoint. Given how things were then, it was moving in a life forward way. So we say: 'Oh, of course. And no wonder I'm still doing this irrational thing.' Or: 'No wonder I'm afraid of that situation.' When we feel it in that mode, the old stuckness has already changed and now implies new ways; it dissolves into becoming part of something larger.

Madison: The life forward that you're talking about, what actually *is* that? What is it that lives forward through us?

Gendlin: Well, you say 'what *is* that?' For me there is no simple 'is', rather an is*ing*. There is always also an implying, not only what occurs. Everything implies *and* occurs. In the new model, occurring generates a new implying. 'What lives us' is like saying where does living come from? It comes from *under*. The living that I know from the inside comes from under, but I can feel it coming. I can distinctly feel it, and when I have no energy I can feel the '*not*-coming'. Then I try to find and appreciate why not, so then it can come. As long as I'm still alive it keeps coming and forgiving all the things I did wrong, and makes me all over again each minute. It's a very distinct experience but it surely isn't a separate clear 'what'. I can sense further down than I can understand, further than a felt sense because a felt sense is already a datum, already a 'something', so it goes lower than that and I don't know how far it goes.

Madison: Can we go any further with trying to describe this?

Gendlin: Well, pure description of anything isn't really possible. Philosophy started 3000 years ago with the realization that anything can be described in many ways. Observing and describing doesn't settle any issue. In my view, any description carries forward; describing is a further forming. But okay, can we say more about it? Well, there's a universe. And the universe has us in it. Some people seem to think about the universe as though it didn't have any people in it. But the only one we know about has us in it as well as dogs and horses and flies and everything else. So *that* universe is what we're talking about with this 'under' – I don't know what else to say except that it's very palpable. But my 'don't-know' is not an agnostic don't know. It's not a religious don't-know either but it's closer to that because it's a very palpable universe for me, but only where I fade into it. I can't claim how far it goes or what it's all about.

Madison: So where you fade into it, and I'm tempted to say 'where it lives through you' . . .

Gendlin: It lives me, yes.

Madison: Okay, so when you have the experience of something carrying forward, that is an experience of 'this living through you'?

Gendlin: It's certainly an experience of the living. Of course the living happens through us, but that's already hypothesizing two separate entities. This larger 'it' lives through 'us', but you don't gain anything by making it something different, something over there. That way it's less. You can call it God or the universe or the unknown, or the endless or anything you want to call it. Often, to save myself from false reverence, I call it 'God or whatever the fuck that should be called'. This takes care of any sort of over-reverence. I mean I'm reverent of it but not the way you would be in front of a king or a dictator. I don't believe in that kind of treading softly. If it makes you smaller and weaker, it's not right.

Madison: So is there a way of saying 'that' without referring to an 'it'?

Gendlin: There should be. A better way is to say that it's palpable to me, and there the 'it' crept in again. All the words bring the current model of little separate unit things. There's nothing wrong with saying 'it' if we refer to it via the body. Then it's palpable and not separated. The 'palpable' body experience I won't give up.

Madison: So are you saying 'it's a palpable *knowing* of some kind?' How can we talk about this 'palpable' process?

Gendlin: Well, how can we talk about this thing that I mean by 'something palpable' without seeming to know more than we really know? When we talk about 'what is a person' I say the same kind of thing, I like to say 'A person is . . .' and then any way you finish that sentence will be wrong. Don't finish the sentence! And yet a person *is*, persons are perfectly obvious to me. I am one, I'm looking at one, it's clear to me that you're in there coming out and if you don't like 'in there', it doesn't matter how we say it, we're sitting here palpably and I'm feeling you. Sartre was lovely on that. There's no way you can't feel someone looking at you, it's totally different from a chair or a statue or any other thing. This 'looking-at-you' has the palpable 'what is a person', to me. And then if you want me to claim that I *know* what that is, then the word 'know' has to have a more experiential meaning.

Madison: When that palpable feeling is carried forward, it moves . . .

Gendlin: When you say 'feeling' it can be misunderstood as a little subjective unit inside a person. Of course I mean a feeling, but for me feeling is a verb, it's a sequence, and it generates time. The feeling isn't a thing here that's feeling something else over there. Every life process, no matter how primitive, is some kind of environmental interaction. And by interaction I mean something like what Heidegger meant by being-in-the-world, except he didn't have a body. He was working away from the old model where all these things are entities either subjective inside us or objective outside us. He said we are (what I call it) 'interaction' with Being. I say we are always already living in our real situations with our bodies, whatever we may know or say. Interaction is first; then you can also have two different things derived from it. So feeling is an interaction process.

Madison: When your body releases because you've said something accurately enough, that is an example of carrying forward: shifting, typically feeling more expansive and less constrictive in some way, lighter – and that difference is palpable.

Gendlin: Yes, absolutely.

Madison: So, it's almost as if the '*it-that-is-ising*', knows the direction. Almost like it's pushing for a particular way and when it gets it, it's a bodily relief.

Gendlin: Yes, absolutely.

Madison: How does it know the way?

Gendlin: Well, it's very complicated [laughter] and I'm not finished with it either. I don't know if one can get finished with that question, the way I know you mean it. But first of all let's say it's an *ising* and that's how it is an *it* if it is an *it* at all. So it's not the old kind of 'it' because it is a process, an 'ing'. And how does this ising know how to push for the right thing for me?

Madison: Yes.

Gendlin: It's stubborn all right. It won't move till something right comes, but it doesn't have that already formed. And when you get a little step right, it implies further. It makes a process of steps you can trust. I wouldn't trust any one spot, except that each spot along that process is necessary so that you can get to the further ones.

Madison: Yet *it* seems to know a direction.

Gendlin: Yes. But 'direction' isn't something painted on the ground, like north south. The direction of this funny process may change and circle around and go all ways, and what's really clear is that life is really like that. So it's not just this mysterious universe living through me. For example, I suggest something to a client but it's worthless until something comes from the client that corrects me: 'Well no, rather . . .'. When what I'm pointing to comes back directly from there, then we're moving. Until that happens *even* my good suggestions aren't worth much. And knowing that allows me to make many suggestions because my client typically knows that I mean the suggestion as a question 'Could it be something like this?' If I've been heard and nothing comes in response, I drop it. It doesn't move us in the life forward direction now.

But in another sense you were asking something mysterious that I can't answer. The simplest kind of life already is this implying and your question means that. You call it 'direction'. I can explain how implying works. For example, why my theory 'knows' the next steps before I can even think the damn thing. The living interaction process always implies ahead of anything formulated. The *ising* process knows what I should think. I can sense what I haven't gotten to yet. But if you want me to ask why the living process can be like that, then you're at some border. And that goes off into religious territory or if you don't need to assert that, then we would stop right there.

Madison: And I'm really fascinated by that.

Gendlin: But let's not treat it as a *not*-knowing. Let's take how we directly find it here, and make our concepts from that. Then we know a lot. 'Direction' is like that. When I have a conflict between this *or* that, I check inside and I say 'I don't have to get torn up between this *or* that, because I know what I want. *I want the right thing.*' I don't know what it is yet, but I'm no longer split; I'm all whole again. The process is restored and can move on. Processing that way is much more likely to let something better come.

Madison: We're calling it 'this thing' now, and you talk about it as though it is an *ising* of particular values.

Gendlin: I would say that the values are derivatives from this process. The ancient values are derivative from this process. The kind of justice or mercy, that you really believe in, end up coming only *from here*. So I wouldn't say that the process is in accord with values, I'd say that values are in accord with it.

Madison: I agree. To say it's in accord with values makes it sound as though it's governed by the values that we have already up on the shelf.

Gendlin: Yes, right, as though the values are there first and it matches them.

Madison: Yes, I would say that it has *valuing* implicit in it.

Gendlin: Yes, so now the question is what does 'has implicit in it' mean. Of course there is valu*ing* if life is always organizing *itself* forward. That's what we then abstract and call valuing.

Madison: Yes, it's not neutral. *Ising* has a specific kind of interest, that's why it has a directionality.

Gendlin: Yes, if we take your concept 'directionality' as 'pointing to whatever it does'.

Madison: It doesn't just say 'oh anywhere' and take you into a dark depression as easily as towards more expansive living.

Gendlin: No, exactly.

Madison: So it has implied in it a kind of valuing, a kind of concern or interest.

Gendlin: Absolutely, and far superior to the culture, any culture. But don't abstract some thin strand from it. Some people might want to stick this *ising* on a hook and call it 'survival' and everyone will say oh that's what we always said, 'it's self-preservation', but that's only a thin abstraction.

Madison: So implicit in the directionality of the carrying forward is the experience of life valuing itself.

Gendlin: Absolutely, something like living for it's own sake or living for living is clearly there. But 'valuing *itself*' sounds like it values nothing else. With philosophy we can turn that around, and see all valuing coming from the process of living which is interaction with everything. We have to break out of that old model where living is just inside a body-structure. That would be much less, just some *thing*. I'm often concerned with getting a certain result in a particular situation; I care about the situation rather than about me. Then I am annoyed when *it* doesn't care about that, only about *me* and *my* quality. It says, 'You're not in the right mode. The situation would go better if you were.' But *I'm* never sure of that. It annoys me that it doesn't care about that situation like I do [laughter]. I try to split the situation off from me, but of course it cannot be separate from me. So yes to your question, it has its own broader purpose.

Madison: Yes. Like it has its own self-interest.

Gendlin: Yes.

Madison: It's an experience of life's self-interest but not as an isolated entity and not abstract as though life was concerned about itself *in general*.

Gendlin: Right, not like that. It's concerned with each creature, and that's so peculiar because you've got trillions of insects and each one is a whole story. But on the other hand there is also this *interplay* with the society, the community, the relationship or the pair, more than an individual. That context is bigger than the individual but the individual is also bigger than that context. Only individuals think and feel beyond what the society already teaches. You're always more than the relationship, but the relationship is also more than you. If you start to talk about your unclear issue to another person, if that's a particular kind of person, you're going to feel and think more than you could alone. But it will still be from you; in addition to that, any useful content you get from that person is something else. You and the relationship are both bigger than each other.

Madison: So if I apply what we've been saying to the topic of 'choice', for example, I think that your perspective is that choice is something that is sensed from the inside?

Gendlin: Yes, everyone can find this bodily experience. Of course we also need to know about the particular topic. We need to be aware of the cultural warnings that we might not feel. We need to develop other dimensions of being human, if we are weak in some of them. But in any situation, if we also attend inside the body we find the unclear implicit experience, many steps and soon a whole field of detail. Without that we cannot make good choices. With it doesn't *guarantee* a choice that we're happy with later; but it's much more likely than without it.

Madison: So me as the person sat here in the way that I concretize myself, I can say that I chose X, and yet the '*ising*' through me, if I give it attention, beckons me in a different direction.

Gendlin: Yes, it might.

Madison: So in a sense it has its deeper meaning and in a sense it challenges the 'me' I identify with. So when we talk about choice and values, it depends upon where it's coming from. I can choose to ignore that *ising*, and pay the price of that or I can choose to follow that direction and the step-by-step unfolding that comes from it, and potentially pay a different price.

Gendlin: Yes, but I would reverse the order. When you set yourself up separately and call choosing between them the 'choice', you're cutting yourself off from the implicit experience. I would want *first* to have *both* values in interplay with that deeper sense. I don't think that is an either/or. When you are in touch with it, the process lets you know much better what 'you' want. So there is a back and forth between the process and what we first thought we preferred. They very often come out together. But if they don't, *then* we may have to deal with that. But I wouldn't say you ever want just the one *or* the other. I would always have liked to be able to say 'I want whatever's right', which is a lot like the old tradition of 'whatever is God's will, I'll do that'. But there are times that God says, 'No buddy, you can't just shove it off on me. You're on the scene and you know what's going on. You've got to make the choice.' But we can make it in interaction with this *ising* process.

Madison: So can you imagine a concrete situation where a person might go through the *ising* process, the carrying forward, and get to a point where they can see the sense of what life wants for them, and yet there's another value that was also implicit in that whole process and that makes the person choose to do something else?

Gendlin: Well there's a worse case, that's when I can't manage to do it. That's a much worse case, and a frequent kind. In many situations we can't work up the energy or the courage, or find little possible steps to do, so we just suffer. A typical case is when a person is in a bad relationship that they can't imagine themselves without, so even if they get to the point of feeling the rightness of leaving they still stay. Then others say that was the person's choice. When they say 'choice' they assume we can just do either. But I know you are asking if there could be *another* value and yes, there could be another value. You want to retain choice? Okay [laughter].

Madison: I want to say that even to pay attention and to be guided by this process is itself a choice and a valuing.

Gendlin: Yes, I have to agree with you. But if one *first* 'chooses' some kind of interplay back and forth with the experiential level, then I can respect another choice. And I don't think that either the process or just going ahead will guarantee a good result.

Madison: And because it's an unfolding process, some of the sensing of the process is always an implicit sensing of the rightness of when to act.

Gendlin: Yes, and that's tough for some people. It's not automatic that people who sense this *ising* also sense the timing, especially if the timing is sensitive. Another thing is that some people never find a time for action. They always examine it some more and have great insights and never *do* anything. . . . *You would think* that people who experience the unfolding couldn't miss how action and timing are a part of it. But many people do. We're only at the beginning of this new kind of thinking and all these new ways (is my excuse). So don't be discouraged, it's very exciting. There are all these loose ends to it. And you've kept the importance of choice, yes.

Madison: And it's absolutely clear to me that this is a different version of choice from the therapist who challenges their client 'Well you have a choice here, X or Y'. That's totally different because that's only the beginning of a whole process into the implicit.

Gendlin: You can almost be sure that in those terms, X and Y, that neither of them is right at this moment.

Madison: If one of them were right the client would probably have already . . .

Gendlin: Yes, it would smoothly have happened already. We need not waste time between two wrong choices; we can spend it with how to get to another possibility. Sartre posed, *either* joining the resistance *or* caring for his grandmother. But abandoning her or shirking the fight are both wrong. In the intricate detail of any real situation there are endless possibilities. Perhaps you stay home and make it a safe house. Your grandmother might pass undetected to deliver messages. Traditional ethics classes teach students to be insensitive to evil, spending half the class time trying to feel that they really could torture someone, and half the time trying to feel that they could allow innocent people to be blown up, instead of knowing that there have to be better ways, more detailed than either of those. When they are both wrong, just say 'I want something else' and then you can begin to sense for new possibilities. Many more choices open up from the bodily living in the situation.

Madison: So what is the difference between what you've been saying here and Rogers's self-actualizing tendency?

Gendlin: Well his idea was more general and broad and without any detail. I don't have anything against it unless you stop with it.

Madison: I'm also thinking that it depends partly upon what we mean by 'self'.

Gendlin: Oh yes, the self has to be derived *from* the self-actualization process. I'm constantly reversing that order. Don't start with the entity. If you have to know *what* your self is before you can find self-actualization, then forget it. The 'self' is a self-responding process, not an entity or a what. Experience is always already the process. Then we can make entities from it. We are the carrying forward process. If there is such a thing as self-actualization then you would have to find it *in you*.

Madison: And that's a particular experience of self. I'm thinking about the first part of what you said – that you turn towards your*self*.

Gendlin: Okay, yes. You find yourself already feeling some way and responding to it and then talking to yourself about it. So what part of all of that do you want to be the self? The whole process of feeling and finding and then explicating, that's all the self? I could agree with that.

Madison: When you talk about the life forward direction you talk about it as a *positive* direction. Can you say what you mean by positive in this context?

Gendlin: The process expands what we mean by positive. You can't just walk up to it and claim that it's positive. *It's* going to change what you mean by positive. In the new kind of thinking we let our concepts have their logic, but we *also* let them refer to the process which is not yet formulated. It is much more than what each culture separates out and emphasizes. It includes you and me and our actual situations, and a lot of things like how the light reflects and how colours are, so it's much broader than what positive and negative mean in any culture or as far as we've individually developed.

Madison: When I read your phrase 'positive life forward direction', I read that as meaning it's positive in the way that the felt shift just *feels* positive, lighter, expansive, a relief, energizing. It's positive in the way that those qualities feel positive.

Gendlin: Yes, but not *just* feelings inside, we are interactions in the world. Just feelings and qualities seem to leave us stuck in some phenomenological subjectivity. I'd rather say it *is* this way than it *feels* this way. I'm already in something larger and subtler and lighter, I'm already *there*, responsive to fresh details and more capable of perceiving possibilities. If I turn that into a feeling, then I've lost it again. Just 'feeling lighter' seems to lose all that. I know you didn't mean just inside. If anyone after experiencing it prefers the opposite then let's hear from them, because I've never met anyone who did.

Madison: Yes, that's an important point. So much of what you are saying is really empirical. We've done this over and over and this is how it is.

Gendlin: Absolutely. It's very empirical. It's *extremely* empirical for me. I love theory and I love philosophy but it's extremely empirical. Everything depends upon you actually *doing* it.

Madison: I want to make a distinction between what you're saying and the imposition of what I would call a false optimism or positivity. I experience rosy optimism as oppressive because it covers up my actual experience.

Gendlin: Oh yes, I recognize what you mean. When I'm trying to hold onto something real please don't give me something 'pink', because then I'll lose what's really a hard-won move forward. Another aspect is how this process gets burdened with theological concepts. I'm not against theology but I am against hanging heavy weights onto a process that doesn't need that. And, just optimism is an insult to anyone who suffers. But just pessimism is an insult to life. I think life itself has meaning; the person looking at me has meaning.

Madison: Yes, but it depends on how we use the word *meaning*. Through the falling away of received meanings and the loosening of life assumptions we can find a vast open space. If I ask myself 'What is the meaning of this open process?' I have asked myself in a way that presumed there is meaning. The question itself already biases me to try to set it explicitly. How can I ask that question without embedding a bias towards meaning?

Gendlin: Yes. I don't blame you for not wanting to use the word 'meaning'. But every word can block what one is trying to show. One needs new phrases in which the word cannot mean the old thing. You can retrieve a word by fresh phrases that arise from experience. This *ising*, this energy flow, this life producing, has more meaning than I can define. In that phrasing, 'meaning' can no longer mean something defined. We do, I believe, need the sustaining of more than we are in control of and often that juncture is crucial. I can remember that I don't have to do it all alone. There is a huge difference between saying life is meaningless, and saying the meanings fall away because you're in touch with more than defined meaning. To me those are almost opposite senses of 'meaning'. When you sense the palpable meaning, *then* the other meanings can fall away. But don't take the other meanings away from people; just losing them won't give them the open space.

Concluding remarks

Through our exchanges in the interview above, it is clear that there is much affinity between Gendlin's thinking and existential practice. However, as existential therapists, we are only now beginning to explore how Gendlin's views challenge and enhance our practice. In the interview above, it is clear to me that Gendlin's comments can be applied to the moment-by-moment practice of existential therapy. In my understanding, the carrying forward of experience is more intricate than stand-alone psychological theory or stage models and therefore guides clients, therapists and supervisors along a path that opens out and expands in unpredictable ways (Madison 2009). The therapist, grounded in and listening from their own felt sensing, in turn invites the client to notice over and over again their palpable body in order to check the rightness of words, concepts, interventions, and interpretations. Felt sensing interweaves with storytelling, challenging, explicit relational moments, and all else that happens in therapy. Gendlin's philosophy and his comments in the interview above thus offer the foundation for a contemporary form of existential practice, an *experiential*–existential therapy that carries us forward in terms of offering a holistic real relationship, when much of therapy seems to be thinning into technique and objectification.

References

Gendlin, E. T. (1981) *Focusing*, New York: Bantam.
Gendlin, E. T. (1997a) *Experiencing and the Creation of Meaning: A Philosophical*

and Psychological Approach to the Subjective, Evanston, IL: Northwestern University Press.

Gendlin, E. T. (1997b) *A Process Model*, New York: The Focusing Institute. Also available at http://www.focusing.org/process.html.

Gendlin, E. T. (1999) 'A new model', *Journal of Consciousness Studies*, 6 (2–3): 232–237.

Gendlin, E. T. (2003) 'Beyond postmodernism: from concepts through experiencing', in R. Frie (ed.) *Understanding Experience: Psychotherapy and Postmodernism*, London: Routledge.

Gendlin, E. T. (2008) 'Planks', Unpublished web discussion paper.

Gendlin, E. T., Beebe, III, J., Cassens, J., Klein, M. and Oberlander, M. (1968). 'Focusing ability in psychotherapy, personality, and creativity', in M. M. Shlien (ed.) *Research in Psychotherapy: Vol. III*, Washington, DC: American Psychological Association.

Heidegger, M. (1962 [1927]) *Being and Time*, trans. J. R. Macquarrie and E. Robinson, Oxford: Blackwell.

Madison, G. (2001) 'Focusing, intersubjectivity, and therapeutic intersubjectivity', *Review of Existential Psychology and Psychiatry*. 26 (1): 3–16.

Madison, G. (2009) 'Evocative supervision', in E. van Deurzen and S. Young (eds) *Existential Perspectives on Supervision*, London: Palgrave.

Madison, G. (2010) 'Focusing on existence: five facets of an experiential–existential model', *Person-Centred and Experiential Psychotherapies*, 9 (3): 189–204.

Merleau-Ponty, M. (1962) *Phenomenology of Perception*, trans. C. Smith, New York: Humanities Press.

Merleau-Ponty, M. (1964) *Primacy of Perception*, trans. C. W. Cogg, Evanston, IL: Northwestern University Press.

Sartre, J.-P. (1956 [1943]) *Being and Nothingness*, trans. H. E. Barnes, New York: Philosophical Library.

Chapter 7

Applied existential psychotherapy

An experiential psychodynamic approach

Betty Cannon

Introduction

It has often seemed to me that existential therapy lacks adequate experiential interventions to allow clients to move through the kinds of changes that existential philosophy regards as possible – or to work with embodied consciousness in a way that truly does justice to the lived body as understood by existential philosophers. Over the past 20 years I have been developing and teaching an approach that combines existential philosophy with techniques and theoretical understanding drawn from experiential therapy and contemporary psychoanalysis.

This approach, which is now called Applied Existential Psychotherapy™ (AEP), often facilitates deep level bodily experienced change. AEP cannot be called psychoanalytic because it does not use interpretation or free association as primary techniques – and it does not accept the concept of the unconscious as a determining realm apart from consciousness.[1] Yet it is psychodynamic in working with the childhood origins of current difficulties, intrapsychic (or self-self) conflict, transference, countertransference, resistance and the defences – and it agrees with the relational or interpersonal emphasis of much of contemporary psychoanalysis. Of course, AEP reinterprets these psychoanalytic principles from an existential perspective. And it uses techniques drawn from experiential therapy, especially Gestalt therapy and body oriented psychotherapy, to work with both historical and contemporary material. It is existential, especially Sartrean, in its understanding of human reality as translucid and free – and in its emphasis on the psychological instant as containing seeds for transformation and change.

In this chapter, I will first discuss the theory and methodology of AEP and then present an example from a dream session followed by a brief conclusion.

Clinical theory

The psychological instant, purifying reflection and the possibility for change

What is the basis for change in psychotherapy? Behaviourists say it is changing one's conditioning. Cognitive behavioural therapists say it is changing one's thoughts. Freud says it is making the unconscious conscious, which happens as the analysand free associates or follows the fundamental rule of saying whatever comes to mind and the analyst strategically interprets unconscious wishes and conflicts. British object relations theorists and many other post-Freudian psychoanalysts have extended Freud's understanding of what must be made conscious to include earliest relations with others who 'mirror' who and what we are. The therapist, as a catalyst for change, must mirror differently. I have reinterpreted this material along Sartrean lines in my book on *Sartre and Psychoanalysis* (1991). Basically, I think that Jean-Paul Sartre's idea of 'the look' explains the mirroring and other relational needs discovered by many post-Freudian psychoanalysts much more coherently than does Freudian drive theory.

More recent relational psychoanalysts have located the potential for change in the therapeutic relationship itself. 'Co-created' by client and therapist, it is the source of the 'corrective emotional experience' that allows one to view self and world differently. While I largely agree with this view, which is being buttressed by a deluge of current brain and infant research, I take issue with some of the relational analysts' postmodern social constructivist views. My own perspective on this is Sartrean. While Sartre in his later philosophy recognizes the impact of language and culture on the formation of an individual's way of relating to self and world (see Cannon 1991: 162–222, 255–288), he nonetheless never abandons the moment of freedom, of self-world making, that makes change possible.

Hence it is to Sartre's ontology (philosophy of being) as set forth in *Being and Nothingness*, augmented by *The Transcendence of the Ego*, that we must look for a basic understanding of the psychology of change and transformation. Sartre himself says toward the end of *Being and Nothingness* that 'the final discoveries of ontology' must become the 'first principles of psychoanalysis' (1972: 735). It is through these that we discover the self as free agent. For Sartre, basic human reality is not a solid something with psychic structure and content – conscious or unconscious. Rather it is 'nothing' – no thing, nothingness. It is not even an 'I' since the personal pronoun is an invention of linguistic reflective consciousness. It is instead a relationship with Being based on the recognition that consciousness is not its objects. At its most primitive level, this world-making process is probably simply the bodily feeling of being here rather than there – simple presence to being. It is basic intentionality in the phenomenological sense of world engagement – consciousness of this or that object.

Sartre calls basic gut-level awareness 'prereflective' consciousness – a term that has been interestingly taken up by some contemporary psychoanalysts to describe processes that they regard as not quite conscious or even as unconscious (Stolorow and Atwood 1992). Sartre would say that these processes are conscious, and hence accessible to reflection, but that they are not yet known (and may often never be fully known) on a reflective level. Sartre later came to call this non-reflective realm *le vécu* or lived experience. It always overflows the possibility for reflective understanding.

Reflective consciousness, as distinguished from prereflective consciousness, arises when one turns and attempts to make a (quasi) object of the self. An insuperable gap, the gap of nihilating consciousness, will always exist between the self reflecting and the self reflected on. Reflective consciousness itself consists of several possible stances toward the self: accessory or impure reflection and pure or purifying reflection. Impure reflection involves the attempt to assign to myself a nature or solid sense of being in a vain search for ontological security. It is the source of the construction of the ego or self as object. This construction is aided and abetted by others, who also desire this reliability and who are forever naming who or what I am. Impure reflection is always contaminated by the looks, touches and words of the original powerful others. It is the source of many misconceptions about the self and much human misery in the form of interference with spontaneity and creative living.

Although we are probably first aware of reflection in its impure form, the existence of impure reflection is predicated on pure reflection. Sartre says that pure reflection is both 'the original form of reflection and its ideal form' (1972: 218). It is the original form because it must be there for reflection to be possible at all. It is the ideal form because it is the 'simple presence of the consciousness reflecting to the consciousness reflected on' (1972: 218) without the distortions arising from the need to make oneself into a solid, object-like self. Sartre says that it 'keeps to the given without setting up claims for the future' (1957: 64). Because impure reflection is so much more common, pure reflection 'must be won by a sort of catharsis' (1972: 218).

Sartre names this catharsis, or standing apart from the self, purifying reflection. He says that nothingness can be revealed neither to prereflective consciousness nor to accessory reflection but 'is accessible only to the purifying reflection' (1972: 273). Purifying reflection is a way of winning back pure reflection. One must attempt to take the position of simple presence to self. This includes presence not only to previously unarticulated prereflective experience, but also to the reflective distortions that one has adopted (and continues to adopt) as ways of dealing with the original others and other life circumstances.

Purifying reflection may lead to what Sartre refers to as the psychological instant. He describes this as a moment of 'double nothingness' in which self and world change together (1972: 600). I find that I am no longer what I was in the interpersonal/sociomaterial world with which I have been familiar, and that I am no longer in the process of becoming what I was about to become in an interpersonal/sociomaterial world that is no longer familiar. I take a different perspective on both past and future. It is as though I am suspended over an abyss, grasping in order to let go and letting go in order to grasp a new way of being in the world. The psychological instant is not an instant or a moment in any static sense, since time is a continuous flow, but it is a radical redirection of one's 'project [or *project*, throwing oneself forward out of the past toward the future] of being'.

Hence the emergence of the psychological instant almost inevitably involves existential anxiety. Clients often describe themselves at such moments as 'standing on the edge of an abyss' or as feeling 'different', 'odd', 'strange', 'weird' or 'disoriented'. Moments of double nothingness allow one to become aware that one is not a thing, but a relationship with being, and that one can choose and rechoose that relationship. Frederick S. (Fritz) Perls, the best known founder of Gestalt therapy, claimed that Gestalt therapy was an existential approach. And this is so in large part because Gestalt therapy emphasizes freedom and nothingness. Perls describes 'nothingness' as the 'fertile void' out of which new possibilities may spontaneously emerge. From this perspective: 'Nothing equals real' (1980: 61–62). He agrees with Sartre that the flight from nothingness (or freedom) is an act of reality distortion or bad faith.

Although AEP encourages clients to claim their freedom, it also recognizes that we are not free from the givens of our world. The other form of bad faith, as described by Sartre, is overemphasis on freedom. This is the idea that I am free absolutely outside the circumstances of my life or the world I live in. We are neither facts in a world without freedom nor free in a world without facts. Instead we are bodily grounded and free in situation, which is a combination of what the world brings and what I make of what the world brings. We experience the world and our history, but we choose what we make of them.

Part of embracing our freedom involves a reorientation to both the lived past that has not been reflectively examined, but that still profoundly impacts us, and the reflectively worked over or 'thematized' past (Sartre 1972: 200) – as they are being currently folded into the present/future we are bringing into being. To the extent that it explores difficulties arising from childhood in great depth, AEP is highly psychodynamic (perhaps even psychoanalytic) in its approach. At the same time, AEP is highly experiential. It seeks not so much a reflective reconstruction of the past as it does an active bodily oriented experiencing of the impact of the past as it colours the present moment – and the encouragement of experiments in which the client tries out something new.

AEP also recognizes that encountering nothingness is freeing as well as anxiety provoking. Profound change involves a recovery of spontaneity and lightness. Like British object relations theorist D. W. Winnicott, AEP defines effective psychotherapy as 'two people playing together' (1985: 38). Where one of them (hopefully the client) is unable to play, it involves learning to play. Play allows us to explore the interstices between reality (what is there) and what we make of it – to reorient ourselves to what is and to open to new possibilities for what might be. AEP encourages clients to experiment with new possibilities and to reclaim their freedom in an embodied way. Indeed, as Sartre says of existential psychoanalysis, the aim of AEP is 'to repudiate the spirit of seriousness' (1972: 796) – the idea that we are weighed down and controlled by the material world and the accidents of our history – in favour of the spirit of play.

Methodology

Facilitating the appearance of the psychological instant

What form does this 'playing together' take in AEP? The methodology is largely drawn from experiential therapy – though the depth of exploration of the past is certainly psychodynamic and the premises for adopting interventions existential. Experiential interventions are used to explore both the past and the client–therapist relationship more thoroughly in AEP than in some other experiential approaches. Yet the AEP therapist, like the experiential therapist, minimizes interpretation in favour of facilitating a process in which the client comes to embrace disowned feelings and wishes through experiencing them. Where we do interpret, our guesses are offered as our own fantasies (to be confirmed or disconfirmed by the client) about what is going on – rather than as the truth about the client's experience.

In AEP we also attempt to come up with experiments that allow the client to entertain the radically new – to find release from the constraints of the past and previously held constructs about who or what self and world are like. This process is highly creative and often quite playful. Sartre says that existential psychoanalysis must be 'completely flexible and adapt itself to the slightest observable changes in the subject'. This is so because the existential analyst's 'concern here is to understand what is individual and even instantaneous [as in the appearance of the psychological instant]' (1972: 732). AEP therapists attempt to follow this guideline in making interventions. It requires a great deal of presence on the part of the therapist. The experiential interventions used in AEP are flexible and oriented to this particular client at this particular moment in therapy. They include awareness of gestures, facial expression, posture, breath, voice and movement as well as verbal content and process – and experiments with these to explore what is and to try out something new. Exaggerating a gesture, movement or habitual body stance, or trying out its opposite, may lead to unearthing its meaning and/or to experiencing a new way of being.

Where language is explored, it is often worked with as process rather than content – and always with the intent of reclaiming agency. One way to do this is to encourage the client to turn nouns into verbs, past talk into present talk, questions (used as avoidance) into statements, evasive language into more concrete specific language. For example, suppose the client says to a partner or other group member, 'Don't you know that [question] I have sometimes had [past talk] the feeling [noun] that I'm kind of [evasive language] in love [noun] with you when you say things like this [evasive language]?' The therapist might suggest the rephrase, 'I love you when you tell me I'm great.' Experiments with reversing statements (e.g. 'I am not very sexual' to 'I am very sexual') can be another way of expanding meaning and reclaiming disowned experience. All this is done playfully rather than seriously – as experiment rather than as prescription for correct discourse.

AEP also relies heavily on a dialogical approach, borrowed from Gestalt therapy, but modified to include a deeper exploration of how the past impacts the present. This is the famous 'empty chair' technique in which the client identifies a conflict with self or other, and creates a dialogue between the conflicting characters. Sometimes the characters are elements in a dream. They may even be parts of the body. The dialogue often deepens to family of origin issues, allowing the client to experience past choices in the immediacy of the present dialogue and to experiment with new ways of feeling and being. A return to the present dilemma tests whether the experiment was effective in lifting the transference – allowing the client to begin to relate differently to self and world. Often resistance and defences are encountered along the way. These are explored as intentional bodily lived experience. Fear that manifests as a particular defensive stance may be newly experienced as an action that was probably effective in the past but may no longer be useful.

The process actually is much more complicated than this, involving attention to the client–therapist relationship as well as to conflicts with self and other outside the therapy. Some clients work with their issues more directly in the therapeutic relationship, finding in the therapist the obstructive other of their childhoods and working through this to a new (one would hope) more authentic relationship with self and others. Others use the therapist more as an ally in working with outside dilemmas – which may also involve transference, resistance and reworking the lived past as it colours the present. One way of working may be more prominent at one stage of therapy and the other at another – or this may shift from one session to the next or even within a single session. As the client moves toward a moment of radical transformation, we pay particular attention to existential anxiety as it heralds and accompanies a profound shift in that person's way of being in the world.

The dream as an existential message: 'The Skeleton Rib Cage'

Fritz Perls was fond of saying that the 'dream is an existential message'. What he meant was that dreams give us a message about what we need to look at in our lives. The dream consciousness is saying: 'This is my existence.' AEP, like Gestalt therapy, does not attempt to reduce the dream to an interplay of disguised unconscious forces that refer to the distant past – though dream work may lead to an understanding of how the lived past underlies the present and distorts current relationships. AEP regards the dream not as a substitute formation but as another kind of consciousness, perhaps more connected with artistic creation than with rational discourse. Hence the dream's 'existential message' is not deciphered or interpreted in terms of universal symbols or unconscious repressed childhood wishes or any other reductionist line of inquiry. Instead dreams are allowed to speak for themselves. We enact (and embody) rather than interpret the dream, a technique borrowed from Gestalt therapy.

First the client tells the dream in the present tense. Then the therapist identifies the characters in the dream (including people, inanimate objects, places, houses, and the dreamer) and invites the dreamer to create a dialogue between dream characters by role playing significant characters and conflicts. Often the therapist works with a complex dream by asking the dreamer which portion of the dream draws the client more or 'has more energy' for him or her – and uses that as a starting point for the exploration. Each character is assumed to be part of the dreamer or to point to an aspect of the dreamer's existence. Analysis is replaced by synthesis or integration. Defences often appear as physical objects – for example, a 'wall' of denial. Conflicts between characters are identified and expanded upon. The dream often deepens to family of origin issues, issues involving disowned parts of the self, or issues in the client's contemporary life. We do not simply stay with the action of the dream. Often it is expanded and worked with so that the dreamer gets to experiment with new ways of being and acting. New 'characters' may appear along the way; often possibilities for change may be indicated by a dream character who points the way.

'The Skeleton Rib Cage' provides an example of work with a dream that leads the dreamer to a psychological instant of profound change. Diane, the dreamer, is a former student and colleague who volunteered to make a demonstration videotape.[2] She has done much prior work with family of origin issues. Although she is not a student of existential philosophy, she is peripherally acquainted with it. She has not read Sartre's *Being and Nothingness*, though one might swear that she has from the language she uses in working with the dream.

Diane begins by narrating her dream in the present tense. As it turns out, it has two parts. In the first, she finds herself standing behind Dick, her husband, who in reality had died several years earlier leaving her with a rather complicated estate to untangle. In the dream, she is trying to rip off a snake that has coiled itself around him. There is a feeling of 'ominous dreariness' in the 'weather' of this part of the dream. Then the dream scene shifts and Diane finds herself holding a skeleton rib cage, which is suspended off the ground. Diane makes an expansive rounding motion with her arms as she introduces the rib cage – as though she is reaching her arms around it. She continues to make expansive lifting movements and gestures, which I often mirror, when she talks about the rib cage throughout the session.

Although I might have been tempted to offer an interpretation based on Diane's feelings about Dick's death and the untangling of the estate, I instead invite Diane to create a dialogue between herself as the Dreamer and the Skeleton Rib Cage – the part of the dream that she says holds the most 'energy' for her. She begins the dialogue by playing the Dreamer, who asks the Rib Cage some questions. When she switches chairs, I invite her to sink into and embody the Rib Cage. Fairly soon she experiences an impasse, saying she feels that this work 'isn't going anywhere'.

I suggest that Diane stay with the dialogue. I have her try out a sentence stem, speaking as the Rib Cage: 'I have the power to . . .'. Then the Rib Cage says: 'I have the power to lift you out of dreariness.' As the dialogue continues and the Rib Cage describes its beneficial functions, I ask what 'part' of Diane it is. The Rib Cage replies: 'I am the part of you that is alive at all costs. I am the survivor.' I suggest, following the storyline of the dream, the statement: 'So I can lift you out of impossible situations' – to which Diane (as the Rib Cage) agrees. This leads me to explore whether the Rib Cage may stand for a defence (perhaps denial) originating in the Diane's original family scenario.

Although the Rib Cage acknowledges that it has been around for 'a long time', we discover that this line of inquiry essentially goes nowhere. When Diane again switches chairs to play the Dreamer, she once more stops and says: 'I'm not feeling much.' I reply: 'Just sit with it and see what you do feel.' Later Diane says that this was an important juncture in the work since she would not have discovered the meaning of the dream if we had abandoned the role-play here. As the dialogue continues, she says she doesn't want to be 'rescued' by the Rib Cage. I explore to see if she is letting go of a defence, but this doesn't seem to be the case. Then, after a long pause, she says: 'There's something else I'm feeling about this. I'm feeling a real expansiveness. This is why I'm having difficulty identifying the feelings because the feelings are not heavy. . . . They're light. . . . And I'm very comfortable in navigating the heavy dreary feelings. What I'm feeling is the absence of problem.' Remembering how much tragedy and unrest Diane has experienced in her life, I respond: 'And that's an unfamiliar place.'

Now we see what Diane has been resisting: the lightness given physical representation by the floating Rib Cage. As a character, it was indicative not of a resistance to psychodynamic material relating to the past: instead Diane, in losing energy in the dialogue, was resisting the emergence of something new. At this point I begin to suspect that Diane is moving into an existential moment. I ask, gesturing toward the other chair: 'So now, what do you want to say to this energy?' She says: 'I find it fascinating how light you are.'

I spend a little time encouraging her to experience this new lightness and reflecting the shift she has made, commenting that she can always go back to the 'snakes and the drama and all that' if she should want to – that she has a choice. She says that it's interesting how none of those things stood out in the dream – what stood out was the Rib Cage. I invite her to feel her own (bodily) rib cage. She makes the same encompassing motion with her arms and hands as she says she feels 'supported' by her rib cage. She says it doesn't feel 'limiting' but 'kind of structural'. She no longer feels what she has described as the 'drama' of the snakes. She says: 'I'm just open. I feel what I don't know how to describe – other than saying it's expansive. I guess if there's going to be a name for this, I guess it would be called freedom.' I reflect this.

I ask: 'And as you feel free, what happens?' She says, motioning backward over her right shoulder: 'There's a memory of tension.' She goes on: 'But is there really tension? I don't think so. It's almost like nothingness [she has her hand on her stomach].' She seems a little giddy and goes on to say: 'I don't know how my mind will allow this.' I say: 'Just keep your mind out of it for a little.' She says: 'Okay, 'cause I could imagine that the mind wouldn't like this place.' She goes on to reflect: 'This is the strangest session I've ever had.' I say: 'Just let it happen. You wanted to stop it several times.' We laugh. She says: 'It's just really odd.'

I invite Diane to stand up, thinking that she might try out this expansion with her feet on the ground and moving around so that she gets a sense of what it is like to really live from this place. As she walks around, she says: 'This nothingness . . . it's refreshing. It's light because it's nothing. . . . It's like a whole different reference. Being free from family dynamics.' As she sits down again, she says: 'This is a very odd session for me.' I reply: 'You're in a new place.' She says: 'It doesn't get caught in the emotional body of things. It's just like energy and nothingness. It's really simple. I feel really simple. Isn't that odd?' I ask if it's nice. She says: 'It's wonderful!'

She again starts to feel some apprehension. She describes feeling a 'residue' from the past, as she gestures backward over her left shoulder. This happens several more times. Each time she moves through it, with my support, back into the expansion.

At one point, when the dream dialogue seems complete, I move into the other chair to sit facing Diane directly. She says she has a 'sense of being really found and really lost at the same time. I'm lost here because I've never been here. There's this sense of nothingness but there's also some solidness.' Soon she again feels the pull of the past. She decides this comes from feeling she should be 'doing something, shaping something, making something happen'. We move forward in our chairs to make stronger contact. I say: 'And if you don't?' Diane says what she's learning right now is that this is 'great'. She again muses: 'This is very strange.'

I ask what it would be like to act from this place. She says she would explore and experience more. I ask her to put this statement into the present tense. She says: 'I am experiencing more and I'm exploring. And I'm not feeling restricted.' We spend a little time emphasizing and supporting this new place she is in. She comments: 'So aliveness is bigger than drama.' Because she had previously identified being alive with drama, she didn't recognize these new feelings when they started to emerge. After another round of fear ('People could get mad at me for being'), she says she feels like a 'fresh piece of clay or an empty canvas or an empty page in the type-writer'. I say: 'This sounds like something waiting to develop.' She says: 'That's really phenomenal.' I say: 'I'm glad we didn't stop.'

She says: 'Yeah, I was really uncomfortable. I was uncomfortable with nothing.' I ask: 'What about now?' She says: 'It's nice because it's bigger. There's more potential.' But she says it's still unfamiliar. 'Even what's between my ears isn't familiar right now.' She goes on to say: 'This stuff really does work. It's interesting how you can go through all that mud and come up into clean water – crystal clear water. It's like a letting go of anything that doesn't work.' She quotes her grandmother, who is 104, who says: 'If it works, you'll know it. If it doesn't work, you'll know it.' I ask if this [our work together] is working. She says: 'This has always worked. But to be in this new place is really working. Because it's like a life I've never experienced before. It's a life force I've never experienced before.' Pointing backwards with both thumbs, she says she no longer experiences the 'tin cans' of the past clanking behind her. She sums up her experience in one word: 'Freedom' – emphasizing this by nodding her head yes. In the rest of the tape, we discuss the session.

Viewers have told me that they feel the expansion and giddiness and anxiety of Diane's prolonged moment of 'double nothingness' as they watch the tape. As for myself, I felt privileged and delightfully surprised to participate with her in this experience. Diane, viewing the tape several months later, said that this was the 'hardest session I have ever done' because it was so disorienting and demanding of her to reside in what Fritz Perls calls the 'fertile void' and Sartre 'nothingness'. As it turned out, it was a very productive moment, since it allowed Diane to move into a new, more playful and expansive space in her life. Four months later she said that the shift was still holding.

Conclusion

'The Skeleton Rib Cage' illustrates the dialogical technique and body-oriented relational emphasis of AEP as these help to facilitate a moment of profound change. By the end of the session, Diane embraces the spirit of play and repudiates the spirit of seriousness – fulfilling in that moment what Sartre says is the aim of existential psychoanalysis. She may backtrack from this. But one doubts that she will again take herself quite so 'seriously' – or that she will choose to continue to engage without insight in the 'dramas' represented by the snake scene earlier in the dream.

This session does not illustrate the whole spectrum of AEP work. AEP frequently addresses everyday dilemmas, rather than dream work. In the early and middle stages, it may look very different from this session. Initial stage work often involves much more attention to establishing safety and a good working relationship. Middle stage work often pays more attention to transference, countertransference and family of origin issues than are apparent in this session. What Diane's dream does demonstrate in almost pure form is the aliveness and relationally oriented immediacy of AEP work – and its capacity to evoke the appearance of the psychological instant in which the client makes a new choice of a way of being in the world.

Notes

1 The distinction made here is not quite so clear when comparing AEP with contemporary psychoanalysis as it is with classical psychoanalysis. Contemporary relational and intersubjective psychoanalysts are very aware that it takes more than making the unconscious conscious to effect psychoanalytic cure – and that some of what it takes is not even verbal. Furthermore they discuss the unconscious in ways that often make one think more of Sartre's idea of prereflective consciousness than of the Freudian unconscious. And others before them (Winnicott, in particular) had doubted the efficacy of interpretation alone in working with certain deep level developmental issues.

2 A slightly edited version of this video can be viewed on the Boulder Psychotherapy Institute website: www.boulderpsych.com.

References

Cannon, B. (1991) *Sartre and Psychoanalysis: An Existentialist Challenge to Clinical Metatheory*, Lawrence, KS: University Press of Kansas.

Perls, F. S. (1980 [1969]) *Gestalt Therapy Verbatim*, New York: Bantam Books.

Sartre, J.-P. (1957 [1937]) *The Transcendence of the Ego*, trans. R. Kirkpatrick and F. Williams, New York: Farrar, Strauss and Giroux.

Sartre, J.-P. (1972 [1943]) *Being and Nothingness: An Essay on Phenomenological Ontology*, trans. H. E. Barnes, New York: Washington Square Press.

Stolorow, R. D. and Atwood, G. E. (1992) *Contexts of Being. The Intersubjective Foundations of Psychological Life*, Hillsdale, NJ: The Analytic Press.

Winnicott, D. W. (1985 [1971]) *Playing and Reality*, London and New York: Tavistock Publications.

Chapter 8

R. D. Laing revisited

A dialogue on his contribution to authenticity and the sceptic tradition

M. Guy Thompson and John M. Heaton

Introduction

R. D. Laing was one of the twentieth century's most controversial psycho-analysts and, at the peak of his fame in the 1970s, he was the most widely read psychiatrist in the world. Renown of that magnitude is dependent on the happy coincidence of multiple factors, including the right message at the most opportune time. In an era when authority figures of every persuasion were suspect, the counterculture movement of the 1960s entrusted this disarming Scotsman to explain to them how they were being manipulated by the very people – their parents, teachers, and other authority figures – they had been most influenced by and dependent upon. Laing's searing portrayal of the duplicitous and oftentimes mystifying politics of everyday life, which he outlined in one explosive bestseller after another (e.g. Laing 1960, 1961, 1967, 1970, 1971) made him a social icon for a generation of psychology students, intellectuals, and artists in European and American academic circles.

In this exchange of perspectives, Michael Guy Thompson and John Heaton, both friends and colleagues of Laing's, will engage in an exchange of opinions addressing their respective views about the core of Laing's existential assessment of the human condition. Their dialogue will focus on the role that authenticity played in both his personal and professional life, and the way that the sceptic philosophical tradition both influenced and illuminated critical aspects of his thinking and clinical philosophy.

R. D. LAING'S AMBIGUOUS CONCEPTION OF AUTHENTICITY
Michael Guy Thompson

Ronald Laing was alternately a wonderful man and a terrible man and his struggle to determine the nature of authenticity, to articulate precisely what he believed it entailed, and to measure up to that standard in his personal and professional behaviour brought out the best and the worst in him.

Despite Laing's affinity with Jean-Paul Sartre and the significant influence that Sartre had on many of Laing's ideas, his conception of authenticity relied predominantly on the thinking of Friedrich Nietzsche and Martin Heidegger. In order to understand Laing's radical take on what it means to be authentic and the extremes of behaviour he adopted in this pursuit, it would be instructive to first review the basic points that comprise Nietzsche's and Heidegger's respective views on this existential principle. Given the space I have available I will be brief.

The currently popularized notion of authenticity that has swept contemporary America and Europe tends to reduce it to more or less whatever one *feels* as opposed to what one *thinks* about the matter at hand. This view originates with the Romanticist philosopher Jean-Jacques Rousseau who objected to the emphasis his contemporary Enlightenment thinkers assigned to the role of rationality at the expense of feeling states, which Rousseau believed were essential to artistic expression. This is a simplification, but Rousseau's critique was rooted in the notion that individuals have an inner self that is hidden and for the most part comprised of feelings that say a lot about who a person genuinely is, so the more in touch a person is with his or her feelings the more authentic that person is said to be. This view suggests that the more authentic a person is, the more pleasing, kind, and compassionate that person will be to others. In other words, the authentic person is a *kinder* and more generous person, the kind of person you might want for a friend. Carl Rogers is a contemporary champion of this vision of authenticity.

Now Nietzsche and Heidegger would have none of this, first because they did not believe in the notion of a self, so for them there could be no 'inner core' of feelings to get in touch with; and second, however one may wish to characterize the subjectivity or human nature of a person, there is no discernible or even necessary relationship between authenticity and ethics of the kind Rousseau implied. From this angle, behaving authentically may make one extremely controversial, as both Nietzsche and Heidegger[1] demonstrated in their personal conduct. For Nietzsche the authentic person is one who is not afraid to face up to the fundamental alienation of everyday life. Such a person was embodied in Nietzsche's conception of the *Übermensch*, usually translated into English as superman or overman: a person who will arrive some day in the future and come to grips with his deepest fears and embrace reality for what it is, however difficult or threatening it may feel. Nietzsche loved the Greeks and though he rejected the conventional view of morality – that we should conduct ourselves by a set of rules that are dictated by a God or society – Nietzsche devoted much of his thinking to the topic of personal values (or character traits) and what kind of values are important for the *Übermensch* to embrace. Like the Greeks, Nietzsche believed that courage was the greatest virtue for the authentic person to cultivate and he saw the *Übermensch* as a courageous, even heroic figure. This is because it entails a special kind of courage to go against society's dictates and to follow the beat of one's own drum, which is more or less how Nietzsche wished to conduct himself.

It is telling that Laing's most famous and polemical book, *The Politics of Experience* (1967), where he rails against contemporary society as a toxic wasteland, is a homage to Nietzsche's *Thus Spoke Zarathrustra* (2006), one of Laing's favourite books. Courage is another theme to which Laing referred countless times, noting that, etymologically, the root of the word means 'heart', implying that the original sense of being courageous was *openheartedness*. Laing often suggested that behaving authentically takes courage or guts and that on a deeper, more profound level to behave authentically entails opening one's heart to another person. Laing believed that such an act assumes courage because placing oneself in such a vulnerable situation is an extremely risky thing to do because when we love we put ourselves at the other person's mercy.

Heidegger's conception of authenticity was indebted to many, including Kierkegaard and Nietzsche, but he also took the concept in new directions and made it very much his own. Heidegger rejected Nietzsche's romantic characterization of the heroic *Übermensch* and argued instead that all human beings are necessarily *inauthentic* pretty much all the time, because this is our lot in life and the essence of our anxiety-prone human condition, from which we can never entirely escape. Despite our condition, we can nonetheless relieve ourselves of our plight, if only momentarily, with acts of authenticity, in moments when we are able to rise to the occasion. But most of the time we are caught up in the pursuit of our daily affairs, trying to get ahead in our unremitting inauthentic fashion, and simply coping with life as best we can. We court popular favour, compete for promotions to further our ambitions, seek to enhance our reputations and 'look good' professionally, all the while slyly lying when it suits our purposes and when being truthful might prove embarrassing, or worse. In effect, we get caught up 'in the crowd' of our own making, whatever crowd or circle we identify with and comprises our world, so that the crowd becomes the arena of our inauthenticity rooted in our self-identity. Unfortunately, our success at this endeavour is all too often the source of our estrangement from ourselves, where our authenticity is situated.

From Heidegger one gets the sense that we are imperfect, fallen creatures. One also gets the sense of a profound loneliness that is co-extensive with authenticity in both Nietzsche and Heidegger. Sticking to your principles and doing what you believe is right often comes at the expense of political expediency and may cost you not only public favour but also the very friends who expect you to serve their interests. Both Nietzsche's and Heidegger's meditations on authenticity had a profound impact on Laing's conception of and relationship with the matter. For Laing, the capacity to be honest about our inauthentic transgressions and own up to them could be just as authentic as conforming to Nietzsche's and Heidegger's characterization of authenticity! As we shall see, this exegesis of Laing's extension of authenticity also planted a seed of confusion for him that became a source of inconsistency.

What were the basic elements of authenticity in Laing's thinking? Laing couldn't stand people whom he thought 'fake', who put on airs and pretended to be who they were not, who were too timid to speak up for fear of making fools of themselves, when they tried to impress you as something or someone they were not. On the other hand he admired those who exercised effort and courage to at least try to be themselves, which was not an easy thing to do in Laing's intimidating presence. Laing was never really comfortable with people, and much of his preoccupation with the nature of the true- and false-self dichotomy in his first book, *The Divided Self* (1960), speaks to his preoccupation with the inherent *falsity* that people erect around themselves in order to fit in with society. This is a tributary of inauthenticity that Laing derived from Sartre's conception of *bad faith*.[2] According to Laing, they pretend to be someone they are not and become alienated from who they genuinely, if unconsciously, are. Both D. W. Winnicott (1976), one of Laing's supervisors in his psychoanalytic training, and Sartre (1981) influenced his use of this terminology to convey his early thinking about authenticity, though Laing abandoned these terms as his thinking evolved. Yet Laing never wavered from his distaste for what he termed 'putting on airs' and the kind of pretence that Kingsley Hall and the other Philadelphia Association houses were so adept at stripping away. Laing's conception of Kingsley Hall was explicitly designed to pare away the inherently false currency of social niceties, proper manners, and common courtesy that are the standard of social relations in virtually every culture on earth – except for Kingsley Hall![3] For those of us who lived in such places, the idea was to simulate the same types of interaction with other members of the household (regardless how psychotic or disturbed) that one would more typically experience in psychoanalysis. This meant dispensing with small talk entirely and speaking from the heart with the same sense of urgency, reflection, and honesty that you would in therapy. The effect was disconcerting, even transformative, and served as a rite of passage into the life of the 'Laingian community'.

On occasion, Laing could be confrontational and by contemporary standards even cruel in the way he sometimes got in someone's face to call them on this or that breach of genuine relating, a tactic he adopted from Esalen Institute techniques that were practised in Big Sur, California in the heyday of the 1960s encounter group movement. Yet he could also be uncommonly gentle, kind, and sensitive; it depended on what he drew from in a given moment. Perhaps the most important litmus for Laing's characterization of authenticity derived from the golden rule: *Do unto others as you would have them do unto you.* I cannot recall another expression that I heard him refer to more frequently in terms of basic human decency, as a rough and ready guide to I-and-Thou relating. In his seminars, Laing would sometimes read from the Lord's Prayer, influenced, I believe, by a book of Aldous Huxley's on the subject, where he critiqued each line of the prayer to give it a contemporary interpretation. Laing was particularly taken with the part of the prayer that speaks of *trespassing* against one's neighbours and the need to forgive both those who trespass against oneself as well as one's own trespasses against others. Laing seemed particularly sensitive to crossing that line, when therapists, for example, including psychiatrists and psychoanalysts, trespass into that space of vulnerability of their patients that is not always therapeutic, but potentially injurious. The concept of trespass seems to be the one irreducible element in Laing's critique of psychiatric and other forms of therapeutic practice that runs through the entirety of his published work. Though his rhetoric was sometimes brutal, Laing didn't seem to care how many psychiatrists and psychoanalysts he alienated, and he paid a heavy price for speaking out against the kinds of manipulative clinical interventions that even today typically pass for normal. The contemporary clinical establishment has still not forgiven him for it. I consider this pretty heroic stuff and a con-temporary example of Nietzsche's admonition to 'philosophize with a hammer!'. It didn't win Laing many friends.

This raises the question: what are we to make of a man who at the time of his death in 1989 had managed to damage his relationships with most of his closest friends and colleagues as a consequence of his unpredictably hostile and erratic behaviour, who delighted in intellectually bullying those closest to him, whose drinking and drug use (marijuana and LSD) drove him to behave so irresponsibly over the last ten years of his life that it was apparent to those closest to him that he was systematically compromising his legacy – a new standard for ethical clinical behaviour that had taken him more than two decades to develop? For those of us who knew Laing and adored him, witnessing this process was a painful affair, and we remain haunted by this perplexing legacy of a man to whom we owe so much yet understand so little. Was Laing's penchant for bullying a form of unmitigated boorish rudeness masquerading as a radical therapeutic intervention? Or was it a manifestation of genuine authentic self-expression, true to his personal values (which were by their nature guaranteed to confuse and intimidate) and which he believed to have therapeutic value?

According to John Duffy, one of Laing's oldest friends from his youth in Glasgow, Laing had been 'a kind, sensitive, and loving young man, a really outstanding individual who was different than the rest, caring and gentle' (Mullan 1997: 100–101). He observed that Laing changed over the years and became increasingly self-absorbed and sometimes brutal. Some of this Duffy attributed to Laing's first, unhappy marriage to Anne. But later after Laing married Jutta, his boorish behaviour escalated and encroached into their friendship. Laing's drinking escalated and he became increasingly self-absorbed and belligerent. Eventually Duffy had enough of it and ended their friendship, much to Laing's shock and dismay.

What Duffy was complaining about was familiar to all of Laing's close friends and associates: the drinking, the baiting, bullying and aggression, in a word, crossing the line – *trespassing*. Yet, Laing often argued that such expressions of turmoil were intended to be *authentic*, that it wasn't a case of being drunk or out of control, but rather a method to his madness in the tradition of William Blake – 'the road of excess leads to the palace of wisdom' was one of Laing's favourite adages. Such accounts were often bewildering because Laing usually apologized for such breaches as if to say he hadn't meant it, while on other occasions he might insist he was provoked and merely 'teaching a lesson'.

An example of the latter was recounted by Maureen O'Hara, a follower of Carl Rogers who helped organize a one-day public event in London featuring Laing and Rogers and their respective cronies (Mullan 1997: 314–322). The event itself was uneventful, but the evening before was a night the participants would never forget. Laing and Rogers had never met, so Laing invited Rogers' group to his home the evening before the workshop to get acquainted. From the moment they arrived at his home an air of discomfort invaded the room. Rogers' group introduced themselves while Laing and his group sat in stony silence. Finally, as the silence became unbearable, Laing announced: 'If you [Rogers] and I are to have any kind of meaningful dialogue, you are going to have to cut out the California "nice-guy" act and get to something approaching an authentic encounter.' The two groups exploded into argument and Laing eventually suggested they go out to dinner to cool off. At the restaurant Laing immediately isolated himself from the others and proceeded to get drunk, much to Rogers' and his group's discomfort. As other customers entered the restaurant Laing shouted, 'See that bald-headed man sitting there?' [pointing to Rogers] 'Well, he's not a man, he's a *pairrrson*!', alluding to Rogers' most famous book, *On Becoming a Person*, in Laing's taunting Scottish burr. As the room fell into stunned silence, Laing ambled over to O'Hara's table and poured some Scotch into her empty water glass. He asked if she liked it and she said she did, thinking this was a gesture of rapprochement, at which point he spat into her drink and asked, 'Well, how do you like it now?' O'Hara tossed the drink in Laing's face and the situation devolved into pandemonium.

Though the groups eventually patched things up and went on with the programme, the damage had been done; Laing and Rogers never spoke again. Later, Laing explained to me that making Rogers and his group feel uncomfortable by his extreme behaviour was his way of teaching them something about authenticity in a way they seemed incapable of being, because they were so *nice* and artificially 'appropriate'. Laing's position was that anything goes when it comes to stripping away such artificial niceness whenever and wherever one meets it, no matter how much trespassing is required in order to get the message across. In her account of this story, O'Hara tells us that after her initial shock, in the following months she came to see Rogers in a fundamentally different way and became so disturbed by his 'artificiality' that she eventually severed her relationship with him; all because of the way that Laing had 'opened her eyes' to what she had heretofore been blinded. However many people Laing managed to alienate that evening, for O'Hara it was an awakening and even a life-changing experience!

Laing was a mass of contradictions. He was essentially a solitary figure with a profoundly spiritual centre that fuelled his quest for authentic relating with both himself and with others, especially with people whom he treated; yet he pursued fame and notoriety in a way that was difficult to reconcile with an authentic engagement with the world. It is perhaps ironic that Laing's last and unfinished book was devoted to love, a topic that was central to his conception of authenticity. Heidegger allowed that none of us is perfect and that we cannot be authentic all (or even much) of the time; simply being honest about our darkest moments may be the most authentic act at our disposal. But following Kierkegaard (1956), Laing insisted that love is essential to authentic relating with others, and that *Caritas*, or charity, is the epitome of such engagement. He also argued that hate is consistent with, and sometimes indistinguishable from, love so that acts of cruelty may be deemed authentic if that is how a person genuinely feels in the moment, in counterpoint to Rousseau's characterization of more benign feeling states at the core of the self.

In his biography of Laing, John Clay (1996) notes that Laing used to have a painting of Breughel's *Fall of Icarus* hanging on the wall of his consulting room on Wimpole Street in the early days of his practice. Anthony Clare interprets Laing's choice of this famous Greek myth as particularly, if unconsciously, relevant, in that Laing also flew too close to the sun, as a consequence of his elevation to the status of a guru. I believe that even in his frequent acts of rebelliousness Laing was convinced he was simply being faithful to his capacity for what measure of authenticity he was capable of accessing. In a way, I admired this about Laing, his inability to grovel, to act the part. So long as this hurt no one but himself, I saw something heroic in his inability to pander to the crowd. I think I even loved him for this and I will always admire his tenacity, if not his inconsistency. When it comes to crossing the line and trespassing on others in the name of teaching them something about how to become more authentic themselves, I believe Laing was engaged in acts of aggression that are difficult to reconcile with his views about *Caritas*, peace on earth, and the like. However complicated and contradictory Laing's legacy remains, we owe him a debt of gratitude for the courage it took to fashion a conception of authenticity that is as illuminating as it is disturbing and, perhaps necessarily, contradictory.

LAING, AUTHENTICITY, AND SCEPTICISM
John M. Heaton

In order to make sense of my critique of some of Michael Thompson's remarks on Laing and authenticity I will first give an outline of my under-standing of Heidegger on authenticity. Authenticity has become a key word amongst existential therapists, indicating that it is something good that we should strive for, a key ethical term. Of course they are entitled to use the word how they wish, but I want to argue that for Heidegger, at any rate, it was much more problematic. His distinction between authenticity and inauthenticity was a question rather than an answer; he was interested in the relation between the two and questioned the assumption that we ought to be authentic all the time. Most therapists, including existential ones, want answers; philosophers mostly question and a good one asks highly pertinent ones.

Heidegger followed the *path* of phenomenology; he came to question some of Husserl's assumptions, but, nevertheless, phenomenological ques-tioning was the path that led him to the question of Being (Heidegger 1972). In one of his later works, he claims that *errancy* arises from 'out of truth'; the true, when it is understood as 'what is correct', has degraded errancy into incorrectness. Correctness is an unacknowledged metaphysic and distorts the 'way' of truth (Heidegger 2006: 93–94). He was critical of too ready labelling of what is correct or not in phenomenology; to err is human.

The distinction between authenticity and inauthenticity is introduced early on in *Being and Time* (1962), since it is crucial to his theme that *Dasein* be understood as *my own*. This way of being is contrasted with 'falling in' with a crowd of my own making, as Mike mentioned above (p. 111), and also with relating to myself and others as if they were objects which are merely there, present-at-hand. Such a self-relation would be inauthentic as it denies the way in which *Dasein is* its possibilities, rather than merely having them. However, we may need at times to objectify ourselves and/or others; for example, when the doctor and I discuss the pain in my knee. Are we behaving inauthentically? Most of us sometimes chatter to other people; is this necessarily 'idle' and inauthentic? Is being idle always something bad which we should avoid? Can we always draw a distinct line between chatter that can be evaluated negatively and chatter that is positive? As Heidegger wrote later, inauthenticity is not a mere *lack*, a privation, but a fully fledged mode of existence (Heidegger 1962: 388; 339).

Authenticity and inauthenticity are possibilities of *Dasein* (Heidegger 1962: 236; 191). A temptation is to believe that we can gradually make a transition to authenticity during the course of our life or perhaps during psychotherapy. Should the aim of existential therapy be to make us more authentic? Many philosophers and most existential therapists take this moralizing attitude to authenticity, certainly Laing did, most of the time, as Mike shows. We and our patients *ought* to be more authentic, follow Laing, the model of authenticity. I disagree and think the relation between authenticity and inauthenticity is far more subtle than the simple-minded dichotomies of conventional morality. Heidegger, if read carefully, took a very nuanced view of these concepts (Staehler 2008: 293). He did not think it correct to be authentic.

Heidegger wrote: '*Authentic-Being-one's-Self* does not rest upon an exceptional condition of the subject, a condition that has been detached from the "they"; *it is rather an existentiell modification of the "they" – of the "they" as an essential existentiale*' (1962: 168; 130). So authenticity is not separated from inauthenticity in any simple way, but is a modification of inauthenticity.

Authentic being-towards-death is an existentiell possibility of *Dasein*. Some would claim that is the most authentic relation possible and some existential therapists have seen this as the ultimate end of existential therapy. Heidegger, however, shows that authentic being-towards-death cannot be characterized 'objectively' (1962: 304; 260). Heidegger, however, claims that it shows *Dasein* that its inmost possibility lies in giving itself up: in shattering all clinging to ideas and beliefs about itself and others that it may use to prop itself up. We cannot authentically say: 'I have achieved it', or claim that anyone else has done so. We cannot have it as an aim of therapy. Thus, for example, to search for a true self is a fantastical undertaking.

Authenticity is not a position that can be arrived at, possessed, and taught. What would teaching it mean? Of course we could try and define it, tell the person to read Kierkegaard and Heidegger and their commentators. They might end up knowing a lot about authenticity but would they understand what it is to be authentic? Could they make a transition from the inauthentic to the authentic by this way of knowing? Is it conceivable to make a transition from inauthenticity to authenticity? Is there continuity between them? Is one a simple negation of the other?

Authenticity and inauthenticity differ from one another perspectively, they are not metaphysical opposites, like good and bad. They are foci rather than polarities. They are orientational and perspectival within the structure of human living. They depend on one another, along with other terms and meanings in a person's life. That an authentic person is nevertheless inauthentic is the quintessence of practice. There is no privileging of authenticity as opposed to inauthenticity, as independent of one another. They cannot function without one another. Some people may no doubt be enslaved and fettered by their inauthenticity. But the human condition is such that we cannot eradicate it, due to the fundamental limitations of our life with one another.

There is a long and ancient tradition that ponders this question. Probably its beginning in the western tradition is in Plato's *Parmenides*; Plato discusses 'the sudden', as the category of transition. What is sudden is a category of the between, which is neither here nor there, neither in being nor outside it, placeless, *atopos*. So the sudden must be thought of as placeless, irreducible to being and nonbeing. I do not know how familiar Laing was with the *Parmenides*, but he was certainly familiar with Dionysius the Areopagite; he could quote parts of his *Mystical Theology* from memory. Dionysius worked in the Neo-Platonic tradition and one of its most valued books was Proclus' *Commentary on Plato's Parmenides*. This has been influential down to Hegel, Schelling, Kierkegaard and Heidegger. They understood the sudden as the 'instant' of salvation. Laing was even more familiar with Kierkegaard who, in *The Concept of Anxiety* and other works, discusses the instant, using the metaphor of the 'glance of the eye' (*Øie-Blick*). Here *nothing* becomes visible. Seeing, in this sense, is not representing but receiving, and receiving what cannot finally be received. Heidegger discusses the *Augenblick* which is translated in *Being and Time* as the 'moment of vision'. He defines it as: 'That Present which is held in authentic temporality and which is *authentic* itself, we call the "*moment of vision*"' (1962: 387; 338).

I think anyone who is even vaguely familiar with this tradition would see the absurdity and what Kierkegaard would call the *daemonic* element, in Laing's bullying behaviour as to who was authentic and who was not. The point of the 'instant' is an event that is not analysable on the horizon of presence. The instant is to-come, prior to any expectation. Laing's hierarchical and teleological attitude to it, his tendency to classify some people as superior, as they are authentic, whereas most of the world is wretchedly inauthentic, is deeply antagonistic to the tradition to which he gave verbal support. I think his biography, *Mad to be Normal* (Mullan 1995), is rather sad as it reveals his tendency to view people in terms of their authenticity or lack of it, his obsessional tendency to search for it in people, and his disappointment at finding so few authentic ones. He never seemed to waver in his belief that he was authentic!

I disagree with Laing on the question of the relation between honesty and authenticity. Laing, as Mike rightly says, put great emphasis on honesty. This in itself is suspect. It is con-men that emphasize how honest they are. Telling people bluntly what he thought of them was seen as being honest and authentic. This is an appalling confusion. Some Christians may have genuine (authentic) deep feelings about the Bible. But does this entitle them to thrust it down the throats of other people? Laing was something of a missionary too, assuming that what was important to him must be important to all.

Are people interested in being enlightened by us? Should we go round trying to convert them to our beliefs? Can we be sure our beliefs are true? Most people judge others by their actions, not their beliefs. I remember one of my early confrontations with Laing: he asked me to help him look in second-hand bookshops for some of his valuable books, which had been sold by his first wife in a pique of anger. As we were looking, he mentioned something he thought was inauthentic about me. I was angry and told him he was as bad as the psychoanalysts he had trained with, who think they know what everyone 'really' means and what everyone is 'really' up to. I added that I did not put much weight on his opinions of people, for why had he married such a horrible woman who sold his books unasked? He never tried preaching authenticity to me again.

Laing was a great connoisseur about other people's inauthenticity. He was an extremely good storyteller and would have me in fits of laughter in describing and imitating famous psychiatrists and psychoanalysts he had met, how they would be anxious to meet him out of envy, be very polite and 'interested' but at the same time obviously hating him. I knew Charles Rycroft, Laing's analyst, quite well. After Laing's death he would talk to me about him. He thought Laing was an interesting case of male hysteria, which is rather rare. He added that he would have treated him rather differently now than he did when he was younger. Many would baulk at the diagnosis of hysteria, but I think Rycroft had a good point. Hysterics, in his meaning of the term, have great difficulty in differentiating between what is a genuine feeling and what is not; in a classical case, whether they are 'really' in love or not. Mike writes that Laing could not stand people who pretended to be who they were not. But, as it has often been pointed out, people we can't stand are often too near our own weakness for us to understand.

I do not think Laing was helped by the general atmosphere amongst psychoanalysts and other therapists. There is a deep tendency, widely encouraged, to identify with the beliefs of a particular therapist, particularly a famous one. I have heard analysts proclaim that Freud, Jung, etc. were geniuses and anyone who questioned them either did not understand them or suffered from envy or some sort of repression. There was no attention to the logic of their theories, or empirical evidence as to their truth. Laing would often complain to me how he could say any rubbish he felt like and large audiences of psychologists and therapists would love it, the greater the rubbish the more authentic it showed him to be! No wonder the poor man took to drink. I asked him why he continued to prostitute himself like this. Once he said he needed the money, mostly he could give no answer. It was a stupid question; of course he could give no answer.

Authenticity is nothing to do with a particular state of mind or superiority or inferiority. It is ridiculous to point to someone and say: 'You are inauthentic and ought to be ashamed of yourself!' Unfortunately, in the world of psychiatry and psychoanalysis, there were many who would take this as a gospel truth when pronounced by Laing, and so hang around him in the hope he would one day pronounce them as authentic. Authenticity is not something that is present-at-hand; it is not a matter of correctness.

Why Laing was so wobbly on this matter I cannot say. He was highly ambivalent about authenticity. He was a great admirer of Montaigne and knew Merleau-Ponty's essay on him (1964). Montaigne was deeply influenced by Ancient Greek Pyrrhonian scepticism and Laing called himself a 'provisional sceptic' (Mullan 1995: 310), which is quite a good name for Pyrrhonian scepticism, a radical scepticism that is sceptical about scepticism! Montaigne did not preach Pyrrhonian scepticism, which would have been totally alien to its spirit, but wrestled with it, restated it, and took his distance from it. He often talked about his own weaknesses and faults. For him, scepticism is a philosophy constantly in suspense, affirming no opinion or dogma other than that of perpetual enquiry. He was open to the infinite and indefinite play of the mind in relation to possible objects, the elusive flow of thoughts. He is usually taken to be an extraordinarily genuine, authentic man. As Merleau-Ponty noted, the words 'strange', 'absurd', 'monster', and 'miracle' recur most often when Montaigne speaks of man. The self is, in the end, 'the place of all obscurities, the mystery of all mysteries' (Merleau-Ponty 1964: 198). To him, as well as for Laing, what we need in therapy is 'not self-satisfied understanding, but a consciousness astonished at itself at the core of human existence' (p. 203).

PERHAPS AUTHENTICITY IS NOT POSSIBLE TO DEFINE
Michael Guy Thompson

I more or less agree with John Heaton's assessment of Laing's selective interpretation of Heidegger's multifaceted meditation on the relationship between authenticity and inauthenticity. As I noted earlier, Laing's application of how he depicted a more authentic way of relating was at times inconsistent, if not contradictory. That being said, it also seems to me that John, in his more 'correct' rendering of authenticity, is being a little rough on Laing in suggesting that he was self-serving in the manner that he used authenticity as a licence, for example, to behave any way he liked. I want to argue that Laing had more integrity than that. Moreover, though Nietzsche and Heidegger were seminal influences on Laing's conception of authenticity, he was also influenced by myriad other philosophers, including Buber, Kierkegaard, Scheler, Montaigne, Sartre, Hegel, Schopenhauer, and assorted Christian and Buddhist thinkers. At the end of the day Laing made his conception of authenticity very much his own with a unique and characteristic sensibility. This sensibility in turn guided Laing in his contribution to the existential tradition and clinical application. Clearly psychotherapy, existential or otherwise, has an objective that philosophy does not. At its essence, it is a contract between two people, one of whom is being paid for the benefit of the other. The value of psychotherapy as well as psychoanalysis is couched in many ways, but what all treatments share in common is that something should change for the patient who has invested so much in it. If Laing (and other existential practitioners) believed the dynamic between authentic and inauthentic ways of relating was a useful way of couching the outcome of such endeavours, that seems no less justifiable a way of articulating it as any other. I don't believe Laing ever stated that people ought to be more authentic than they are; he was merely trying to bring their attention to the possible costs of not being aware of such matters.

As John pointed out in his illuminating critique of Heidegger's conception of authenticity, the concept resists definition and necessarily requires from each of us our own relationship with it; not only in terms of understanding it, but more importantly, in the manner that we live it. I don't believe that Laing ever claimed that authenticity was a kind of contest. If anything, he tried to be quite honest about his own faults and limitations, even indiscretions, in his characterization of his role in the therapeutic relationship. He even admitted to wondering whether the people he typically saw in therapy were more together than he was! This kind of honesty represented a conception of authenticity that Laing was quite good at, and was consistent with a sceptical frame of reference. If anything, he frequently went out of his way, in virtually every public lecture of his that I attended, to state that he did not consider himself to be any healthier, or more sane, and by implication, more authentic than the people he treated in his clinical practice. It seemed to me that the point he was making was that the capacity to *be who you are*, and to level with your patients accordingly, just might be the most therapeutic way of connecting with them, on a man to man basis, as he was fond of saying.

I agree with John that, for Heidegger, authenticity is a very ambiguous concept, but I'm not certain that it follows Laing did not grasp this, nor that Laing relentlessly focused on whether he and those around him were behaving authentically. Laing was perfectly aware of the inherent problem in determining what is or isn't authentic relating. And embracing the fact of one's very human station as an inherently inauthentic creature was a conclusion that Laing took for granted, both in himself and his patients. Laing's critique of his own critique concerning authentic modes of existing is itself a Heideggerian sensibility in its essence. Naturally, Laing was not going to address this question in the same manner as Heidegger. Laing was interested in situating his questioning in an explicitly clinical setting, one with which Heidegger was not concerned. That being said, I agree with John in suggesting that Laing's goal, unlike Heidegger's, was to raise one's awareness to what it means to live one's life in an inherently inauthentic fashion and to use psychotherapy as a means to becoming more authentic wherever possible – and desirable. This doesn't, however, constitute a 'moralizing' perspective, but a practical one. Our lives are improved by virtue of becoming acquainted with this distinction. One is still free to choose what seems right, expedient, or even necessary, without invoking an ought in the equation. That a state of mind or being is desirable does not render it moralistic. It seems to me this is precisely the point of an existential-based way of approaching psychotherapy.

I know that my time is running out, and I wish we had more space to carry our conversation further. I want to close with a statement as to Laing's legacy and his contribution to the existential clinical tradition. Most people know Laing from his many publications, and others from the extraordinary attention paid to his clinical experiments at Kingsley Hall and the subsequent houses that continue to operate to this day. It seems to me that these houses epitomize a more authentic way of establishing a therapeutic relationship with those who are usually too vulnerable to fend for themselves, and who seek a safe haven from those determined to 'treat' them whether they want treatment or not. This levelling of the playing field between 'doctor' and 'patient' was as radical an idea in 1965, when Laing established Kingsley Hall, as it is now. However complicated and contradictory Laing's legacy may be, every one of us owes him more than we can ever repay. And the world, despite having drifted away from environmental explanations for the causes of psychotic disturbance, owes him a debt of gratitude for bringing the treatment of the mentally disturbed from the back wards of mental hospitals onto the front covers of newspapers and magazines where they have remained ever since. Despite his faults and, at times, disgraceful behaviour, he was also, as his old friend Rollo May once remarked, 'on the side of the angels'. He persuaded an entire generation, including myself, to put our money where our mouth is and enter the cruel fray of the mental health establishment – an oxymoron if there ever was one, and play a role in helping those who are too vulnerable to help themselves. And for that we should be eternally grateful.

AUTHENTICITY AND GREEK CYNICISM
John M. Heaton

Perhaps the crucial remark which shows the difference between Mike Thompson and myself is: 'That a state of mind or being is desirable does not render it moralistic. It seems to me this is precisely the point of an existential-based way of approaching psychotherapy' (p. 122). There is a crucial difference between a state of mind and a state of being. A state of mind is a matter for psychology. A state of being is radically different, this is studied by philosophy. From Aristotle to Heidegger it has been pointed out that the nature of being is the central problem for philosophy. To confuse the two is to fall into psychologism, which unfortunately many existential therapists do.

Let me illustrate this in the case of authenticity. A famous incident of Laing's occurred in Chicago (A. Laing 1997: 169). He was being shown round a mental hospital and came across a young girl, diagnosed as schizophrenic, who was naked and rocking herself, refusing to speak to anyone, in a corner of her room. He immediately undressed, went into her room, and sat beside the girl. Soon she started to speak to him, a human contact had been made. Now I would say this was an authentic act on Laing's part. Why? Because it worked – the girl was obviously in a state of despair and he managed to make human contact with her which is a difficult thing to do. Furthermore, to see that it was so, we do not need to look into either the girl's mind or Laing's – their state of mind is indifferent to us. This type of act was characteristic of Laing.

Now what about his 'disgraceful' behaviour, many incidents of which were reported by his son (A. Laing 1997), and by Mike in his treatment of Carl Rogers? Was that authentic? I would say no, because he was not properly attuned (*gestimmt*) to the people he was with, and so to himself, at the time. The people involved were not interested in being 'enlightened' by Laing, so felt he was merely being rude or abusive. Note that this judgement is not about Laing's state of mind but about the effectiveness of his actions.

Laing admired Nietzsche greatly. Nietzsche thought that Cynic scepticism is a necessary step to any new order. He wrote: 'The modern Diogenes – Before one seeks a human being, one must have found a lantern. Will it have to be the lantern of the Cynic?'; 'The highest one can reach on earth is Cynicism' (both quoted in Desmond 2008: 231–232). Much of Laing's writing (especially Laing 1967) and behaviour are reminiscent of the Cynics.

The ancient Cynics were notorious for outrageous behaviour, especially satire on the vanity of civilization. Thus Diogenes, a famous cynic, one day went out into the marketplace at noon with a lighted lantern, 'seeking a human being' (Desmond 2008: 21). This was a quote that Laing liked. Once Diogenes was visited by Alexander the Great, who found him lolling in the sun. The king offered him his choice of gifts. Diogenes replied dismissively: 'Stand out of my sun' (Desmond 2008: 2). Diogenes once did not behave well at a dinner and the guests called him a dog, so he lifted up his leg like a dog and urinated on them (p. 88).

There are many stories of Cynics' behaviour. They would have sex and masturbate in public, make rude and witty jokes, have fantastical humour and public antics, and satire of rich elites. Was this authentic? Yes, if it was timed appropriately and they were attuned to people. Cynicism flourished in the Greek and Roman world from about the fourth century BC until about 529 AD when the Christians destroyed all pagan religion. Cynics were to be seen in the city streets, country roads, and would associate mostly with ordinary people but at times with kings and even the Roman emperor himself. They were mostly wanderers, with almost no possessions, who made it their business to chastise people for their greed, vanity, and lack of courage. Their aim was to live as close to nature as possible, to be self-sufficient and free.

When we judge authenticity we are not concerned with the state of mind of the participants but with their actions and their attunement to others. This is a matter of judgement, not definition or analysis of the mind. Thus many saw the actions of the Cynics as just crazy. Others were deeply impressed. The Cynics often changed people's lives.

Lastly I want to emphasize the relation between authenticity and integrity. Nietzsche sought to show that we each have a perspective on the world, that the world for us is the horizon of interpretive meaning within which judgements can be true or false. It is wrong to imagine we can dissociate from the world and judge it impartially – a position that many psychiatrists and psychoanalysts take. To use Kierkegaard's terms, the ethicist lacks 'subjective truth'; he imagines he can be a universal spectator of himself and others and so judge actions from a universalist point of view, what is now called a 'view from nowhere'. So he lacks integrity, he is estranged from his being in the world. Laing, however he expressed himself, was Laing.

Notes

1 See Thompson (2004, 2006) for a detailed examination of both Nietzsche's and Heidegger's respective views on authenticity.
2 See Sartre (1981) for a thorough discussion of bad faith and its relationship to psychotherapy.
3 See Thompson (1997) for a description of how a typical post-Kingsley Hall Philadelphia Association household functioned in its adherence to Laing's treatment philosophy; I lived in a house of this kind, at Portland Road, for four years, from 1973 to 1977.

References

Clay, J. (1996) *R. D. Laing: A Divided Self*, London: Sceptre Books.

Desmond, W. (2008) *Cynics*, Stocksfield: Acumen Press.

Heidegger, M. (1962 [1927]) *Being and Time*, trans. J. R. Macquarrie and E. Robinson, Oxford: Blackwell.

Heidegger, M. (1972 [1969]) 'My way to phenomenology', trans. J. Stambaugh, in M. Heidegger, *On Time and Being*, New York: Harper and Row.

Heidegger, M. (2006 [1997]) *Mindfulness*, trans. P. Emad and T. Kilary, London and New York: Continuum.

Kierkegaard, S. (1956 [1847]) *Purity Of Heart Is To Will One Thing*, trans. D. Steere, New York: Harper and Row.

Laing, A. (1997) *R. D. Laing A Life*, London: HarperCollins.

Laing, R. D. (1960) *The Divided Self*, London: Tavistock Books.

Laing, R. D. (1961/1969) *Self and Others*, New York and London: Penguin Books.

Laing, R. D. (1967) *The Politics of Experience*, New York: Pantheon Books.

Laing, R. D. (1970) *Knots*, London: Tavistock Books.

Laing, R. D. (1971) *The Politics of the Family*, London: Tavistock Books.

Merleau-Ponty, M. (1964 [1960]) 'Reading Montaigne', trans. R. McCleary, in M. Merleau-Ponty, *Signs*, Evanston, IL: Northwestern University Press.

Mullan, B. (1995) *Mad to be Normal: Conversations with R. D. Laing*, London: Free Association Books.

Mullan, B. (ed.) (1997) *R. D. Laing: Creative Destroyer*, London: Cassell.

Nietzsche, F. (2006) *Thus Spoke Zarathrustra: A Book for All and None*, trans. A. Del Caro, Cambridge: Cambridge University Press.

Proclus (1987) *Commentary on Plato's Parmenides*, trans. G. R. Morrow and J. M. Dillon, Princeton, NJ: Princeton University Press.

Sartre, J.-P. (1981 [1943]) *Existential Psychoanalysis*, trans. H. Barnes, New York: Philosophical Library.

Staehler, T. (2008) 'Unambiguous calling? Authenticity and ethics in Heidegger's *Being and Time*', *Journal of the British Society of Phenomenology*, 39: 293–313.

Thompson, M. G. (1997) 'The fidelity to experience in R. D. Laing's treatment philosophy', *Contemporary Psychoanalysis*, 33 (4).

Thompson, M. G. (2004) 'Postmodernism and psychoanalysis: a Heideggerian critique of postmodern malaise and the question of authenticity', in J. Reppen, M. Schulman and J. Tucker (eds.) *Way Beyond Freud: Postmodern Psychoanalysis Evaluated*, London: Open Gate Press.

Thompson, M. G. (2006) 'Vicissitudes of authenticity in the psychoanalytic situation', *Contemporary Psychoanalysis*, 42 (2).

Winnicott, D. W. (1976 [1960]) 'Ego distortion in terms of true and false self', in D. W. Winnicott *The Maturational Processes and the Facilitating Environment*, London: Hogarth Press.

Chapter 9

The existential 'therapy' of Thomas Szasz

Existential, yes; therapy, no[1]

Keith Hoeller

The present work [*The Myth of Psychotherapy*] is an effort to complete the demythologizing of psychiatry begun in *The Myth of Mental Illness*. As mental illness is the core concept of what psychiatrists allegedly study, so psychotherapy is the paradigmatic practice in which they supposedly engage. The task of psychiatric demythologizing would thus remain incomplete without scrutinizing the ideas and interventions that psychiatrists designate by the term *psychotherapy*.

(Szasz 1978: xv)[2]

Psychiatrist Thomas Szasz is best known for his attempt to dismantle the so-called 'medical model' of psychology. After being rejected by numerous psychiatry journals, his essay 'The Myth of Mental Illness' was published by the *American Psychologist* 50 years ago (February 1960). 'My aim in this essay is to ask if there is such a thing as mental illness, and to argue that there is not' (1960: 113).

In his book *The Myth of Mental Illness: Foundations of a Theory of Personal Conduct* (1961), Szasz announced that the purpose of his 'destruction' of the theory and practice of *involuntary* psychiatry was to create a new kind of *voluntary* psychotherapy:

I should like to make clear, therefore, that although I consider the concept of mental illness to be unserviceable, I believe that psychiatry could be a science.[3] I also believe that psychotherapy is an effective method of helping people – not to recover from an 'illness,' it is true, but rather to learn about themselves, others, and life.

(1961: xi)

Szasz's monumental task reminds us of Heidegger's task to 'deconstruct' metaphysics in order to clear the way for a retrieval of being; likewise, Szasz had to deconstruct the entire history of psychiatry in order to retrieve the promise of a non-medical psychotherapy as originally practised by Socrates and Plato. Yet Szasz's positive contributions to the theory and practice of psychotherapy have been neglected.

Already in an early paper Szasz suggests that the ideal therapeutic relation would be one of 'mutuality', which 'requires an awareness of the other person as a human being exquisitely *distinct* from oneself, and yet *like* oneself' (1956: 220). Szasz continued to develop the idea of a non-paternalistic psychoanalysis as a relation between legal and social equals. In a classic paper, co-authored with Marc Hollender, he discusses 'three basic models of the physician–patient relationship', predicated on different dynamics of status and power: the Activity–Passivity Model, in which the active doctor operates on a passive patient; the Guidance–Cooperation Model, in which 'the patient is expected to "look up to" and to "obey" his doctor', and the model of Mutual Participation 'predicated on the postulate that equality among human beings is desirable' (1956: 587). Szasz and Hollender note that this model 'is essentially foreign to medicine' and that 'the physician may be said to help the patient to help himself' (p. 588). This model depends on the agreement between doctor and patient as to what is good and bad: 'Without such agreement it is meaningless to speak of a therapeutic relationship.' These and other reflections led Szasz to develop in *The Ethics of Psychoanalysis* (1965a) a type of 'therapy' that would naturally flow from his critique of 'mental illness'. In *The Myth of Psychotherapy: Mental Healing as Religion, Rhetoric, and Repression* (1978) he sought to replace the pseudomedical term 'psychotherapy' with an expression issued from the philosophical approach of Socrates – 'Psychotherapy as the cure of souls' (1978: 28).

The development of an autonomous psychoanalysis

Szasz *et al.* (1958) highlight two different strains in nineteenth-century psychiatric thinking: Kraepelin's attempt to classify mental illnesses as organic diseases (which must be eradicated, just as pathogenic bacteria are to be eradicated from the body); and Breuer and Freud's new psycho-analytic technique, which introduced 'the first genuinely communicative relationship (in a medical setting) between doctor and patient' (Szasz *et al.* 1958: 526). Szasz felt that Breuer and Freud had thus invented a secular, modern version of the priest–penitent relationship:

> I was interested in psychotherapy, in what seemed to me the core of the Freudian premise – and promise, which unfortunately, never material-ized as a professional code. Freud and Jung and Adler had a very good idea – that is, that two people, a professional and a client – get together, in a confidential relationship, and the one tries to help the other live his life better.
>
> (Wyatt 2000: 8)

In Freud's initial practice, Szasz says, 'there's no coercion. It's entirely contractual. The client pays' (Sullum 2000). But Szasz believes that, partly through remaining wedded to 'the self-contradictory proposition that psychoanalysis is both a dialogue and a treatment' (1998: 9), Freud contradicted the promise of psychoanalysis:

> He sacrificed it by betraying confidentiality, by creating training analysis, by creating child analysis, and so on. It immediately became a thing where the premise was that the therapist knows more about the patient than the patient himself. There was a kind of manipulation, exploitation involved.
>
> (Sullum 2000)

Unfortunately, Freud chose the paternalism inherent in the pseudo-medical model, which postulates that behaviour is not freely chosen; rather, it is the product of unseen (and unconscious) forces over which the individual has little or no control. Since the person is neither aware, nor in control of himself, he is therefore dangerous. It then becomes necessary that the doctor play the role of the police and resort to force, fraud, and coercion, if necessary, in order to protect the individual from herself and others. Szasz saw that one of the first steps in developing an autonomous psychotherapy was therefore to make therapy itself autonomous from medicine.

Since the 1940s, there had been a burgeoning field of non-medical counsellors, therapists, and social workers of many theoretical persuasions. But the American Psychiatric Association's (APA) official position was that psychotherapy was a medical enterprise: it should either be practised by doctors, or practised under the supervision of doctors. The APA had mounted a nationwide campaign to prevent clinical psychologists from obtaining licensure by the states. Since Szasz was convinced that psychiatry was not in fact a legitimate medical science, psychotherapy too should not be a medical specialty. In 1959, Szasz entered the debate between psychiatrists and psychologists and threw his weight behind the movement for non-medical therapy. He argued that it is 'scientifically indefensible' to restrict therapy by alleging it is a form of medical treatment: therapists deal with 'problems in living'.

Prior to *The Myth of Mental Illness*, Szasz exhibits little familiarity with existential philosophy and psychology. In a phone conversation, Szasz told me that much of his early knowledge of existentialism came from reading Karl Jaspers (personal communication, April 2010). The first edition of *The Myth* (1961), however, does cite several existential philosophers, including William Barrett, Simone de Beauvoir, Martin Heidegger, Karl Jaspers, Walter Kaufman, Søren Kierkegaard, and Friedrich Nietzsche. He also discusses 'existential analysis' as 'the third major nonorganic school of European psychiatry', citing Ludwig Binswanger and Rollo May. Yet he is quite dismissive of both existential philosophy and psychology, arguing that existential psychologists, in turning their backs on psychiatry and the medical model, were abandoning the psychosocial sciences as well, and all for a philosophical movement of dubious scientific and moral value (1961: 95).

It is significant that this criticism is entirely missing in the revised edition of *The Myth of Mental Illness* (1974b). Indeed, immediately after *The Myth*, Szasz begins to regularly cite many of the existentialists in a positive manner. Szasz became more familiar with existentialism when, in the 1960s, an editor of *The New Republic* asked him to review some of Camus's works for him (personal communication, April 2010).

'Human Nature and Psychotherapy: A Further Contribution to the Theory of Autonomous Psychotherapy' (1962) reads much like an essay in existential philosophy, with references to Camus and Sartre. Szasz speaks of 'Moral Man' who is autonomous and able to make choices and decisions. He describes five fundamental moral dilemmas that each of us must face: (1) Autonomy Vs. Heteronomy; (2) Domination Vs. Submission; (3) Meaning Vs. Futility; (4) Individuation Vs. Group Identity; and (5) Socialization Vs. Alienation.

Szasz's 'autonomous therapy' is based upon this existential view of human nature. Therapy should not be about either predicting or controlling human behaviour; it should be about understanding it. And coercion and force are inimical to understanding:

> In the study of man, control, in any absolute sense, can be neither a legitimate scientific aim, nor a reasonable criterion of the value of theory . . . if our aim is understanding, we must eschew power, for it is a hindrance, not a help in understanding our fellow man.
>
> (1962: 281)

Szasz saw Camus as 'a secular moralist' who had succeeded 'in delineating the outlines of an ethic of personal autonomy', and given us 'an ethic that is at once humanistic and humble' (1965b: 33). He admired Camus's clear sense of limits or moderation: 'It is clear who must set the limits for man; himself, and if not he, the State. But who must set the limits for the State?' (1965b: 33). Indeed, Szasz pinpoints 'The Moral Dilemma of Psychiatry' as the decision about autonomy or heteronomy (1964). The psychiatrist must ask himself: Whose side are you on? Is your goal to do the bidding of others by controlling a person who has been sent to you? Or is your goal to help a person understand themselves on their own terms?

The ethics of psychoanalysis

Where does this leave us with respect to describing and understanding what so-called psychotherapists do with their patients or clients? It leaves us with the challenge, first, of having to unmask the false medical conceptualization of the psychotherapeutic enterprise; and, second, of having to recast it in a nonmedical, nondiagnostic, and nontherapeutic framework and vocabulary.

(1974a: 521)

In *The Ethics of Psychoanalysis* (1965a) he lays out the principles of what he calls 'autonomous psychotherapy'. He points out that the term 'psycho-analysis' may be misleading. But he wanted to call attention to its possibilities, and to avoid any neologisms. In *The Myth of Psychotherapy* he overcomes his reluctance and suggests a new word for psychotherapy that comes from the Ancient Greeks: *iatroi logoi* (healing words). Therapists would be called *iatrologicians*, specialists of the art (not science) of rhetoric (1978: 208).

While psychiatry traces the history of psychotherapy back to the Ancient Greek doctor Hippocrates, Szasz identifies its creators as his philosophical counterparts: Socrates and Plato. The Socratic method of dialectic was the first kind of 'psychotherapy': it consisted of two people asking questions about important matters of life such as justice, courage, friendship, love, knowledge, wisdom, and of course the ideal society.

Ultimately, Szasz came to conclude that he could no longer call himself a psychoanalyst:

> Many years ago, I ceased to identify myself as a psychoanalyst. Why? Because I wanted to be faithful to my belief, which I have held ever since I knew anything about psychoanalysis, that *psychoanalysis is a moral, not a medical, activity.*

(2003b: 53)

Szasz proposes a unique kind of contract between two free, equal, competent, consenting adults. It is oral, not written, and 'the participants understand that neither legal nor even social sanctions are available for punishing the party who breaks the contract' (1965a: 105). If the client breaks the contract, the therapist is free to terminate it; if the therapist breaks it, the client is free to terminate. Szasz realizes that 'many of the practices psychoanalysts engage in – such as child analysis, training analysis, prescribing drugs, hospitalizing the patient, communicating with the patient's spouse, would all be prohibited by such a contract' (1988: x).[4]

Szasz says that his practice does not include diagnosis, writing letters excusing the client's behaviour, communicating with employers or with the courts. If the client wants someone to know she is in therapy, she can provide a copy of her cheque or invoice. He does not do couples or any kind of group therapy. He does not see children. He doesn't take insurance or any third party payments. He doesn't even take notes. Indeed, virtually the entire book is a lesson in what not to do, and it advises therapists to set aside their training and nearly everything they do with and to their patients.

So, what does Szasz do in therapy? What approach does he use? Where does one go to get trained, or how does one learn to be a Szaszian therapist? Where can one find some of his famous 'case histories' testifying to the wonders of his new brand of therapy? Where is the evidence that Szasz's method and techniques are more effective than other methods of therapy? Who are the famous disciples of Szasz? All of these questions issue from the framework of medicalized psychotherapy: like the myth of mental illness, psychotherapy is a metaphor that has been literalized. 'Psychotherapy is conversation, and conversation is not treatment' (1974a: 517). It is the concept of disease that leads to the concepts of diagnosis and treatment. And treatment leads to the idea that there are 'techniques' that can be specifically applied to each disease. Szasz's thesis is that:

> The practice of analytic technique issues from the personality of the analyst and can never be distinct from it. In this respect, the analyst's technique differs radically from techniques of medical healing, but is similar to such personal habits as honesty and politeness . . . it is not something that he can pick up or discard at will.
>
> (1965a: 39)

This makes psychotherapy analogous to education and teaching. Indeed, Chapter 3 of *The Ethics of Psychoanalysis* is entitled 'Psychoanalytic Treatment as Education'. Yet Szasz never abandoned his belief in the healing power of a professional relationship. He ends 'Cleansing the Modern Heart' with a section on 'The Ethical Duty of Psychoanalysis', summarizing 'the moral and political–economic core of, and the social conditions for the psychoanalytic situation' as follows:

> They are: the inviolable privacy of the professional–client relationship; the client's willingness to assume responsibility for his behavior and pay for the service he receives; the analyst's willingness to eschew coercion justified by the legal–psychiatric principle of the 'duty to protect' (the client from himself and the community from the client); the legal system's willingness to exempt the analyst from this principle (at present an integral part of the mental health professional's legal and social mandate); and the public's willingness to accept that a secure guarantee of privacy and confidentiality, similar to that granted the priest, as an indispensable condition for the proper conduct of psychoanalysis as a secular 'cure of souls.' These conditions are absent in the therapeutic state. The result is a tragic loss of liberty for client, 'therapist,' and society.
>
> (2003b: 59)

The existential 'therapy' of Thomas Szasz

In *Existentialism*, Mary Warnock emphasizes that the term 'existentialism' 'does not designate a system or a school; there are some philosophers who might be described as Existentialists but who would reject the title; others who might be surprised to be so described' (Warnock 1970: 1).

> We can say that the common interest which unites Existentialist philosophers is the interest in human freedom. They are all of them interested in the world considered as the environment of man, who is treated as a unique object of attention, because of his power to choose his own courses of action. . . . They aim above all to show people *that they are free.*
>
> (Warnock 1970: 1)

Freedom is thus the first shared characteristic of existentialism. The second one is that in the realm of human behaviour 'causation is an illusion' and that all the existentialists have a 'missionary spirit':

> They want the facts about human freedom, as they conceive them, to be not merely accepted, but absorbed by each person for himself, so that when he has absorbed them, his whole view of his life will be different.
>
> (Warnock 1970: 2)

It is, therefore, 'a committed and practical philosophy' that is primarily concerned with ethics, questions of right and wrong.

More recently, Thomas Flynn lists five key themes which 'depict a family resemblance . . . among these philosophers': (1) existence precedes essence; (2) time is of the essence; (3) humanism; (4) freedom/responsibility; (5) ethical considerations are paramount (Flynn 2006: 11). Since Szasz has repeatedly defined his two major themes as freedom and responsibility, his kinship with existential philosophy, which has grown stronger over the years, should be self-evident. His books and articles repeatedly cite existential writers such as Chekhov, Dostoevsky, Kafka, and Tolstoy, and he regularly uses the word 'existential' as an adjective (Stadlen 2003: 233–234, note 10).

Since Szasz's critique of the pseudomedical model has been intended to return psychotherapy clients to the status of free and responsible adults, non-medical therapists of all types, but especially existential therapists, ought to welcome him with open arms. Szasz himself writes:

> My views on psychotherapy have been influenced by existential philosophers, a debt I have acknowledged. Also, to the best of my

knowledge, I was the first medically trained psychoanalyst in the United States to condemn the opposition of American psychoanalysts to non-medical analysis and psychotherapy. For these reasons, it seems to me that my writings ought to appeal to existential analysts.

(2003a: 203)

Indeed, Szasz has long served on the editorial boards of the *Review of Existential Psychology and Psychiatry, Journal of Humanistic Psychology*, and *Existential Analysis*. Yet while Szasz has undoubtedly embraced existential *philosophy*, there has been a tension between Szasz and existential *psychotherapy*. Szasz has pointedly criticized existential psychiatrists and therapists on two counts: the employment of the term 'antipsychiatry'; and the use of force and fraud. As we have seen, he has rejected the terms 'therapy' and 'analysis' with all of their medical implications.

Szasz has criticized the existential psychiatrist R. D. Laing for the discrepancy between his views and his actions, most recently in his book *Antipsychiatry: Quackery Squared* (2009). Szasz objects to the term 'antipsychiatry' because it is in effect a smear word. It is akin to calling all people who oppose paedophilia by Catholic priests 'anti-Catholic'. Szasz believes that Laing and Cooper diverted attention away from his own critique of the heart of psychiatry and that he himself then became tarred by the anti-psychiatry brush.

Szasz adds that 'many psychiatrists and psychologists identified as existentialists embrace psychiatric brutalities, which I reject' (2003a: 204), and furthermore that few existential therapists have been willing to publicly condemn and repudiate the twin pillars of psychiatry: involuntary commitment and the insanity defence. He specifically cites Boss's use of involuntary treatment, Heidegger's refusal to condemn the National Socialism and Nazi psychiatrists, and Sartre's refusal to criticize the Soviet Gulag and the 'systematic murder of mental patients by French psychiatrists during the Occupation' (2003a: 204).

In *Insanity*, while Szasz credits both the humanistic and existential psychologists for bringing the concept of intentionality to the fore, he points out that:

> To my knowledge, not a single will psychologist or existential psychiatrist has criticized the cognitive–ethical absurdities of the insanity defence or urged its abolition, raising doubts about the sincerity or seriousness of their belief that persons conventionally regarded as insane possess free will and are therefore responsible for their behaviour.
>
> (1987: 231–232)

What, then, is existential therapy? In *Freedom and Destiny*, the existential psychotherapist Rollo May asks: 'What is the purpose of therapy?' (1981:

18). He rejects 'adjustment' because it 'means that the therapist is the psychic policeman for the society, a role that I, for one, heartily detest' (p. 19). May believes that freedom – not happiness – is the number one goal of therapy:

> I propose that *the purpose of the psychotherapy is to set people free.* . . . I believe that the therapist's function should be to help people become free to be aware of and to experience their possibilities.
>
> (pp. 19–20)

My own view is that 'perhaps more than any other type of therapist, existentialists do not shy away from philosophical questions' (Hoeller 1990: 198):

> Psychotherapy is one of several contemporary ways of asking the question of the ultimate meaning of life, in other words, 'How should I live?' This question is intimately entwined with questions of meaning, ethics, and politics. . . . The purpose of psychotherapy is to show the client, sometimes by example, that there are other ways to be and other choices that can be made. Choosing always involves risk, however, as the human condition always contains an element of the tragic, and this is what makes humans noble.
>
> (Hoeller 1990: 197)

Szasz has not escaped criticism from several existential therapists. There are two main criticisms of Szasz intended to show that he is not an existential therapist: the first is that his insistence that mental illness is a myth stems from a kind of Cartesian dualism; the second is that there are times when therapists should break confidentiality to force 'treatment' on their clients.

In an exchange of views in the journal *Existential Analysis*, Burston argues that 'Szasz is *not* an existentialist when it comes to the mind/body issue' (2004: 219). Hetherington says that 'he is unashamedly dualistic in his thinking, proclaiming that illness "can affect only the body" so that "there can be no mental illness"' (2002: 229). Stadlen notes that 'the reader is told, in advance, that Szasz's "thinking" is "dualistic", and that Szasz is not "ashamed" of this, though by implication he should be'; similarly, the term 'proclaiming' implies Szasz's lack of well-considered argumentation (Stadlen 2003: 217).

Though Burston says that 'the phrase "mental illness" is actually a thundering contradiction in terms, which perpetuates and inscribes the Cartesian mind/body dualism in the discourse of the mental health professions' (Burston 2004: 219), he also says that 'decades of research on psychosomatic, psychophysiological, and psychoneuroimmunological disorders indicate that Szasz's dicta are predicated on a distinction between mental and physical disease that is completely untenable' (Burston 2004: 219). Yet he does not reference a single such study, let alone one that would disprove Szasz's claim that 'minds' cannot be sick except in a metaphorical sense – Szasz's key point.

As far as enforced treatment is concerned, when Burston says he is opposed to involuntary hospitalization because a therapist who uses coercion 'cease(s) to function as a therapist', he seems to be agreeing with Szasz on a fundamental point. But he hastens to add that if people other than the therapist should involuntarily commit someone, it 'cannot be helped. Some things are more precious than the therapeutic alliance' (Burston 2004: 228). He adds that 'similar constraints prevent us from maintaining complete confidentiality when a client's behaviour poses a grave risk to another human being' (Burston 2004: 227). If a therapist fails in his duty to warn, she 'becomes an accomplice to mischief and murder' (Burston 2004: 227).

Burston is strongly opposed to Szasz's idea that we have a right to be a danger to ourselves, that is, a right to suicide. He writes that an anorexic teenager or young adult 'has not yet lived, and to allow such a one to take her own life "freely" without attempting to alert or assist her family in any way is perverse, in my view' (Burston 2004: 227). Furthermore, 'by valuing life above the principle of confidentiality, we are making an ethical judgment – the wrong one, in Szasz's view; the right one, in mine' (Burston 2004: 227).

But why should therapists play the role of policeman? Priests take a vow, supported by law, of absolute confidentiality as to what they are told in the confessional. The attorney–client privilege also protects the client by preventing his attorney from breaking his obligation of confidentiality. Burston states that while priests rightly have such a responsibility to keep quiet, therapists have none, since they are not, as Szasz claims, 'secular priests' or 'confessors'. He does not explain why therapists should play policeman, but priests and attorneys should not.

These existential therapists, and others like them, either do not see, or do not care, that there is a fundamental contradiction between an existential philosophy dedicated to the freedom of the individual and a medical model that is dedicated to denying people that very same freedom.

Conclusion

Szasz, with his focus on freedom and responsibility, has remained more faithful to the key tenets of existential philosophy than many existential therapists. He has not only preached the gospel of freedom, but he has also practised it. Yet he is no more a 'therapist' than Socrates was a 'Sophist'. He no more does 'therapy' than Socrates practised 'sophistry'. His own dialogical 'cure of souls' can only be metaphorically – not literally – likened to 'therapy', and only with qualifiers. But if we understand 'therapy' in his terms as the ethical practice of a philosophical dialogue, then I think it fair to say that Szasz has developed an exemplar of existential 'therapy' that remains true to the principles of existential philosophy. He has, however, deliberately broken with all of the vestiges of the pseudomedical model. He wants nothing to do with the idea that psychotherapy of any type belongs within the health professions: 'The psychiatrist *qua* health care professional is a fraud' (2009: ix).

Unfortunately, many existential therapists and analysts have placed their primary fidelity in the traditional idea of psychotherapy as a quasi-medical enterprise involving diagnosis and treatment, and they refuse to see their clients as free and responsible adults. The pseudomedical model is still alive in some existential therapists, where it still serves as a justification for the breaking of confidentiality, and the use of coercion, force, and fraud in order to protect clients from themselves and society from their clients. While Rollo May detested the idea of playing 'psychic policeman', many existential therapists have embraced this role. There is no doubting the commitment of such existential therapists to psychotherapy. But there is ample reason to doubt their commitment to existentialism. If existential philosophy is to serve merely as pseudohumanistic rhetoric for the therapeutic state, then existential therapy has ceased to have any attachment to its philosophical roots.

I believe that an existential 'therapy' is still possible. But it will look more like Szasz's model than what has heretofore been called 'existential therapy':

> Let us, then, ask: What is existential psychotherapy *not*? My answer is: It is not a treatment for a medical ailment, it is not any kind of 'health service'. This view rests on two pillars. One is an extension and application to existential therapy that mental illness is not an illness and psychotherapy is not a treatment. The other is a critical analysis of the adjective 'existential,' in 'existential therapy'.
>
> (Szasz 2004: 128)

Szasz is challenging existential therapists to make a choice between existentialism, with its commitment to the fundamental value of human freedom, and therapy, with its commitment to the medical model and the denial of this freedom. For nearly three quarters of a century, existential therapists have rather unexistentially refused to make this choice, thinking they could have their cake and eat it. Szasz saw the contradiction in Freudian psychoanalysis between the idea of a free, voluntary dialogue between equals, and the paternalistic medical model that denied both freedom and responsibility to its victims. He has now highlighted the same contradiction at the heart of existential therapy.

Is existential 'therapy' a philosophical enterprise between equals based upon freedom and responsibility? Or is it a pseudomedical enterprise between two unequals based upon a deterministic theory of human nature and the use of deceit and force. Are people free and responsible for their behaviour, or is their behaviour the product of unknown and uncontrollable forces? Existential philosophers long ago decided on the former. It is high time that existential 'therapists' did so too.

In *States of Mind*, Jonathan Miller asks: 'So you're saying that whoever finds themselves distressed should seek relief from some ethical source, rather than from some medical one' (1983: 290). Szasz replied:

> Yes, that's right. It's a mistake for people to seek relief for existential or spiritual difficulties through technological means. . . . I hold all contemporary psychiatric approaches – all 'mental health' methods – as basically flawed because they all search for solutions along medical–technical lines. But solutions for what? For life! But life is not a problem to be solved. Life is something to be lived, as intelligently, as competently, as well as we can, day in and day out. Life is something we must endure. There is no solution for it.
>
> (Miller 1983: 290)

Notes

1 I am grateful to Thomas Szasz, Jeffner Allen, Greg Madison and Laura Barnett for their many helpful comments and suggestions on this chapter; I am of course solely responsible for its contents.
2 All references in this chapter will be to Szasz, unless otherwise specified.
3 A social, as opposed to a natural, science. Szasz later abandons this idea and says that therapy should be an art.
4 Szasz does not prescribe medications as he is not engaged in a medical enterprise. As a libertarian, however, Szasz favours allowing any competent adult to take any drug they want – indeed he believes that all drugs should be *legalized*.

References

Burston, D. (2004) 'Szasz, Laing, and psychotherapy', *Existential Analysis*, 15 (2): 218–229.
Flynn, T. (2006) *Existentialism: A Brief Insight*, New York: Sterling.
Hetherington, H. (2002) 'Comprehension and apprehension: lucidity and existence tension', *Existential Analysis*, 13 (2): 221–237.
Hoeller, K. (1990) 'Existential psychotherapy', in J. K. Zeig and M. Munion (eds) *What Is Psychotherapy? Contemporary Perspectives*, San Francisco: Jossey-Bass.
Hoeller, K. (1997) 'Thomas Szasz's history and philosophy of psychiatry', *Review of Existential Psychology and Psychiatry*, 23: 6–69.
May, R. (1981) *Freedom and Destiny*, New York: Norton.
Miller, J. (1983) *States of Mind*, New York: Pantheon Books.

Schaler, J. with Mastroniani, A. (2004) 'Bibliography of Thomas Szasz', in J. Schaler (ed.) *Szasz Under Fire The Psychiatric Abolitionist Faces His Critics*, Chicago: Open Court.

Stadlen, A. (2003) 'A poor model for those in training', *Existential Analysis*, 14 (2): 213–244.

Sullum, J. (2000) 'Curing the therapeutic state: Thomas Szasz interviewed by Jacob Sullum: Thomas Szasz on the medicalization of American life', *Reason*. Available at https://reason.com/archives/2000/07/01/curing-the-therapeutic-state-t.

Szasz, T. (1956) 'On the experiences of the analyst in the psychoanalytic situation: a contribution to the theory of psychoanalytic treatment', *Journal of the American Psychoanalytic Association*, 4: 197–223.

Szasz, T. (1959) 'Psychiatry, psychotherapy, and psychology', *AMA Archives of General Psychiatry*, 1: 455–463.

Szasz, T. (1960) 'The myth of mental illness', *American Psychologist*, 15: 113–180.

Szasz, T. (1961) *The Myth of Mental Illness: Foundations of a Theory of Personal Conduct*, New York: Hoeber-Harper.

Szasz, T. (1962) 'Human nature and psychotherapy: a further contribution to the theory of autonomous psychotherapy', *Comprehensive Psychiatry*, 3: 268–283.

Szasz, T. (1964) 'The moral dilemma of psychiatry: autonomy or heteronomy?', *American Journal of Psychiatry*, 121: 521–528.

Szasz, T. (1965a) *The Ethics of Psychoanalysis: The Theory and Method of Autonomous Psychotherapy*, New York: Basic Books.

Szasz, T. (1965b) 'Portrait of a secular moralist', *New Republic*, 27 November: 32–33.

Szasz, T. (1974a) 'The myth of psychotherapy', *American Journal of Psychotherapy*, 28: 517–526.

Szasz, T. (1974b) *The Myth of Mental Illness*, New York: Harper and Row.

Szasz, T. (1978) *The Myth of Psychotherapy: Mental Healing as Religion, Rhetoric, and Repression*, Garden City, NY: Anchor Press/Doubleday.

Szasz, T. (1987) *Insanity: The Idea and Its Consequences*, New York: Wiley.

Szasz, T. (1988) *The Ethics of Psychoanalysis: The Theory and Method of Autonomous Psychotherapy*, Syracuse, NY: Syracuse University Press.

Szasz, T. (1998) 'The healing word: its past, present, and future', *Journal of Humanistic Psychology*, 38 (2).

Szasz, T. (2003a) 'The secular cure of souls: "analysis" or dialogue?', *Existential Analysis*, 14 (2): 203–212.

Szasz, T. (2003b) 'Cleansing the modern heart', *Society*, May/June: 52–59.

Szasz, T. (2004) 'What is existential therapy *not*?', *Existential Analysis*, 16 (1): 127–130.

Szasz, T. (2009) *Antipsychiatry: Quackery Squared*, Syracuse, NY: Syracuse University Press.

Szasz, T. (2010) Personal communication.

Szasz, T. and Hollender, M. (1956) 'A contribution to the philosophy of medicine: the basic models of the doctor–patient relationship', *AMA Archives of Internal Medicine*, 97 (5): 585–592.

Szasz, T., Knoff, W. and Hollender, M. (1958) 'The doctor–patient relationship and its historical context', *American Journal of Psychiatry*, 115 (6): 522–528.

Warnock, M. (1970) *Existentialism*, New York: Oxford University Press.

Wyatt, R. C. (2000) 'An interview with Thomas Szasz, M.D.: Liberty and the practice of psychotherapy', available at http://www.psychotherapy.net/interview/Thomas_Szasz.

Chapter 10

A dialogue on dialogue

Mick Cooper and Ernesto Spinelli

We knew that our chapter could be one of two possibilities. First, we could write *about* dialogue. Second, we could attempt to *engage in* dialogue by beginning a 'dialogue on dialogue' and experiencing the uncertainty of that journey, where it would lead us and who we would feel ourselves to be through that journey. We have opted for the second choice and can only hope that readers experience something of the exciting sense of dialogue that we each experienced throughout the process.

From Mick

What is it that allows for a space to be created in which dialogue can happen? What kind of relationship needs to exist, if any, for dialogue to occur? I don't think you need to know someone: dialogue can emerge in a first meeting. But I feel there needs to be some kind of common language – and difference, in the sense that there needs to be something 'more than' what either holds already. It seems to me that dialogue is pulled apart when two people are wanting to take it in different directions. So common purpose seems to be one of the preconditions of dialogue: both parties need to want to have a dialogue – blindingly obvious at one level, but also, probably, critically important. So if, in entering this dialogue, I am solely concerned with impressing you, or with proving that I know more about dialogue than you, then dialogue, at that point, isn't going to be possible.

For me, a central element of the nature of dialogue is an interchanging, or an interpenetration, of perspectives or views. It's about me both expressing to you how I see things, and also taking in your views, being able to digest that, and, critically I think, allowing myself to be changed as a result of that; or, at least, being open to being changed. So, for us to have a genuine dialogue, we both have to be open to being changed by the other – or even want it: to learn, but also to be willing to teach.

From Ernesto

Whew! An *awful* lot in there and I'm not sure to what to respond. So I'll try taking a Gadamer-inspired route through this. Bear with me. Van Deurzen writes the following:

> The word, dialogue, literally means conversation, or if we go back to the Greek roots of the word, 'verbal consideration' or even 'dispute'. It does not mean a conversation between two partners: that would be duologue. It is therefore, interestingly, originally not the opposite of monologue. 'Dia' means 'through' and 'logo' means 'to talk'; dialogue is thus about talking through some issue, it is about working one's way across something with words.
>
> (1992: 15)

I think that this distinction is obviously relevant to the enterprise of psychotherapy in general and existential therapy in particular. It acknowledges that dialogue has an intentional focus.

Gadamer contrasted two types of dialogue: (1) dialogues that have been pre-set in their intention or direction by at least one of the participants: and (2) dialogues whose focus, intent and direction only emerge through the dialogue itself. All dialogues, Gadamer acknowledged, find a direction, but there exists a truthful quality to a dialogue that shapes its own form and focus (i.e. type 2) that cannot be experienced in the dialogue that is being actively directed toward a certain pre-set goal (i.e. type 1). One consequence of entering the second form of dialogue is that:

> the way one word follows another, with the conversation taking its own twists and reaching its own conclusion, may well be conducted in some way, but the partners conversing are far less the leaders than the led. No one knows in advance what will 'come out' of such a conversation.
>
> (Gadamer 2004: 383)

So, in responding to your initial points, I'm trying to remain open to the possibilities of this second type of dialogue; in part because it interests me, in part because I think that this is the dialogue that existential therapy claims to offer. Although I'm not sure how many existential therapists truly do offer it: it requires of the participants a receptive stance toward any unforeseen possibilities that may arise, and hence the abdication of the security that comes with the sense of directing change, 'doing it right', or of 'the expert's' superiority of knowledge and status.

Gadamer points out that we in the west have placed substantially more significant value upon the first type of dialogue, which dominates our understanding of how to go about discerning truth. It underpins the dominant mode of conducting research and lies at the heart of our methodological assumptions. However, Gadamer then throws down the experiential gauntlet and says, in effect: 'Okay. You claim to favour the first over the second type of dialogue, but look at your own life experience. Consider those dialogues that have truly impacted upon and shaped your life, that you return to as being meaningful, unforgettable and life changing. Now what do you see? Isn't it far more likely that these dialogues are more akin to type 2 than to type 1? But if so, why are we – and especially those "we's" who claim to be interested in understanding, meaning and truth – so dismissive of any investigation that is steeped in this type of dialogue? I suspect that, once again, an answer might lie in the implications of attempting to adopt type 2: insecurity, loss of expertise status, uncertainty of the impact of the investigation on the investigator. I think this parallels exactly your statement about dialogue as both being prepared to being changed by the other and wanting "to learn, but also to be willing to teach".'

The other day I was reading a fascinating paper by Max Velmans that looks at how we have attempted to define consciousness. He argues that what he terms 'materialist theory' (exemplified by people like Daniel Dennett) presupposes that:

> information about brain and behaviour obtained from a third-person perspective is scientific and reliable, while first-person data about conscious experience tells us nothing about its ontology at all. European phenomenology and classical Indian philosophy assume the opposite to be true. Accordingly, their investigations of consciousness have been primarily phenomenological. Within modern consciousness studies there are also many intermediate theoretical positions with associated research paradigms that take both the existence of the material world and the existence of consciousness seriously, for example viewing first- and third-person investigations of the mind/brain as complementary sources of information about its nature.
>
> (Velmans 2009: 141)

When I read this, it seemed to me that Gadamer's distinction on dialogue was being expressed yet again, but that a third position was emerging that both acknowledged that distinction and valued what each approach has to offer. If we look at the state of psychotherapy research, we can see that the dilemma posed by Velmans in the quote above is also valid *but* that, as yet, no significant 'intermediate theoretical position' has been postulated, let alone attained a substantial degree of acknowledgement and respect. In theory at least, existential therapy stands as an exemplar of first-person inquiry. Indeed I have long argued that doing existential therapy is in many ways the equivalent of conducting structured phenomenological enquiry and in this sense the therapy (and/or the dialogue) *is* the methodology (Spinelli 2005, 2007).

Thinking about dialogue, I went back to a talk that Szasz gave to the Society for Existential Analysis and I found this quote from Freud:

> Words are the essential tool of mental treatment. A layman will no doubt find it hard to understand how pathological disorders of the body and mind can be eliminated by 'mere' words. He will feel that he is being asked to believe in magic. And he will not be so very wrong, for the words which we use in our everyday speech are nothing other than watered-down magic.
>
> (Freud, cited in Szasz 1992: 2)

Thinking about our discussion has, I think, helped me focus and clarify thoughts around the distinction between relatedness and relationship. For me, relatedness (the being/world matrix that existential theory claims underpins all possibility of reflective thought and experience) is the foundational grounding upon which the whole of existential theory rests. It is, for me, what makes it such a radical western theory (though to people from non-western traditions it seems a bit simplistic and simple-minded!). It's also what makes it such a damnably difficult theory to talk about – because our very language contradicts its ideas. So, for me, relationships are one form or manifestation of relatedness. I can disavow all relationships and still be expressing relatedness (in fact, it's only through relatedness that I can make such disavowals).

Now, therapists – or most therapists – keep banging on about the importance of the relationship itself. But for me, the dilemma is that there are so many different expressions of relationship – from relatively egalitarian to autocratic – and not only between different therapists, the same therapist experiences being in quite different relationships with different clients, or even at different times with the same client. Now, I've read, and you know better than me about this, that there is no evidence to suggest that any particular kind of relationship provokes any better outcome than any other – yet the relationship is critical to beneficial outcomes. How do we make sense of this?

We can begin by considering relatedness from another angle: relatedness, being-in-the-world, worlding (my own limited contribution [Spinelli 2007]) all serve to place our reflective experience of being within a set of inescapable *contextual* conditions. These contextual conditions provide the structure to all our reflections. But they are also under constant flux and in this sense each being's experience of being is constantly novel and unrepeatable.

So, with therapy, every therapeutic relationship is created within a context (relatedness) in that we say 'now we are doing therapy; now I am a therapist; now I am a client'. The context itself shapes the way of being of the participants. For all we know, the context has already in and of itself provoked many of those beneficial outcomes attributed to the 'doing' of therapy (Spinelli 2007, 2009).

My interest in recent research on the placebo, or 'contextual healing' as it is beginning to be called, arose because the distinction that medical researchers were making between 'instrumental healing' and 'contextual healing' seemed to be exactly pinpointing the dilemma that therapists face. We have, like most doctors and surgeons, assumed that only skills-based interventions serve as the indicators of outcome. Placebo–research contradicts this and proposes that contextual factors are as significant – if not more significant, in that they set the magical context for effective interventions (Spinelli 2009).

If we think of Freud's quote above, we can see that he was getting at something like this. Words are magical within a set context that we call therapy. The words in and of themselves don't hold any magic to them. It is only when the words are expressed and considered within a particular set of contextual conditions, by the *contextualized beings in dialogue* that they act as agents of healing – whether for the client or the therapist or both.

For existential therapy, this raises questions about the therapist's *dialogical attitude or disposition*. Martin Buber's notion of *inclusion* (Friedman 1964) addresses significant aspects of this attitude. Leslie Farber's dialogical concerns centred on *a way of talking* that led both therapist and client toward a 'truthful dialogue' with themselves and one another, the 'whatness' of therapeutic dialogue could 'be about' anything – i.e. the content of the discussion did not truly matter (Farber 1967, 2000). This way of talking is addressed by Gadamer's type-2 dialogue. This is *not* unstructured, non-directional dialogue, but it provokes a different sense of structure and direction which is not open to enquiry along the lines associated with 'evidence-based therapy'. What do you get from all this?

From Mick

Ernesto, thank you for your wonderfully erudite and stimulating correspondence. I have to confess that this is the fifth or sixth time I have tried to reply, each time deleting my response because it felt inadequate. It made me think immediately about some of the potential barriers to dialogue. First, a fear of not being 'good enough', and how this led me to focus on the judgements of our imaginary audience rather than on what you were actually saying. Second, a sense of being overwhelmed by the sheer number of things I wanted to respond to, which instilled in me almost a total paralysis. Third, just a struggle to get into 'flow' in answering you: every answer felt contrived and jarring. Before I could respond in dialogue, I needed to find my voice.

So where to start? First, I think the distinction that you make between 'relationship' and 'relatedness' is a very valuable one. I think it highlights the basic distinction between intersubjectivity as an ontological premise, and intersubjectivity as a concrete, interpersonal activity. These, as you say, are often very confused: it reminds me of some of the confusions that I have experienced in the world of dialogical psychology (e.g. Hermans and Dimaggio 2004) where 'dialogical' is sometimes used to refer to an ontological condition of human being – that we are always-in-relationship; and sometimes to a form of interpersonal communication – contrasted with the act of monologue. So in discussing dialogue and relationality, I think we both agree that it is really important to pull apart the different levels of dialogicity.

I'm also left with a sense that we need to do more unpacking. Let's start by saying that there is an intersubjectivity at the ontological level of human experiencing what, I think, you call 'relatedness'. I think of this particularly in terms of language: that our being is infused with the being of others by virtue of the fact that our very thinking is based upon a socially constructed medium.

Where, I think, this starts to get tricky, though, is if we try and apply this ontological relatedness to actual human relationships, as in the therapeutic relationship. If this is an ontological level of relatedness, it is obviously not something that we can create or not create in the therapeutic relationship. It is simply there by virtue of our human Being. So when you talk about the power of the therapeutic context and relatedness this, I think, must be a different level to the ontological level. However, it is also not so concrete as the level of interpersonal dialogical communication. So already we have three levels of dialogue: (1) an ontological relatedness; (2) the interhuman context; and (3) immediate dialogical encounters with another. Distinguishing between these planes seems useful to me because it means that we can talk about a fundamental intersubjectivity of human being (level #1), even if, as I am increasingly wondering, ontical dialogicity (level #3) may be absent in many circumstances. Do real, concrete people truly meet in dialogue? I think this question deeply haunts me. Is 'relational depth' (Mearns and Cooper 2005) something that is fundamentally shared, or are the moments of experiencing deep connection with an other really moments of fantasized connection, where the self never breaks out into the Other, but remains cocooned in its own being? I think, if I am honest, I am expressing here something of a deep disappointment with dialogue. For me in dialogue, there is a yearning for connection, for touching. Yet, as Buber (1947) writes, there are so many 'faceless spectres of dialogue'.

What does it mean to say that we have truly touched in dialogue? I think, for me, it means that something you said truly impacts on me and changes me: it doesn't just act as an opening for me to say what I was always planning to say – it doesn't simply alter my trajectory; it becomes part of my being. Then we might say that concrete dialogue is the crucible in which sustained human intersubjectivity is formed.

So, for me, dialogue requires me to take towards you some kind of *genuinely unfinished opennesses*, where you may be able to step in and provide some answers: thoughts, concerns and worries, where the answer lies, not within me, but within you. If I share those unfinished opennesses – and they must be genuinely unfinished – then maybe there is the possibility of you becoming part of me.

That takes me back to therapy. Therapy works, perhaps, to the extent that the client reaches out to the therapist with something that is genuinely unfinished: something that the therapist can imprint upon and engage into. I am sure that you have had the experience of working with clients and supervisees where all seems wrapped up and complete, and where there is no real sense of contact. But, perhaps, a client can take from therapy to the extent that he or she can reveal to the therapist some unfinished openness. At an ontological level, that unfinishedness exists as an integral part of being; but whether or not it is communicated is a matter of choice.

As I write this, I come back to the sense of there being so much I want to say to you: I can't hold it all. So here is a question that, for me, is genuinely unfinished: 'What do you do to me that makes this a dialogue, and what do I do to you? What are we to each other if we are in genuine dialogue?'

From Ernesto

Your question has so many implications! The shortest answer I can give is: in dialogue we recreate one another, be it temporarily or in some more lasting fundamental way. In dialogue neither one of the participants emerges from the encounter without some sense of change – personal and interpersonal – and perhaps also a sense of possibility – who I and you and we *can* be.

Now let me focus this on therapy. If there is to be dialogue in therapy, then it can't just be the client who is open to the possibilities you describe. The therapist must be as well, otherwise it will be an 'I–It' meeting. In a therapeutic encounter that is dialogically focused, the encounter is steeped in the uncertain, the 'genuinely unfinished openness' (great phrase!) that you write of. This is risky stuff for both and, as such, it may be that therapy itself is not always the best place for such dialogical encounters. Perhaps a lot of therapy might have to settle for duologues?

What I think can happen in therapy is that the context permits the experience of a differently felt sense of ontic being. Our way of thinking and relating has already shifted just by 'magically' doing therapy and being therapist/client.

However, in every dialogue there is always the sense of possibility and failure. Beckett's: 'Ever tried. Ever failed. No matter. Try again. Fail again.

Fail better' (Beckett 1983: 7). Why therapy is rarely dialogical is because such attempts require a mutual openness to the uncertain possibility. And therapists are not so likely to readily open themselves to the insecurity that this attempt provokes. Seeking directly to change, educate, improve or cure the client prevents the dialogue to which you refer. This is not to say that these enterprises have no impact, nor that the therapist might not be touched and moved and broadly affected (even in a personal way) by the client's responses to these endeavours. But in adopting them the therapist avoids what you term 'the genuine'. The 'I' and the 'you' may be affected, *but* also remain separate. The 'we' that is the sense of relatedness is beyond their grasp.

The current thrust of therapy, it seems to me, is deeply antagonistic to this 'genuineness'. What is being promoted is something else entirely. *But*, as I mentioned above, perhaps 'genuine dialogue' is just too plain disturbing for therapy to embrace (willingly). Or, rather, for what has become understood as therapy to experience willingly.

I have a suggestion here: could we focus on concrete examples from our practice that seem to us to get closest to dialogue?

From Mick

That sounds good, but first I want to share with you where I am at, re-reading this dialogue so far. I had a sense of sadness, and I think it relates to the Beckett quote above. I read again your previous email and realized how much of it I missed, or failed to capture. Actually, there are large chunks of it that I didn't really understand, particularly the issue of contextualization – I don't have a strong felt sense of that, or a visual image, and I think that makes it difficult for me to really know what you are trying to convey here. I wish I could have stopped you and said, 'Ernesto, can you explain that to me?' Maybe one of the barriers to dialogue is not really understanding the other, and feeling too shameful to ask. I lose you, and return back to my own unfinished opennesses.

Maybe, though, the sadness is more about what really happens in dialogue: two men meet in words, each with a passion to share with the other, each immersed and driven by their ideas, each loving and passionate about 'ex-telling' their ideas – not to convince the other, but for the sheer beauty of expansion and elaboration and reaching out through their own truths to an-Other.

I am thinking about a client who comes to see me and who shared about his life. There are unanswered questions – unfinished opennessses – throughout his self-understanding. He wants to understand: why he gets so depressed, why he can't get on with his life, why his relationships consistently break down – will he ever find love again? Mainly, I listen to the dialogue and allow it to unfurl. I can see parallels with my own life, there are personal things that I want to share with him, but that is my story, not his. Sometimes, as I try and understand his experiencing of his world, I get a sense of what might be going on, and share it with the client. Sometimes, it helps him, sometimes, it's wide of the mark: 'Mmm . . . no, it's not quite like that.' The work is helpful for him: he realizes that he needs to end a relationship that is making him feel worse, he starts to consider that maybe the end of other relationships wasn't his fault. He talks through, and stops trying to avoid some painful early experiences.

Now, two questions: (1) Is this dialogue (or duologue)? (2) Does that matter? On reflection, I think it is dialogue. Why? Because I am taking his discourse into myself, digesting it, feeling my way into his world – and, critically, my response to him emanates from this immersion (indwelling?). Is this a good definition of dialogue: that one's response emerges from one's immersion in the other's world? But then, his response does not necessarily emerge from an immersion in my world, and I am not sure it needs to – he is learning, developing: I am facilitating that process. Yet for me to be of any value, by definition, he must be digesting something of what I am sharing – so something dialogical is also happening that way around.

You say that the therapeutic encounter is steeped in uncertainty and risky. Am I taking the risk in that example? And what does it really mean? Is it even helpful? I do share my honest sense with this client – I don't lie to him – but I don't share everything I honestly feel. Sometimes I take a bit more of a risk: my sense is, sometimes he appreciates those responses, sometimes they don't seem to be particularly helpful. But I am definitely, in the main, constrained – and I am also focused, in the sense that my responses are orientated towards what I believe will be helpful to the client. So this is not the Gadamer type-2 dialogue that you mentioned. There are elements of it, in the sense that the client has space to share whatever, however, but we are orientated towards a particular goal – improvements in the client's well-being. Actually, it's ironic that, at the present time, I'm working on a pluralistic framework for counselling and psychotherapy with John McLeod (2007, 2010) which is orientated very much towards specific goals – what clients want from therapy – and sees this as the focal point of the therapeutic dialogue – very much Gadamer type 1!

Another part of our pluralistic approach is that different clients want, and benefit from, very different things, and that there is no one 'healing element' for all clients. And I do believe in that very passionately. So, for the client above I think what has helped him most is being able to develop a greater understanding of himself, so that he feels more in control of his life, and has the capacity to make different choices that don't reinforce the same patterns of behaviour. I think the dialogue here has been helpful: it's meant I've got a good understanding of his world and helped to clarify it to the best of my ability; and I also think a sense of connection between us has been important to him.

Reflecting on my own experience as a client: the last time I went to therapy, I was struggling with some god-awful anxieties, and I just, mainly, wanted a space to talk everything out in a way that was as incoherent as it felt. I didn't want to have to make sense, I didn't particularly want any answers, any reasons: just incoherence, blurting, connecting with the actuality of my fragmentary lived-experience. Essentially, space not to be a professor but a complete mess, so that I could be a half-decent teacher and dad in the rest of my life. She was a new (for me), person-centred therapist, and I really loved working with her. She was warm and friendly, very genuine, but basically got out of the way and helped me feel that it was okay just to incoherently splurge things out – it was an 'enormous psychological space', as my colleague Dave Mearns (Mearns and Cooper 2005) would say, where I could do whatever I needed to do. That was until the last session: when we talked about how it had been for me, I shared all this positive feedback. The therapist acknowledged that, and said she was surprised because she felt I had never really allowed myself to connect, deeply, with her – we'd never explored our relationship. I was, mainly, hurt – but also a bit disappointed and angry that it felt she had not really understood what I wanted (or who I was). I don't think I wanted dialogue, certainly not mutuality, just space to connect with myself.

But, of course, it wasn't just connecting with myself that was important, but communicating that to an other, and feeling that it was deeply received and accepted. Maybe what was most healing at that time was a sense of being radically myself in all that awfulness and extremity, and having it quietly witnessed (no, more, imbibed). It was not that I wanted to inflict this awfulness on my therapist, or even to feel that I wasn't alone with it: I think it was the process of the deep and consistent sense of being taken in, in all my incoherence and fragmentation, that meant that, after each session, I came away feeling a bit more okay about myself and able to cope with life.

From Ernesto

I share your sense of sadness. I suspect that the sadness is an expression of connection that appears and disappears so seemingly haphazardly but which, nonetheless, serves to remind us of what we can experience 'in the between'.

I also want to suggest that 'not understanding' is not the problem or the obstacle. Rather, it is what we associate with not understanding – self-criticism, shame, punitive thoughts, etc. – that leads us away from that connection or openness. I can think of times in my life where not-understanding felt glorious and awakening because I didn't judge myself for not having understood, and embraced this non-understanding being that I was being.

To me, these moments of accepting embrace, whether with an external other or with that other (or others) who provide my internal dialogues, is *the* great promise of therapy. And, here, I think, we may have reached a point where there exist some possibly significant disagreements between us regarding therapy.

More and more, I've come to a way of practising therapy as a therapist that is, quite simply, a conversation. I've actively pursued a process of divesting my self as therapist of as much of the mystique we therapists give ourselves. I remain scrupulously professional, I think, but I also have come to reject many of the barriers we seem to think are so important – the anonymity, the silence, the focus on certain topics as opposed to others, etc. I try to speak openly and clearly with my clients so that a process of clarity, of digging into what one 'means' in an embodied way rather than just a verbal or cognitive way becomes more possible. I feel that, in many ways, my attempts to simplify the process of therapy have served to simplify me as well. More and more I feel like the Peter Sellers character in the film *Being There* who basically can only make simple superficial statements which are then read into by those around him so that they become 'deep thoughts'. This, for me, is the biggest difficulty I am facing in my work with clients – because they are clients in therapy they persist in assuming that the simple things I might be saying are full of deep, hidden meanings. I don't blame them for this, of course. In their position, I would be doing, and have done, the same. I can see how this frustrates, upsets and at times can discourage clients, how they can and do impose misunderstandings. Some have even felt hurt and angered. Knowing this, why do I then persist with this? In general, I think clients look for answers to their life problems from another. This search leads them to assume that the statements which the other makes must contain an implicit instruction, demand, or critique. I think that most of the time, in most dealings with others, this view is absolutely correct; hence I can see that their expectation in sitting down with a therapist is that they will get more of the same. My attempts at simplicity and demystification serve as means *for me* to stop trying to provide and receive what is expected. I used to think that the main purpose of such an enterprise was that it would clarify the other's world and provide a means to that *immersion* that you write about. While I agree that it can do, I have stopped thinking that it is this immersion-into-the-other's-world that is of critical value within therapy. I want to propose, instead, that it is a much more foundational, fully embodied experience: *the accepting embrace of self and other as each is being in that moment of being*. In other words: the very focus of our discussion – dialogue.

So, for me, the indwelling is an outcome rather than an aim. I see it more as accepting/embracing/being with whatever is occurring without defence or pretence. This stance seems to me to provoke a shared sense of being that can at times border on the uncanny. It's a sort of merging and in those moments of merging, the experience not only of indwelling but, perhaps as importantly, dwelling in one's own embodied being is shared.

As I write this, I am aware that it sounds like I've gone off the rails and am spouting some new age rubbish. For me, these moments are not at all 'soft and sweet', they are hard: tough truths come to light – not always easy or pleasant to retain. But I do believe that it is in and through these moments that clients grasp a sense of themselves in a far more honest and truthful manner and, through this, become open to new possibilities of being. So for me it's maybe paradoxically about abdicating all attempts at immersion.

I agree entirely that 'different clients want, and benefit from, very different things', but also remain of the view that what underpins the different wants, and the possibility of their fulfilment through therapy, is this dialogical experience. I guess that I'm taking dialogue as a sort of portal for a way of being with one's self and with another that permits a shift away from how one most typically is, or always is, or must be with, one's self and with another. This is where the 'context' comes in; perhaps your sense of missing what I'm saying occurs because you suppose that there is more to what I'm saying than I intend.

It's back to what I wrote earlier about placebo effects, I'm afraid. To some extent, psychotherapy has addressed these factors by referring to non-specific factors, or embedded shared factors that appear throughout all forms of therapy. I also think that when therapists speak of the power of the relationship itself they are acknowledging the contextual features inherent in any act of therapy. But some critical points are still being missed.

I want to suggest that from the very moment of acknowledgement of this new relational context, *before anything is done*, a lot has already occurred that provides the possibility of therapeutic change. *What* is it that has happened so mysteriously? I think it is precisely *the accepting embrace of self and other as each is being in that moment of being*. I experience being 'me' differently through the unusual context I find my self in. My self is shaken and stirred by this context and so I can explore, reconsider – and *reconfigure* – this self within this context which challenges the assumptions about being that I may have previously maintained. How much of that reconfiguration is lasting or can be 'exported' to my more typical contexts remains open-ended; though the way I am experiencing myself *now* may well shake my previous stance at least to the extent that I can no longer believe in it as the *only* stance available to me.

My words seem inadequate and more likely to confound rather than illuminate. At the same time, though, I am also aware that as I was writing them, I was writing them with you and me in mind, that I was not immersed in you or in me but that it was more like being *immersed in the experience of the possibility of a mutual immersion*. It felt like what we are calling 'dialogue'.

From Mick

Dialogue seems to need digestion, consideration and response. It is amazing that there is so much here, like an enormous tangled ball of string: different leads, different ends, different strands and possibilities. I feel that if I pull on one and keep going with it I can write something: if I try and untangle the whole ball, I never get going.

I love what you say about 'accepting embrace', although, of course, it takes me straight back to Rogers (1957) and his 'core conditions' for therapeutic change. What's new here, though, is the idea that accepting embrace and dialogue are, essentially, synonymous. Is that true? I think I agree with you that a deep sense of acceptance is a precondition for dialogue to occur: I can't think of a time when I've felt in dialogue with another where I haven't felt a deep sense of acceptance. For me, subjectively, the experience of dialogue is this one of articulating, and connecting through, that which is at the edges of awareness: the unspoken, the implicit, the semi-conscious. And it is only with the expectation of accepting embrace from the Other that I can feel safe enough to draw out these threads. The more I feel deeply and fully accepted, the more I can pull out that which is unspoken: and also that which inspires, interests, excites and intrigues me. I guess we become habituated to the things that we are used to saying or communicating; that which is at the edge is novel, and calls forth a novel response from the Other – it makes dialogue come alive. Also, without that Other accepting me, it seems unlikely that they are going to engage with what I am actually communicating to them. Their acceptance allows them to engage and empathize deeply with me: to pull out further my own strands of thought, and to help me develop and evolve my ideas.

Is the experience of dialogue *the same as* the experience of accepting embrace? I'm not so sure about this. I am thinking about times when I can feel deeply accepted, but also not particularly stimulated or interactive. For dialogue, it feels to me like something more is needed – is it risk, challenge, input from the Other? Maybe the key here is something about difference? I need both accepting embrace, but also some kind of difference to engage with. I guess another way to put this would be that 'dialogue emerges when there is an expression/exploration of difference within an accepting embrace?' I think there is something key for me about the necessity of both these things existing, and that the greater the acceptance (across difference), or the greater the difference (within a context of acceptance), the greater the dialogue.

At the same time, some of the times in my life that I would most emphatically characterize as dialogue have been ones in which there has been a core recognition of similarities – though with the central difference that the other person and myself are different people, and we are not merging into one. I always remember the point made by Buber (1947) that, to have dialogue, you cannot be the same as the Other, for to bridge to another you need to have difference. So thinking about this, it seems to me that one of the key qualities of dialogue is this experience of 'bridging': whether across ideas or across people. And the accepting embrace that you describe seems a key precondition to that: providing us with the safety to move backwards and forwards without worrying about getting hurt.

The image that comes to my mind is of those lovely little (iron?) bridges in Venice, and of people walking, excitedly, with passion and purpose, backwards and forwards over them. Words that come to mind are 'exchange', 'excitement', 'movement', 'play', 'journey', 'aliveness'. And I have a sense of standing at one edge of the bridge and looking down at the canal from one perspective; and then crossing over and looking at it from another perspective. And then chatting to someone. And then going to another bridge to have another look; and chatting more, and coming back; and moving on. (This probably sounds inane, but that is what comes from an expectation of being acceptingly embraced!)

An interesting question for you: What would your image for dialogue be?

To take it back to therapy, I think our similarities here are much greater than our differences. Like you, I feel that I have moved further and further away from trying to conform to established therapeutic conventions and rituals. I just see myself as me, Mick, trying to help someone, as best I can, get what they want. Nothing cleverer than that. So that image of crossing bridges, chatting with someone, looking at things from different perspectives and having a relatively informal dialogue(?) is exactly what I see therapy as being about – and I hear the same from you. Core to it is that willingness to go wherever with someone, and to hear – and respond to – whatever they are saying. But also, when I think of how this compares to my nondirective colleagues, I think there is something a bit more. Is it a playfulness? A willingness to take a bit more of a lead? It is something about being willing to say to a client, 'Wow, have you seen what is down there?' or 'I'm just not getting what you are describing there', or 'Shall we go over here for a bit?' Of course, having said that, it seems to me so important that this is in response to what the client seems to want and need. I have experienced clients who, I think, feel much more stimulated and engaged when I am joining in with the discovery, while others just want me to shut up, so that they can get on with their own processing.

I'm feeling a sense that we are moving towards a natural ending, though I'm not sure we have reached any definitive conclusions. I do feel like we've crossed some bridges together, come to some shared understandings, seen things in different ways, and I've found it a very stimulating experience. Hopefully, readers who have accompanied us on this journey will continue in whatever direction is of interest to them. For me, some of the key questions remain the issue of whether dialogue is a subjective experience or an intersubjective phenomenon: is the dualness of it an illusion, or is it a genuine meeting and encounter that transcends individual entities? I think you generally see it in intersubjective terms, I think I struggle with this question more. In terms of therapy, I think we both feel that dialogue and good therapy are synonymous, but both are struggling to quite find the words for what this really means. It seems to me that that is still the great unanswered question: What is dialogue? Where we both agree is that acceptance is fundamental, but I think I am emphasizing difference a bit more.

From Ernesto

Like you, I realize that a great deal that has been raised and argued will be left to 'dangle' – and perhaps stimulate readers to pursue themselves. So. First, because it was such fun to conjure up, my image of dialogue:

> Projecting a scene out of an imaginary film directed by Francois Truffaut, my mind visualizes a typical French café somewhere in the backstreets of Paris around Clichy. At the table of a seedy bar, sits the young hero, writing distractedly into his notebook. He is a poet and he's in agony because once more the world has rejected him. Suddenly, the whistled tune we are hearing in the background filters through to him and, in spite of himself, he pauses, looks up from his writing, and observes the characters in the café and so many small vignettes of human life: autumn leaves falling and whirling; an accordion player, on his way to earn his living along the café-lined Champs Elysées, limps by; people pass by in groups, couples, or quite alone, hurrying, dawdling, happy, miserable – each and every one of them so singularly, so totally, alive.
>
>   And, at last, we begin to see a smile cracking upon the face of the sad poet because he has just discovered the answer to the greatest of mysteries: he realizes that, regardless of his personal despair, the world chooses to go on, it still welcomes him, provides him with scenes of everyday existence, which he is free to enter. And in this moment of acceptance, he rips up the poem and acknowledges his power, to make and unmake and remake every aspect of his life.
>
>   The whistling becomes overpowering and, as the scene fades out, we see the poet attempt to catch hold of the drift to the tune and begin to hum along to it.

Okay, done! Now, one thing you said regarding the Other set off a sudden sense of 'A-ha!' that really felt exciting for me: you asked whether embrace and dialogue are one and the same. What came up for me was what, for me, is one of Heidegger's greatest insights – that 'by "Others" we do not mean everyone else but me – those against whom the "I" stands out. They are rather . . . those among whom one is too' (Heidegger 1962: 154; 118). As I understand it, Heidegger is proposing that one's very sense of 'I' – or more generally speaking, one's sense of self – is also an expression of 'other-ness'. So, here's what I'd like to propose: when there is that sense of 'meeting the other' which we've suggested lies at the heart of dialogue, the 'other' who is met is not only the external other but also 'the other that I am'. It is an embrace of all (my) being. And in adopting such an embrace, each experiences a 'subjective' acceptance whose 'open subjectivity' is such that it can't be confined to the usual limits of subjective experience but which, rather, reveals the interrelational foundation to the experience of subjectivity.

More prosaically, and specifically related to therapy, it seems to me that the experience of dialogue in therapy permits both client and therapist to experience *the acceptance of their own* 'otherness' as well as the 'otherness of the other'. In this way, either or both participants may have that felt sense of already being different or changed simply through their engagement with the relational dialogue.

How this occurs, as well as its frequency, seems to me to still remain largely a mystery. Our focus on relatedness, relationship, 'core conditions', 'attending skills', etc. are all like the Taoist 'finger pointing to the moon', in that they direct our attention toward that to which we yearn (the moon) but cannot/should not be mistaken – even if they often are – for the focus of our yearning. Personally, I've grown not to mind this mystery at all – but then, I'm still that hippie who, 40 years ago, refused to watch the moon landings because, for him, they ravaged for evermore the mystique that marked humankind's relationship with the moon. Whereas you, more wisely, still have the desire, I feel, to 'know about' – and not just 'know' – so that the pointing finger and pointed-to moon cease to be so clearly demarcated.

From Mick

Although we are coming to an end here, in some ways it feels like we are/I am just beginning to sense what it means, and how to dialogue with each other. For instance, I read your image of dialogue, which I just loved, but I also thought: 'Actually, I don't really understand it, and I need to ask Ernesto what he means by that.' So I think I am beginning to learn that, for me, to engage with you in dialogue means being a bit more 'upfront' and not standing back out of a fear of looking stupid. Also, I really like what you said about the difference between us being around structure vs. laidbackness, and I think that is an interesting one as far as dialogue is concerned. I was thinking it probably needs both: some kind of orientation, but then, within that orientation, an openness to whatever. I have a bit more of a 'structured' and focused perspective on what constitutes dialogue, whereas I think yours is more orientated around spontaneity and flow.

I think we will both agree that it feels fine to leave this dialogue relatively unfinished, with no neat bows tying it up; maybe one day we could carry it further. But for now, lots of questions, lots of threads, lots of uncertainties – a very existential place to stop!

References

Beckett, S. (1983) *Worstward Ho!*, London: John Calder.

Buber, M. (1947) *Between Man and Man*, trans. R. Gregor-Smith, London: Fontana.

Cooper, M. and McLeod, J. (2007) 'A pluralistic framework for counselling and psychotherapy: implications for research', *Counselling and Psychotherapy Research*, 7 (3): 135–143.

Cooper, M. and McLeod, J. (2010) *Pluralistic Counselling and Psychotherapy*, London: Sage.

Deurzen, E. van (1992) 'Dialogue as therapy', *Journal of the Society for Existential Analysis*, 3: 15–23.

Farber, L. (1967) 'Martin Buber and psychotherapy', in P.A. Schilpp and M. Friedman (eds) *The Philosophy of Martin Buber*, LaSalle, IL: Open Court.

Farber, L. (2000) *The Ways of the Will: Selected Essays*, New York: Basic Books.

Friedman, M. (ed.) (1964) *The Worlds of Existentialism: A Critical Reader*, Chicago: University of Chicago Press.

Gadamer, H. G. (2004) *Truth and Method*, London: Continuum.

Heidegger, M. (1962 [1927]) *Being and Time*, trans. J. R. Macquarrie and E. Robinson, Oxford: Blackwell.

Hermans, H. J. M. and Dimaggio, G. (eds) (2004) *Dialogical Self in Psychotherapy*, Hove, UK: Brunner–Routledge.

Mearns, D. and Cooper, M. (2005) *Working at Relational Depth in Counselling and Psychotherapy*, London: Sage.

Rogers, C. R. (1957) 'The necessary and sufficient conditions of therapeutic personality change', *Journal of Consulting Psychology*, 21 (2): 95–103.

Spinelli, E. (2005) *The Interpreted World: An Introduction to Phenomenological Psychology*, 2nd edn, London: Sage.

Spinelli, E. (2007) *Practising Existential Psychotherapy: The Relational World*, London: Sage.

Spinelli, E. (2009) 'Down these mean streets: existential challenges for therapy in the 21st century', *Existential Analysis*, 20 (2): 214–225.

Szasz, T. (1992) 'Taking dialogue as therapy seriously: "words are the essential tool of therapy"', *Existential Analysis*, 3: 2.

Velmans, M. (2009) 'How to define consciousness', *Journal of Consciousness Studies*, 16 (5): 139–154.

Chapter 11

The Viennese School of Existential Analysis

The search for meaning and affirmation of life

Alfried Längle

> He who knows a 'why' for living, will surmount almost every 'how'.
> (Frankl [1967: 103] reformulating Nietzsche)

Historical background

The present-day Viennese School of Existential Analysis evolved out of Viktor Frankl's Logotherapy. The Viennese neurologist and psychiatrist Viktor E. Frankl (1905–1997) called the anthropological basis of Logotherapy 'Existential Analysis' and its practical application in the search of purpose and meaning 'Logotherapy'. Frankl founded this existential school in the 1920s (Frankl 1938, 1973). Logotherapy has been referred to as the 'Third Viennese School of Psychotherapy' following the psychotherapies of Freud and Adler (Hofstätter 1957). Frankl's early interest in psychotherapy led to a personal correspondence with Sigmund Freud when Frankl was in his twenties. However, Frankl did not train in psychoanalysis due to his dissent with Freud over its anthropological foundations. Frankl went on to receive his psychotherapeutic training in Alfred Adler's School of Individual Psychology (Längle 1998a).

During these years of training in the late 1920s, Frankl's psychotherapeutic thinking took shape under the influence of Adlerian teachers Oswald Schwartz and Rudolf Allers (Frankl 1988). Frankl began a lifelong engagement with psychology and psychotherapy, developing a theory to combat what was called the growing 'psychologism' within the field. By 'psychologism' Frankl was referring to a 'pseudo-scientific procedure [that] presumes to analyze every act for its psychic origin, and on that basis to decree whether its content is valid or invalid' (Frankl 1973: 15). Frankl's interests focused on what he termed the 'specifically human' dimension. For Frankl, the intellectual, philosophical and spiritual capabilities of human beings indicate our fundamental need to search for meanings and values. He considered the 'will to meaning' our primary motivation, the active and deliberate search for meaning in our lives. He often contrasted the 'will to meaning' with Freud's 'will to pleasure' and what Frankl summarized as Adler's 'will to power' (Frankl 1985: VII f).

Frankl (1973) wrote his first full manuscript on Logotherapy prior to his deportation from Vienna to the concentration camps in 1941. Frankl (1985) attributes his survival of the horrors of the camps to three things. First, the relationship to his family, a relationship he kept alive in his heart and mind; this included a strong hope that the family would be reunited. Second, Frankl's determination to rewrite his lost manuscript; he attributes the creative and mental challenge of recreating this manuscript from memory as an important factor in keeping him alive. And finally, Frankl acknowledged his strong faith in God. The reconstructed manuscript was written following Frankl's release and was eventually published in English as *The Doctor and the Soul* in 1955. Frankl also reported on the psychic and physical stages experienced by the inmates of the camps. His most famous report became the book *Man's Search for Meaning* (1985).

Frankl had intended Logotherapy to act as a supplement to the psychotherapies of the 1930s rather than a comprehensive theory of its own. Logotherapy emphasizes the suffering that results when meaning is lost, and was thought of as a corrective for a growing trend towards 'psychologism' (Frankl 1967, 1973, 1988). Logotherapy is 'meaning therapy' or a 'psychotherapy centred on meaning' (*logos* means 'meaning' in Greek); and the search for meaning evokes a person's freedom and responsibility. According to Frankl, a person is not merely a physical being with psychological drives: a spiritual dimension (a third dimension of the human psyche in addition to the somatic and psychological dimensions) has to be added to address uniquely human qualities and capabilities that cannot be subsumed under physical or psychological processes. These uniquely human qualities bring us 'into existence'. Through this dimension our life is open to what is possible, meaningful and of value.

In the last 20 years, progress has been made in existential analysis through the work done by the Society for Logotherapy and Existential Analysis in Vienna, particularly in the areas of motivation and methodology (Längle 1990, 1993, 1994; Längle and Probst 1997). Today this form of existential analysis can be considered an independent and major current in psychotherapy. It has evolved from Logotherapy as a supplement to various psychotherapies into a full-fledged psychotherapeutic method (Stumm and Wirth 1994; Stumm and Pritz 2000). Apart from this development, classical Logotherapy continues to be taught in Europe and America focusing upon meaning-related problems (e.g. Lukas 2006). The remainder of the chapter presents an overview of this Viennese form of existential analysis, describing its structural model (the four fundamental existential motivations), illustrated by a case study and commentary on psychopathology.

Viennese existential analysis – overview and aim

The Viennese type of existential analysis can be described as a phenomenological and person-oriented psychotherapy (in many ways it comes close to the theory of Carl Rogers). The word 'existence' lies at the core of existential analysis. Existence, from our perspective, denotes what can simply be called a 'whole' life. From an existential perspective, the realization of human existence is characterized by making decisions; this requires both freedom and responsibility. While an individual's 'existence' is experienced as uniquely 'one's own', the process of coming to a decision is further influenced by the contexts of that individual's particular world. It is not merely the individual's subjective experience that is the focus of this existential analysis. This existential analysis stresses how continuous dialogues, relationships, and mutual influences between the individual and the world around him or her shape a meaningful existence (Frankl 1959, 1973: 160).

Fixations, distortions, one-sidedness and traumas influence an individual's experience, behaviour, emotions and perceptions. The aim of existential analysis is to guide a person towards experiencing their life authentically and freely. This is done through practical methods that help an individual to live with 'inner consent', or the ability to affirm what he or she is doing. We can summarize this aim as: helping people to recognize and come to terms with their behaviour and emotions and live with 'inner consent'. This description resonates with the Rogerian concept of congruence (e.g. Rogers 1961). However, existential analysis places more emphasis on the active decisions and commitments an individual exhibits, rather than the accompanying mood or organismic feeling. Phenomenological analysis of work with patients (Allport 1955; May 1979; Längle 2000) has shown over the years that this inwardly given (spoken and/or felt) consent is a highly complex achievement, wherein the individual brings together all the relevant layers of their existence into one simple 'yes' (what we term affirmation).

Existential theory of motivation

Difficulties in reaching inner consent (such as partial consent or not coming to terms with a particular experience) reveal more about the structure of human existence and the personal needs that enable us to realize life in a fulfilling and rewarding way. As a result of my phenomenological investigations, I find that the structure of existence in my phenomenological investigations analysis is made up of four dimensions and each of these dimensions corresponds to what we call fundamental human motivations. Human existence, according to existential psychotherapy in general, is motivated by more than sexual drives, the drive for power, equilibrium or freedom from tension. All of these common motivations are grouped around the following deeper motivations: finding a basis for being in the world; coming into a close relationship with what we experience as being our life; being oneself, by finding one's identity and authenticity; and reorienting the constant changes within human existence into creative developments of 'becoming', which corresponds to the existential concept of meaning (Allport 1955; Längle 1999, 2003a; Längle and Probst 1997: 149–169). The social dimension is so fundamental that it finds its representation in all four motivations. We are primarily oriented to search for and discover answers in each of these categories. Becoming aware of our 'approach' to life and our existence, and responding to both by giving our personal answer (our consent) is the realization of each of these motivations. These four categories have historical analogies in Binswanger (1958), Boss (1963), Maslow (1954), Yalom (1980) and Epstein (1993), see also Grawe (1998) and a philosophical basis in Heidegger's 'Existentialien' (Heidegger 1962; Längle 2004). Frustration at these deeper levels of motivation leads to disturbing experiences like insecurity, apathy, emptiness, disappointment and boredom, meaninglessness (Frankl 1959; Kolbe 1992; Längle and Probst 1995; Kundi et al. 2003) and can culminate in forms of psychopathology (for a historical overview see Frankl 1997; for a general introduction see Längle 1992a).

Because these four structural dimensions are fundamental aspects of human existence, human activity tends to orient itself (motivate itself) towards accessing, empowering, or strengthening a relationship to them. Therefore, the four structural dimensions of existence can be psychologically categorized as the four 'fundamental existential motivations'. While Frankl considered the search for meaning ('will to meaning') to be a person's deepest and primary motivation, the contemporary theory of this form of existential analysis has found three additional motivations that precede the motivation for meaning (Längle 2008).

1   A person is basically motivated by the *Fundamental Question of Existence*: I am – can I be? Such a question takes into account both the concrete circumstances (facts) of my being here in the first place, as well as my own power to bear or change the actual conditions of my life. To do so we need three main prerequisites: 'protection' –a secure physical and emotional base, space and support from others. A person experiences these to the highest degree when they feel accepted by others. This in turn enables a person to embrace an accepting attitude towards themselves and others. Feeling accepted generates a sense of security about one's very existence. Without the experience of security, a person essentially fights for their very existence. Disturbances at this existential level lead to anxiety problems and form the psychic component of schizophrenia (Längle 1996, 1997).

2 A person is motivated by the *Fundamental Question of Life*: I am alive – do I like this? This question involves one's relationship to life. Do we relate positively to life, are we literally 'attracted' to life, to such a degree that we can give our consent to live? This also means being able to live with pleasure, passion and suffering. The prerequisite of experiencing the value of life is, I would argue, having relationships, taking time and experiencing closeness to what is of value for oneself. These experiences in turn enable a person to devote themselves to other people, to their community, to social action. Feeling and experiencing the value of one's own life resonates with a deep feeling that it is good that 'I' exist (it is good that 'I' am here). Not being able to come to terms with this dimension turns life into a burden; to live without inner consent is the existential equivalent of being depressive (Nindl 2001; Längle 2003b).

3 A person is motivated by the *Fundamental Question of Being Oneself:* I am myself – do I feel distinctive and unique? Do I feel I am allowed and encouraged to be the way I am, to behave the way I do? Do I experience appreciation, respect and esteem for my own worth (Längle 1998c)? These experiences and feelings arise as the result of attention, justice, recognition and appreciation, the respective prerequisites of this dimension. This in turn enables a person to actively 'hold their own', to delineate their own identity from another's and to recognize and respect another person's worth. Disturbances at this level lead to the histrionic complex of symptoms and to the main personality disorders (Längle 2002; Probst and Probst 2002; Tutsch 2003).

4 A person is motivated by the *Fundamental Question of Continuous Becoming and Change*: I am here for a while – to what end? For what purpose? In what greater capacities or contexts do I see myself? What do I live *for*? What is my perspective in a world and life where all is continuously changing – is there a valuable outcome? This dimension of existence deals with our inherent desire to turn our contributions to life into a meaningful whole; to become fruitful in life. A person experiences meaning when they feel they are engaged in worthwhile tasks or are oriented towards possibilities waiting to unfold in the future. This type of 'existential meaning' (Frankl 1973; Längle 1992b) may be found in societal or ambient tasks, worthwhile and needed work, fulfilling valuable duties, adopting positive attitudes towards unchangeable situations, as well as enjoying pleasant situations, encounters, nature, art etc. (Frankl 1973: 42ff.; Längle 2007). A further type of meaning that does not depend upon our own activity is called 'ontological meaning'. This relates to the meaning of being itself (e.g. what is the meaning of my life? Or what is the meaning of having a particular illness?). These meta-questions, if you will, find their answers in philosophy, faith or religion (Frankl 1973; Längle 1998b).

Experiences and feelings at this fourth dimension of existence enable a person to synchronize themselves with the world. In addition, they enable a person to discover and realize his or her unique and personal meaning in each and every situation. Disturbances at this level can lead to an inclination to suicide and dependency (Debats 1996; Längle and Probst 1997).

Existential analysis in practice

This Viennese existential analysis is a phenomenological approach. During sessions, the therapist is guided by what the patient is saying, and no attempt is made to interpret what the patient is saying. Rather, the therapist simply tries to *understand* what is being conveyed from the present context. Further, existential analysis focuses on the establishment of a dialogical exchange between the patient and his or her world (Längle 2004).

This existential analysis views the individual as firmly imbedded in the circumstances of his or her life. As I see it, from an existential analytic perspective, psychic 'disease' is caused by a partial isolation: this means we call disease the constant disturbance in experiencing dialogical exchange and relational connections a person has, subjectively and/or objectively (Längle 1992a). If psychotherapy detaches a person artificially from the connections of his or her life (for example, by concentrating solely on psychic processes like drives, emotions, perceptions, desires, transferences or disease), this will lead in our view to a distortion of human existence as 'whole' (Frankl 1959, 1967; Heidegger 1962; Längle 2004).

Since life happens in the present, existential analysis *begins* with what is currently at issue for the patient. However, all of the patient's experiences, be they from the present or the past are treated in order to 'open a future' for the patient and in order to highlight the possible requirements, the possible options that are necessary to step forward into the future. We have mentioned that existential analysis views human life as 'coming into existence'. How is existence barred?

1   It may be that burdens or specific events of the past come to over-shadow the present. In such cases, existential analysis uses the *biographical method* (Kolbe 1992) – a phenomenological approach to overcoming 'undigested' past events. In contrast to psychoanalysis, the approach of existential analysis is neither archeological (Freud) nor historical: instead of a systematic screening of a patient's past, existential analysis is a 'project analysis' (Sartre 1958), focusing on the future dimension of life, stimulating engagement with its challenges and reflection on its values. This also involves the exploration of those areas of a patient's life that prove to be a hindrance in their present life. Past suffering(s) are the object of existential analytic work only so far as

they obstruct a patient's current life. It should be noted that what may obstruct or hinder a patient's present life may be caused by long-held and life-hampering attitudes towards losses, conflicts or traumas. Existential analysis focuses on these attitudes and how they may in turn produce psychological disturbances and suffering (Längle 1994).

2   Trauma, suffering and distorted attitudes do not constitute the only reason for an unfulfilled life. Those who seek aid and external assistance frequently do not fully realize their own *abilities and resources*. In such cases, existential analysis aims at encouraging a patient's unique abilities, their emotions, self-acceptance and approach towards themselves (Längle 1993, 1994).

3   Some people suffer from a very different deficiency. These patients are not suffering because of past events or an inability to recognize their own abilities and resources, these are patients who lack a '*Why*' in their lives. A variety of experiences, including grave loss and crisis, can lead to feelings of emptiness, to a life lacking in orientation and devoid of meaning (Frankl 1973, 1988; Längle 1992b, 2007).

When a person's life has become hampered, the therapist and patient look for a 'track of life' within the existential analytic dialogue. Therapist and patient try to overcome the impediment of trauma and suffering, and uncover an authentic direction and orientation for the patient. When new possibilities for leading a meaningful life are discovered, existential analysis turns into 'Logotherapy': this means treating the disturbance by assisting in the search for, and realization of, meaning. The following case study will illuminate this point.

A case study

Mrs M, 40 and single, has been suffering from depression for years. 'One day I am certainly going to kill myself. That day is not far off. Nothing doing anyway.' Her despair becomes the central theme for the coming sessions. The 'nothing doing' stands out: she believes that only doing something *useful* can possess meaning. But useful for whom? We begin with this strong conviction about what is meaningful. If life does not correspond to her ideas and wishes, she feels it worthless. It becomes evident how her 'concept of life' is rigid and lacks an open exchange and dialogue with the world. For Mrs M, life should be of service, otherwise it is no life.

This track proves right and leads to her '*pre-existential*' *attitude* towards life as I call it: 'Life must be as I want it – otherwise I won't keep going.' In her anger and defiance she develops suicidal ideas.

Doesn't this attitude show a depressive 'violation' of life in its despair to come to a true life? For who loves what one 'violates'? We speak about the fact that life does not conform to the conditions we would like to impose upon it. Life is never at my service since, in the end, I am here to tackle my life instead of waiting for it ('existential twist' – Frankl 1973). But she remains in thrall to her emotions: 'There is terrible anger in me that life is like that. It was not me, after all, who has brought me into the world. That is outrageous: I am here without being asked and cannot even expect anything.' Our wrestling for a new attitude towards life becomes understandable as the background of her life. For 20 years the patient has held on to the same assumptions, that particular needs have to be fulfilled before she is willing to accept life. She wants to have a partner and children – she is still waiting. In the meantime, she has become petrified in her anger. After years of disappointment, she seeks relief in alcohol and tranquillizers, and since they do not give her peace of mind she longs for death.

In cases where the patient's assumptions and attitudes have made them literally passive, existential analysis, as with many psychotherapies, begins by trying to understand the biography and the experiences that have led to such attitudes. It is of therapeutic value if this woman can come to understand why she has become like this. This would give her greater access to herself and install an inner relationship with herself. These are all procedures for establishing the second existential motivation (the relationship one has to life), that is fundamentally disturbed in depression. Otherwise, how could she give up this attitude with which the greatest part of her life and her failure has been intimately tied up? It is essential through this biographical work to uncover her true struggle for a fulfilling and meaningful life. For the first time she understands that she does not bear sole responsibility for not having achieved a fulfilling life. She begins to understand how the many setbacks and reverses she has suffered throughout her life have hindered her and we come to respect her for not having given up her struggle for a meaningful life. Subsequently we work through these wounds by using the method of Personal Existential Analysis (PEA, Längle 2000; 2003c). As a result she can see for the first time how her life can in fact turn out well.

We also work 'paradoxically' in order to instil in her how vital and necessary it is to gain some distance from her demanding attitudes about life – for they are blocking much of her activity. I ask her: 'What would you do, if you knew from now on that your demands will never be fulfilled?' At this point, the patient has gained a relationship to her life: 'Strangely enough, I think about this frequently. If I knew that I was going to be alone for the rest of my life, I could live more easily. Sometimes I feel annoyed that my desire is so strong.' Haltingly and tentatively, the patient lets herself be guided during the next couple of hours to a new and open (phenomenological) attitude, i.e. to take life as it comes. Only then can she deal with it in a meaningful way. We try out the 'first' existential meaning of life, viz. to make the best out of the givens of existence. I offer: 'Do you want to try just for today to say yes to your life – and with this yes, to turn your life, as it is now, into the partner for whom you have longed for such a long time?' She resolved, though with some hesitation, to renounce any man and to consciously live alone for a whole day. This gave her some breathing space. Soon one day became several days. She started sensing the calm she had been longing for. It was not the calm of annihilation, but a calm arising from the protection against her conditional desires. With her 'conditional' attitude, she had driven life away. Her newly achieved equanimity finally permitted her to become truly alive.

A process such as the one described can take months and sometimes, with particularly hardened attitudes, it can take years. Loosening hardened attitudes requires process interventions like the method of Personal Existential Analysis (Längle 2003c) and structural work, like, in this case, strengthening the patient's relationship to his or her life (second fundamental motivation). This can be achieved through the patient's work on experiencing his or her life as valuable and meaningful.

Conclusion

In the past 25 years, the approach of Frankl's Logotherapy has been expanded through the work of the Society for Logotherapy and Existential Analysis based in Vienna (GLE-International, Vienna). This expansion has resulted in substantial theoretical and practical changes. This form of existential analysis is no longer centred solely on the process of finding meaning, as it was in Frankl's Logotherapy. The theory is broader in scope, based on four fundamental existential themes that give rise to a complex motivational theory, a better understanding of existential contents contained in suffering and a theory of emotions; it also involves the development of the ego-structures and of coping mechanisms, as well as dealing with their fixation which forms what is generally called psychopathology. Frankl's innovative concept of meaning is not overshadowed but incorporated into existential analysis. The development of a specific theory and method of processing painful or traumatic experiences (PEA) supplements the structural model of existential analysis, which consists in the Fundamental Existential Motivations.

This new phenomenological processing method, Personal Existential Analysis (PEA), combined with half a dozen new methods and techniques such as the Will Strengthening Method, the Meaning Finding Method, the Method of Personal Positioning, the Mourning Steps, the Regretting and Forgiving Steps, the Method of Dealing with Aggression, etc., has enlarged the methodology substantially (Längle 1994, 2000, 2003c). The implication of the fundamental existential structures has broadened the application of existential analysis and improved its effectiveness (Längle 1999, 2000; *Existenzanalyse* 2000). These new developments have also completely changed the training programme in structure, self-experience, and duration. It now lasts five to six years part-time. In addition, current research is dealing with understanding personality disorders and subsequent appropriate therapies (Längle 2002). Empirical studies are also currently being undertaken on the effectiveness of psychotherapeutic practice and training, the safeguarding of quality in terms of therapy, and the effectiveness of therapy in hospital settings (Längle *et al.* 2000, 2001).

References

Allport, G. W. (1955) *Becoming. Basic Considerations for a Psychology of Personality*, New Haven, CT: Yale University Press.

Binswanger, L. (1958 [1946]) 'The existential analysis school of thought', in R. May, E. Angel and H. F. Ellenberger (eds) *Existence*, New York: Basic Books.

Boss, M. (1963) *Psychoanalysis and Daseinsanalysis*, New York: Basic Books.

Debats, D. L. (1996) 'Meaning in life: clinical relevance and predictive power', *British Journal of Clinical Psychology*, 35: 503–516.

Epstein, S. (1993) 'Emotion and self-theory', in M. Lewis and J. Haviland (eds) *Handbook of Emotions*, New York: Guilford Press.

Existenzanalyse 2000, 17, 3 Empirical studies in Existential Analysis.

Existenzanalyse 2001, 18, 1 Empirical studies in Existential Analysis.

Existenzanalyse 2002, 19, 2 Narcissism. Kongreßbericht der GLE-International.

Frankl, V. (1938) 'Zur geistigen Problematik der Psychotherapie', *Zentralblatt der Psychotherapie*, 10: 33–45.

Frankl, V. (1959) 'Grundriß der Existenzanalyse und Logotherapie', in V. Frankl, V. v. Gebsattel and J. H. Schultz (eds) *Handbuch der Neurosenlehre und Psychotherapie*, vol. 3, Munich: Urban and Schwarzenberg.

Frankl, V. (1967) *Psychotherapy and Existentialism. Selected Papers on Logotherapy*, New York: Simon and Schuster.

Frankl, V. (1973 [1955]) *The Doctor and the Soul. From Psychotherapy to Logotherapy*, New York: Random House.

Frankl, V. (1985 [1946]) *Man's Search for Meaning*, New York: Washington Square Press.

Frankl, V. (1988) *The Will to Meaning. Foundations and Applications of Logotherapy*, New York: Nal Penguin.

Frankl, V. (1997) *Theorie und Therapie der Neurosen*, 7th edn, Munich: Reinhardt.

Grawe, K. (ed.) (1998) *Psychologische Therapie*, Göttingen: Hogrefe.

Heidegger, M. (1962 [1927]) *Being and Time*, Oxford: Blackwell.

Hofstätter, P. R. (1957) *Psychologie*, Frankfurt: Fischer.

Jöbstl, B. (2002) 'Mein ganzes Leben war nur Leiden', *Existenzanalyse*, 19: 21–27.

Kolbe, C. (ed.) (1992) *Biographie. Verständnis und Methodik biographischer Arbeit in der Existenzanalyse*, Vienna: GLE.

Kundi, M., Wurst, E. and Längle, A. (2003) 'Existential analytical aspects of mental health', *European Psychotherapy*, 4: 87–96.

Längle, A. (1990) 'Existential analysis psychotherapy', *International Forum of Logotherapy*, 13: 17–19.

Längle, A. (1992a) 'Der Krankheitsbegriff in Existenzanalyse und Logotherapie', in A. Pritz and H. Petzold (eds) *Der Krankheitsbegriff in der modernen Psychotherapie*. Paderborn: Junfermann.

Längle, A. (1992b) 'What are we looking for when we search for meaning?', *Ultimate Reality and Meaning*, 1: 306–314.

Längle, A. (ed.) (1993) *Wertbegegnung. Phänomene und methodische Zugänge. Tagungsbericht der GLE* 1+2, 7. Vienna: GLE.

Längle, A. (1994) 'Personal existential analysis', in *Proceedings, 16th International Congress of Psychotherapy IFP*. Seoul: Korea Academy of Psychotherapy.

Längle, A. (1996) 'Der Verlust des Zusammenhalts. Psychopathologie und existentielle Themen in der Schizophrenie', *Existenzanalyse*, 13: 13–22.

Längle, A. (1997) 'Die Angst als existentielles Phänomen. Ein existenzanalytischer Zugang zu Verständnis und Therapie von Ängsten', *Psychotherapie, Psychosomatik und klin. Psychologie*, 47: 227–233.

Längle, A. (1998a) *Viktor Frankl – ein Porträt*, Munich: Piper.

Längle, A. (1998b) 'Zur ontologischen und existentiellen Bestimmung von Sinn. Analyse und Weiterführung des logotherapeutischen Sinnverständnisses', in H. Csef (ed.) *Sinnverlust und Sinnfindung in Gesundheit und Krankheit. Gedenkschrift für Dieter Wyss*, Würzburg: Könighausen und Neumann.

Längle, A. (1998c) 'Guide to the person', *Newsletter of the Society for Existential Analysis*, 4.

Längle, A. (1999) 'Die existentielle Motivation der Person', *Existenzanalyse*, 16: 18–29.

Längle, A. (ed.) (2000) *Praxis der Personalen Existenzanalyse*, Vienna: Facultas University-Press.

Längle, A. (ed.) (2002) *Hysterie*, Vienna: Facultas University-Press.

Längle, A. (2003a) 'The art of involving the person', *European Psychotherapy*, 4: 25–36.

Längle, A. (2003b) 'Burnout – existential meaning and possibilities of prevention', *European Psychotherapy*, 4: 107–121.

Längle, A. (2003c) 'The method of "personal existential analysis"', in *European Psychotherapy*, 4: 37–53.

Längle, A. (2004) 'Dialogik und Dasein. Zur Initiierung des psychotherapeutischen Prozesses und der alltäglichen Kommunikation', *Daseinsanalyse*, 20: 211–236.

Längle, A. (2007) *Sinnvoll leben*, 4th edn, Salzburg/St. Pölten: Residenz.

Längle, A. (2008) 'Existenzanalyse', in A. Längle and A. Holzhey-Kunz *Existenzanalyse und Daseinsanalyse*, Vienna: UTB (Facultas).

Längle, A. and Probst, C. (1995) 'Existential questions of the elderly', in P. Hofmann, G. Wieselmann and H. G. Zapotoczky (eds) *International Conference on Aging, Depression and Dementia*, Vienna: Maudrich.

Längle, A. and Probst, C. (eds) (1997) *Süchtig sein. Entstehung, Formen und Behandlung von Abhängigkeiten*, Vienna: Facultas University-Press.

Längle, A., Orgler, C. and Kundi, M. (2000) *Existenzskala ESK*, Göttingen: Hogrefe-Beltz.

Lukas, E. (2006) *Lehrbuch der Logotherapie: Menschenbild und Methoden*, Munich: Profil.

Maslow, A. H. (1954) *Motivation and Personality*, New York: Harper and Row.

May, R. (1979) *Psychology and the Human Dilemma*, New York: Norton.

Nindl, A. (2001) 'Zwischen existentieller Sinnerfüllung und Burnout', *Existenzanalyse*, 18: 15–23.

Paddelford, B. (1974) 'Relationship between drug involvement and purpose in life', *Journal of Clinical Psychology*, 30: 303–305.

Probst, M. and Probst, C. (2002) 'Narzißmus bei Kindern und Jugendlichen', *Existenzanalyse*, 19: 82–86.

Rogers, C. R. (1961) *On Becoming a Person*, Boston: Houghton Mifflin.

Sartre, J.-P. (1958 [1943]) *Being and Nothingness*, London: Routledge.

Stumm, G. and Wirth, B. (eds) (1994) *Psychotherapie. Schulen und Methoden. Eine Orientierungshilfe für Theorie und Praxis*, Vienna: Falter.

Stumm, G. and Pritz, A. (eds) (2000) *Wörterbuch der Psychotherapie*, Vienna: Springer.

Tutsch, L. (2003) 'Of the phenomenology and therapy of narcissistic personality disturbance', *European Psychotherapy*, 4: 71–85.

Yalom, I. D. (1980) *Existential Psychotherapy*, New York: Basic Books.

Chapter 12

Reasons for living

Existential therapy and spirituality

Emmy van Deurzen

Introduction

Doubts about the meaning of life are arguably one of the major causes of depression and anxiety. Our reasons for living can be surprisingly fragile and often remain invisible to us, until we are in crisis and have to take stock of what really matters. Existential therapy provides a safe space and time to reflect on our reasons for living. Existential therapists have to be very clear about their own reasons for living if they want to provide an inspirational rather than a merely aspirational therapy and enable people to get back in touch with the spirited and passionate life they are capable of.

The word psychotherapy or 'therapy of the psyche' can be taken to mean many things. *Therapy* comes from the Greek verb *therapeuo*, meaning 'I attend to'. And while *psyche* is taken to mean mind, soul, or self, depending on who does the interpreting, the word translates literally from Ancient Greek as *force or breath of life* and by extension refers to the power of human consciousness and the spirit of courage (in Latin *spiritus* means 'breath') that ensure our vitality. And so, our definition of psychotherapy might be that of: *attending to the force of life*. This is strikingly similar to Solomon's formulation of spirituality as the 'thoughtful love of life' (Solomon 2002: ix).

What we make of psychotherapy depends greatly on how we conceive of this principle of human vitality and how well we attend to it. Some consider it to be placed in the physical drive for bodily survival or in the sexual libidinal drive towards procreation. Others see it as the rational striving of the mind towards knowledge, or in a global search for well-being or right living. I have long argued (Deurzen 2002, 2009; Deurzen and Young 2009) that it is vital for existential therapists to be aware of their own values and beliefs as well as those of their clients and to question them. Tracking these at all levels allows us to be aware of how and why some people might miss out some areas of existence.

Therapy as a philosophical project

Attending to our own ways of making meaning at different levels helps us to recognize our therapeutic bias. It stops us working in the dark, assuming too much and coaxing people in the direction in which we are going ourselves. It is only by constantly clearing our perspective that we can depart from the radical point zero required by our phenomenological method. This was Husserl's (1977) objective for the transcendental reduction, which exposes the transcendental ego: to fathom our own biases and to get to the bottom of our self-reflective experience, clearing a space in ourselves from where we are most likely to see to the horizon. This requires us to be explicit about our beliefs, not in order to get rid of them but in order to scrutinize their essence. The word 'spirituality' is apt in this context, for such self scrutiny is a search for the fundamental convictions, ideals, principles and beliefs that are our breath of life and define us. If we refine these to get to their core we reconnect to universal truth. As existential therapists we owe it to our clients to keep cleansing the lenses through which we look at the world. To work truthfully is to be as attentive to our personal observations as to those of others and to gradually puzzle out the picture of reality that, verifiably, has most chance of doing justice to the phenomena in view. Some might have difficulty with such a broad definition of spirituality. They might find it easier to agree with the following definition:

> Spirituality which comes from the Latin spiritus, meaning 'breath of life', is a way of being and experiencing that comes through awareness of a transcendent dimension and that is characterised by certain identifiable values in regard to self, others, nature, life and whatever one considers the Ultimate.
>
> (Elkins et al. 1988: 10)

By this definition, spirituality can still be just as easily socially or culturally based as religiously based, since, for some people, human society and the human being are the ultimate and transcending principle. Humanism, atheism or particularly strongly held political convictions such as Marxism may then function as the equivalent of a spiritual base, as indeed might a commitment to a worldview informed by scientific research. It is quite important to take account of such secular spiritualities, as these are gradually gaining ground (Dawkins 2006; Armstrong 2008; Deurzen 2009) as much as are orthodox or fundamentalist forms of spirituality. For this reason, I often prefer to refer to an ideological or philosophical dimension of life rather than to a spiritual dimension.

The point of all this is to be able to help clients get clarity about the ideas, ideals and beliefs they hold with passion and conviction at the core of their being. Such beliefs are often irrational and deeply emotional. While we might in principle find sufficient reasons for living in the pure pleasure of our physical sensations, in the positive emotions of our relationships or in the simple satisfaction of being who we are, it is unlikely that we will thrive if we have not deeply connected our reasons for living to a more elemental spiritual core of meaning. It is to this core that existential authors appeal. They inspire us with a love of living well in relation to some overarching truth.

Theoretical contributions from philosophy

Kierkegaard's project of reclaiming faith from the church dogmas that he loathed is directly related to his struggles with passion. His leap of faith is a leap into a committed and loving life, which is lived with profundity and personal engagement: to the full. It is passionate inwardness that is the key to such a loving life and such inwardness brings us in touch with what he calls God – which he essentially equates with the principle of Love, which he holds to be everything. 'To defraud oneself of love is the most terrible, is an eternal loss for which there is no compensation either in time or in eternity' (Kierkegaard 1995: 5–6).

Nietzsche's search for a principle to live by is equally poignant, as it is set against the background of the nihilism which he thought had replaced religion. Nietzsche was greatly concerned with the implications of such a nihilistic stance and urged his readers to reflect on the absurdity of this position. 'But how have we done this? How were we able to drink up the sea? Who gave us the sponge to wipe away the entire horizon?' (Nietzsche 1974: 125). Nietzsche wanted to know how people could live without a transcendent principle. His madman in *The Gay Science* is perplexed at the death of God. Much of Nietzsche's work was a search for inspiration in a world deserted by religion, a resketching of the horizon, by transvaluing all established values and thinking from scratch. His solution was for the superhuman to reclaim the will to power for himself by becoming a bridge that could stretch across the gap between animal and God. The principle of the eternal return was his closest formulation of an ethical life, teaching us to live as if each moment might endure forever.

Husserl's road was rather different, as his phenomenology was a scientific project. Yet his search for the transcendental ego (1977) was also a search for the spiritual core of consciousness. This is why it is so often ignored and rejected in spite of the fact that it is what holds his entire theory together. The phenomenological and eidetic reductions deal with the objective world and our mental processes in relation to it, but the transcendental reduction takes us into an entirely different realm: that of clarity about our internal philosophy. 'The fundamental science then becomes transcendental phenomenology, a psychology in the highest sense, a new sense which includes all critique of reason and all genuine philosophical problems' (Husserl 1977: 170).

Such a psychology seeks to systematically contemplate the way in which I reflect upon myself and adopt a particular way of life or come to an ethical deliberation. This is a very different human science model of psychology to replace the established model, which is based in the physical and objective sciences. It is a transcendental psychology that seeks to establish how we arrive at our reasons for living.

Following in Husserl's footsteps, Heidegger became increasingly concerned with Dasein's embeddedness in Being and with the ontological and metaphysical aspects of human being. His notion of *Ereignis*, i.e. the repossession of our being in an actively truthful manner by living with the fourfold of Being, is an example of his attempt to formulate a new metaphysical psychology of existence. It centres on reaching out towards Being in gratitude and plenitude with true awareness of what is. 'Original thinking is the thanks owed for being. That thanks alone gives rise to thinking of the kind we know as retribution and reward in the good and bad sense' (Heidegger 1968: 141).

Jaspers' philosophical contribution (1969) similarly focuses on the description of the 'comprehensive', the overarching principle of Being that transcends all human preoccupations. Tillich's *The Courage to Be* (1952) goes hand in hand with his theological writings and shows a similar focus on that which is beyond us and is shown up as 'ultimate concerns' that we need to learn to encompass. Gabriel Marcel's (1954) phenomenology of 'having' and 'being' and of embodied fidelity to extra temporal ideals is illuminating for existential therapy, even though it is grounded in his strong Christian faith. Buber's (1947, 1970) and Lévinas' (1969) philosophical worldviews, which inform many existential therapists' understanding of the therapeutic relationship, are profoundly influenced by Judaism. If their words are inspirational it is because they draw on these transcendental forces and refer all human problems to an eternal beyond that provides the wide angle of existence. What distinguishes these existential philosophers is their willingness to engage fully with elemental questions, in a manner that is non-dogmatic and remains self-questioning and challenging.

They recognize that if we believe in nothing, we become nothing. Not caring about ultimate truths leads to apathy. If we believe in something and engage with it, commit to it, live it, our psyche reflects this concern and becomes inspired, passionate, alive. Even the nihilistic existentialist authors knew this. Sartre struggled with the transcendental aspects of his worldview and found it hard to formulate the new ethics he had promised his readers. He filled the transcendental horizon of his work initially with a staunch belief in socialist and Marxist principles, but replaced this with a more global dialectics (Sartre 1982). His *Notebooks for an Ethics* (1992a) and his *Truth and Existence* (1992b) are, like de Beauvoir's *The Ethics of Ambiguity*

(1970), a testimony to their secular search for a way of life that works in practice and that is based on dynamic, reflective and dialectical values. Morality starts when we become clear of our own point of view. Perhaps de Beauvoir summed it up best in her essay 'Pyrrhus and Cineas': 'Wherever there is a point of view, there is not nothingness. And to tell the truth, I can take no other point of view but my own' (de Beauvoir 2004: 140).

Our point of view is all we have. The psyche is nothing but reflection, but it is not nothing. We need courage to self-reflect and decide how we want to live. Our ethics has to be constantly tried and tested by our reflected existence. Ethical principles are not theoretical: we have to be able to live by them in practice:

> There is no abstract ethics. There is only an ethics in a situation and therefore it is concrete. An abstract ethics is that of the good conscience. It assumes that one can be ethical in a fundamentally unethical situation. . . . Ethics is the theory of action. But action is abstract if it is not work and struggle.
>
> (Sartre 1992a: 17)

Camus (1954, 1975, 2000) and Merleau-Ponty (1962, 1964) were similarly concerned with the concrete experience of the individual. Personal, meticulous observation, description and reflection replace the magic of transcendence offered by divinity. Engaged perception and reflection open the way towards the recovery or discovery of meaning. This is no longer a meaning assigned by universal and unchanging principles, but one that we create by the way in which we exist and perceive the world.

Practical contributions

This brings us back to the practice of existential therapy, which is the concrete praxis of existential reflectivity on our ways and reasons for living. Binswanger (1963) made history when pointing out to Freud that a therapeutic failure they were discussing together could 'only be understood as the result of something which could be called a deficiency of spirit [Geistlichkeit]' (Binswanger 1963: 1). He was astonished when Freud concurred, saying: 'Yes, spirit [Geist] is everything' (Binswanger 1963: 1). Of course Freud famously went on to add: 'Man has always known he possessed spirit: I had to show him there is such a thing as instinct' (Binswanger 1963: 1). This is critical. Freud's psychoanalysis and behavioural psychology were both phenomena of their time and sought to understand human beings from an objective, natural science perspective. This made them highly reductionist. Inspired as he was by Husserl's work, Binswanger reminded us that what human beings were now most at risk of losing was their spirit.

Spiritedness and passion make life worthwhile and whole. They inspire us and light our inner fire. Many people become desperately confused and depressed when they lose the northern star of the passionate purpose of their life. They feel out of touch with themselves, though they may not know why this is:

> The greatest hazard of all, losing one's self, can occur very quietly in the world, as if it were nothing at all. No other loss can occur so quietly; any other loss – an arm, a leg, five dollars, a wife, etc. – is sure to be noticed.
>
> (Kierkegaard 1980: 32)

Frankl (1964) for similar reasons made *logos*, or meaning, the central plank of his therapy. Unlike Frankl though, Binswanger always kept an eye on the other dimensions of life, which remain important too. Though it is undoubtedly true that when we have purpose and meaning we feel more able to put up with adversity and hardship, life still requires us to deal with concrete reality. The art of living is about weaving the different strands of life together into a meaningful whole that holds us safe. Strands are constantly added and taken away, so that we need to tend carefully to the fabric of our lives on a daily basis, disconnecting, reconnecting and integrating all the time. It is one of the great advantages of ageing that we may experience a growing ability to unite and understand our experience, absorbing the losses and disappointments that inevitably multiply as we mature. Human transcendence is arrived at by reflecting on our experience, rising above it and making sense of it.

Framework for meaning

When meaning is carried by a whole network of significance it is less easily lost. Baumeister (1991) proposed four ways of finding meaning which together form the basis of a well-lived existence:

1 *efficacy*: by showing ourselves able to stand our ground in the physical world
2 *value*: in proving that we are an important part of the social world
3 *self-worth*: through feeling at ease with who we are
4 *purpose*: when discovering that we have a significant role to play in life.

Yet to have such goals and values is not enough: they must be realistically achievable. A good life is invariably a life that is continuously trying to improve itself; it is an ongoing process of re-creating ourselves. This is why recreation, sleep and relaxation are so important: for these are the times

	Umwelt	**Mitwelt**	**Eigenwelt**	**Überwelt**
Physical survival	Nature	Things	Body	Cosmos
Social affiliation	Public	Others	Ego	Culture
Personal identity	Private	Me	Self	Consciousness
Spiritual meaning	Sacred	Being	Soul	Transcendence

Figure 12.1 Different dimensions of the four spheres of existence

when we come back to ourselves and allow new experiences to be absorbed, so that the kaleidoscope of our lives can be transformed to accommodate the new givens. One of the charms of holidays is to be able to take time to rethink our life structures and projects and to fan the flames of our passions and enjoyment, ensuring our re-engagement with levels of life we had come to neglect. This is critical when our existence has become too narrowly focused and is no more than a daily chore. How unfortunate then that holidays are often used to merely distract and divert ourselves from problems we wish to leave behind but find unchanged upon our return. We are all too easily inclined to leave reappraisal to times of crisis when the fault lines of our existence are exposed and old habits break down by force. This is unwise. It is like leaving our homes to degrade without preventative improvements or carefully planned renovations. We are liable sooner or later to see our roofs cave in if we live in this way.

So how do we deal with the challenges of our lives more productively? If we want to live with spontaneity and creativity we need to establish a secure frame, within which we can afford to be more playful. Figure 12.1 shows 16 fields of human existence that need tending. It is arrived at by intersecting the four dimensions of life, namely the *Umwelt* (around-world), *Mitwelt* (with-world), *Eigenwelt* (own-world) and *Überwelt* (over-world) with the four layers of human existence, that are the physical, social, personal and spiritual domains' we thus come up with 16 essential planes of life that each need our attention if we are to thrive. Of course this does not do justice to the interwoven, multilayered and dynamic experiential realities of each day. It is merely a conceptual tool to help us remember and track our multiple reasons for living. Such a map can help us remain calm and clear when clients face confusion and chaos. It points us towards missing sources of meaning and can generate new reasons for living.

Each of these fields represents an entire world in its own right and throws up challenges and contradictions we need to learn to handle. If we combine this model with Baumeister's four ways of finding meaning, we will see that for our lives to make sense we need:

1   To feel effective in our embodied existence in the physical world, in relation to nature and the objects we encounter, whilst feeling part of the cosmos.
2   To feel of value by having confidence in our personal ego, whilst relating with others in the social world, with a sense of belonging to the culture we live in.
3   To feel a sense of self-worth as the individual we are, at ease in that private sphere where we encounter our personal thoughts and consciousness.
4   To feel purposeful in relation to what is sacred; meaningfully and soulfully proceeding to transcend the banality of our lives.

If we learn to master the paradoxes and dilemmas in each realm, overcoming each problem as it unfolds we come to dynamically evolve as human beings and learn to transcend our fate.

Application to therapy

This is precisely what existential therapy is about: to deal with all areas of life that are blocked or have never yet opened up. Therapy is a time when people can reflect on their way of being, elucidate and understand what was previously unspoken and unknown and actively engage with what it means to be human.

People rarely have a good idea of the many different ways in which their lives have become obstructed. They are only vaguely aware that the light of their life has dimmed, but do not know what is possible. Listening to a client's life story whilst attuned to these various layers of existence, we can detect the contradictions and foreclosures they are struggling with.

Gary tells me that he is a company director and is very good at earning a living and providing for his family. He knows he has neglected his own body, spoiling it with too much luxury. His despair is tangible though he is out of touch with it. He fears the ageing process that has ravaged his appearance and his health. Serious medical problems have brought him to therapy: initially he claims he just wants his body fixed. He has been told that therapy may help by allowing him to vent his emotions. So that is all he wishes to do. Yet he speaks of feeling driven and empty all the time. Deep down he knows nothing can be fixed unless he is prepared to start thinking about his life and his own purpose. In Gary's life there is no loving exchange with the things in his world, no organic interaction with nature, no respect for his body. Nor is there any deep connection with the people in his life, including his wife and children. So, even at the physical and social levels, which dominate his life, he is out of touch with most of the fields of existence. At the personal and spiritual levels he lives in a vacuum, with little self-reflection or self-awareness and no real ideals. And as we start our dialogue about his life, Gary very slowly has to learn to reclaim area by area of existence, until he can start making sense of life in an ever more meaningful way. Changes will soon follow this fundamental work of reclaiming his reasons for living.

Like so many others Gary had never imagined that it was possible to find a deeper meaning in his life than doing his duty, earning a lot of money and finding succour in food and drink. Therapy for Gary was therefore not about addressing symptoms but about raising his consciousness of his existence. His symptoms of despairing depression and bewildered anxiety were merely derivative and became irrelevant as soon as he began addressing the issues underneath. It is important that we patiently work out with each of our clients what they are good at and what they have neglected. Each life is a patchwork of contradictions, failed opportunities and as yet unrealized values. Sometimes a psychiatric diagnosis can conceal basic gaps in the fourfold of existence. We have to look through it towards the real preoccupations that each person is struggling with.

Sylvie, who is 25 and was diagnosed with schizophrenia at the age of 17, has hardly been out of her parents' house in the past years. She hides away in order to be safe, unaware that this very hiding creates the turbulence of a frustrated energy that turns on itself. She has populated her tiny universe with a whole array of fantasies and imaginings that have become her reality, though nobody shares this reality. She feels incompetent in the physical dimension. She doesn't dress herself anymore, is too scared to go to the corner shop and has trouble with the most basic routines of personal hygiene. She has a distorted view of the personal dimension and the social one is blanked out entirely, taboo, marked as dangerous (even her parents are unwelcome guests in her space). The spiritual dimension is crowded with wishful thinking, both positive and negative and the fantasy books she idolizes are full of doom and destruction. Sylvie has lost track of who she is and wants to be, can be or will be allowed to be. She sees herself as incapable of coping with the most basic tasks in the public and physical domains and avoids them like the plague. She daren't even dance or swim or ride a bike. Her antipsychotic medication has left her completely 'out of synch' with her own body. Only her books are worth living for, she says. They are her entire universe. The real world is scary and she is fundamentally filled with fear. Therapy is about re-establishing her confidence to explore the world, but this can only be done when she allows herself to deflate her sham security. We work hard at extending her capacity for self-observation and self-reflection, which she is curiously good at, but has never learnt to use in a constructive way. Our discussions focus initially on the reasons why her particular suffering counts for something in the universe. From here she begins to harvest new reasons for living that gradually re-engage her with the world.

No two clients are the same and therapists have to be willing to participate in many different worldviews. We all have different blind spots and sometimes even gaping holes in our lives. Some of us learn to play to our strengths and hide the rest, contenting ourselves with less; some of us give up, giving in to our perceived weaknesses. It is our existential challenge to learn to tolerate losses and disappointments and deal with adversity, understanding that we must content ourselves with doing a good enough job at living, rather than aiming for perfection.

Existential therapy enables people to reclaim authorship of their life and stimulates a renewal of being. It allows people to feel more part of the universe and in charge of their own life at the same time. This is what Heidegger meant by re-owning our life (through *Ereignis*). Typically such awakening involves an expansion into the spiritual domain, after an experience of crisis or transition. Frequently people feel quite confused about this aspect of existence. Their life crises can provide the call of conscience that helps them open up and evolve. Their troubles are not just symptoms of psychopathology but dark nights of the soul, which may lead to enlightenment. When our focus becomes too narrow, our freedom is stifled and our growth stunted. We feel guilty towards life and to ourselves. When life breaks down and brings us chaos, new creativity can emerge and we can take charge of life once more. Of course it is quite possible to remain caught up in this phase of chaos or doubt for too long and to end up having no focus, no engagement and no reasons for living at all. There is the risk of becoming rigidified at such moments and to hang on to formulaic dogmas or orthodoxies instead of exploring new ways of being. This is why it is so vital at those moments to offer a person an elemental search for practical wisdom that can inspire them to make something of their life.

Conclusions

Our clients deserve a therapy that gets to the bottom of their existential turmoil, rather than covering it up. There is no point in providing quick fix solutions that fix nothing. We need to be prepared to think clearly about meaning and being:

> Our experiences in therapy and in groups, it is clear, involve the transcendent, the indescribable, the spiritual. I am compelled to believe that I, like many others, have under-estimated the importance of this mystical, spiritual dimension.
>
> (Rogers 1980: 130)

Rogers, like many other seasoned therapists, came to a more existential view towards the end of his career. Existential therapy, as I have defined it, is a spiritual quest that aims for inspirational rather than aspirational objectives. The existential task is to enable people to search for truth, actively, carefully and painstakingly, through the experience of reflecting on their own position in the world and the possibilities of their existence. This is a search for individual freedom and for the liberation of the human mind from prejudice, blind error and self-deception. In facilitating that search, we give our clients back to themselves and help them reconnect to life.

References

Armstrong, K. (2008) *The Case for God: What Religion Really Means*, London: Random House.

Baumeister, R. (1991) *Meanings of Life*, New York: Guilford Press.

Beauvoir, S. de (1970 [1948]) *The Ethics of Ambiguity*, trans. B. Frechtman, New York: Citadel Press.

Beauvoir, S. de (2004) 'Pyrrhus and Cineas', in M. A. Simons (ed.) *Simone de Beauvoir: Philosophical Writings*, Chicago: University of Illinois Press.

Binswanger, L. (1963) *Being in the World*, trans. J. Needleman, New York: Basic Books.

Buber, M. (1947 [1929]) *Between Man and Man*, trans. R. G. Smith, London: Kegan Paul.

Buber, M. (1970 [1923]) *I and Thou*, trans. W. Kaufmann, Edinburgh: T. and T. Clark.

Camus, A. (1954 [1951]) *The Rebel: An Essay on Man in Revolt*, trans. A. Bower, New York: Vintage.

Camus, A. (1975 [1942]) *The Myth of Sisyphus*, trans. J. O'Brien, Harmondsworth: Penguin.

Camus, A. (2000 [1942]) *The Outsider*, trans. J. Laredo, Harmondsworth: Penguin.

Dawkins, R. (2006) *The God Delusion*, London: Bantam Press.

Deurzen, E. van (2002) *Existential Counselling and Psychotherapy in Practice*, London: Sage Publications.

Deurzen, E. van (2009) *Psychotherapy and the Quest for Happiness*, London: Sage.

Deurzen, E. van and Young, S. (eds) (2009) *Existential Perspectives on Supervision: Widening the Horizon of Psychotherapy and Counselling*, London: Palgrave Macmillan.

Elkins, D. N., Hedstorm, L. J., Hughes, L. L., Leaf, J. A. and Saunders, C. (1988) 'Towards a humanistic-phenomenological spirituality', *Journal of Humanistic Psychology*, 28 (4): 5–18.

Frankl, V. E. (1964 [1946]) *Man's Search for Meaning*, London: Hodder and Stoughton.

Heidegger, M. (1968 [1954]) *What Is Called Thinking?*, trans. J. Glenn Gray, New York: Harper and Row.

Husserl, E. (1977 [1925]) *Phenomenological Psychology*, trans. J. Scanlon, The Hague: Nijhoff.

Jaspers, K. (1969 [1932]) *Philosophy*, three volumes, trans. E. B. Ashton, Chicago: University of Chicago Press.

Kierkegaard, S. (1980 [1849]) *The Sickness Unto Death*, trans. H. Hong and E. Hong, Princeton, NJ: Princeton University Press.

Kierkegaard, S. (1995 [1847]) *Works of Love*, trans. D. F. Swenson and L. M. Swenson, Princeton, NJ: Princeton University Press.

Lévinas, E. (1969 [1961]) *Totality and Infinity: An Essay on Exteriority*, trans. A. Lingis, Pittsburgh, PA: Duquesne University Press.

Marcel, G. (1954 [1949]) *The Philosophy of Existence*, trans. M. Harari, London: Harvill.

Merleau-Ponty, M. (1962 [1945]) *Phenomenology of Perception*, trans. C. Smith, London: Routledge and Kegan Paul.

Merleau-Ponty, M. (1964 [1948]) *Sense and Non-Sense*, trans. H. Dreyfus and P. Dreyfus, Evanston, IL: Northwestern University Press.

Nietzsche, F. (1974 [1882]) *The Gay Science*, trans. W. Kaufmann, New York: Random House.

Rogers, C. R. (1980) *A Way of Being*, Boston: Houghton Miflin.

Sartre, J.-P. (1982 [1960]) *Critique of Dialectical Reason*, trans. A. Sheridan-Smith, London: Verso/NLB.

Sartre, J.-P. (1992a [1983]) *Notebooks for an Ethics*, trans. D. Pellaner, Chicago: University of Chicago Press.

Sartre, J.-P. (1992b [1989]) *Truth and Existence*, trans. A. van den Hoven, Chicago: University of Chicago Press.

Solomon, R. C. (2002) *Spirituality for the Skeptic: The Thoughtful Love of Life*, New York: Oxford University Press.

Tillich, P. (1952) *The Courage to Be*, New Haven, CT: Yale University Press.

Chapter 13

Research

An existential predicament for our profession?

Linda Finlay

Many practising existential therapists seem resistant to research: they neither read it nor do it. Research is seen as taking place in 'academic ivory towers' and as 'irrelevant' to practice. Is this their lack of knowledge or confidence talking? Or, are they expressing unease with – an alienation from – research currently produced? Whatever the cause, the effect produced by the *research-practice chasm* is to shame practitioners, drive them to despair/detachment, and to split the profession. A case in point is the recent National Institute for Health and Clinical Excellence (NICE) guideline in the UK which, on the basis of quantitative evidence, promotes cognitive behavioural therapy (CBT) for managing depression (NICE 2004/7). Such research spearheads policy with pernicious effects: cheaper, quick-fix behavioural answers are favoured rather than longer term explorations of existential struggle. Tensions between modalities are exacerbated as other therapy approaches are effectively excluded in a wider context where rampant market-driven consumerist trends drive us towards reductionist, technical, manualized procedures.[1] Is there a place still for our existential practice or is it time to devise exit strategies?

'Thrown' into a situation not of our choosing, it is tempting to absorb ourselves in everyday inauthentic daily lives and deflect from our existential predicament (Heidegger 1962). Soothed by the knowledge that clients find existential therapy meaningful, even inspiring, we carry on doing what we have always done and do not bother with research. Yet are we not getting caught up in a 'parallel process' where we are marginalizing ourselves in shame (Evans and Finlay 2009)?

Alternatively, when pushed to engage with research for postgraduate study, we risk 'falling' into an 'abyss of meaninglessness' where the comfort of scientific convention and 'box-ticking research' ensures we conform to external requirements.[2] We employ the mechanistic modes of data collection/analysis embraced by positivists – an anathema to us existentialists who prefer more relational, interpretivist forms.

With the closing down of possibilities, I suggest we are facing an existential crisis for the life and soul of our profession as existential therapists.

In this chapter I offer a 'wake-up' nudge. It is time for us to ask basic questions about our role, purpose and meanings, and to confront our responsibilities. We have some stark choices if we are to engage with research: What should our strategy be? What methodologies will safeguard our professional values and identity, ensuring authentic research? I invite you to dialogue with me.

Strategic choices

The effectiveness of CBT, with its short-term interventions and measurable outcomes amenable to being tested experimentally, has been repeatedly demonstrated. Lacking a comparable evidence base, humanistic–existential (and other) therapies are being left behind. The playing field is not level. How should we respond?

Assuming we seek to support the project to engage with research (as consumer and/or producer) we have at least three strategic choices: (1) we can play 'them' at their own outcome measurement game; (2) we can get them to play a different game on the same pitch; (3) we can take our bat and ball into a different playing field altogether.

Playing the outcome measurement game

If we play the game of outcome measurement we would need to find appropriate outcome measures and construct experiments – ideally, the gold standard of randomized controlled trials (RCTs) – to 'prove' that our therapy works. This is easier said than done. We lack the necessary research experience and our longer term existential concerns are not easily measured by focusing on behaviour and experimental means. However, we could bolster our effort by invoking current evidence: for instance, Wampold *et al.* (1997), reviewing research carried out between 1970 and 1995, found that all forms of psychotherapy appear to be equally effective when competently applied. Numerous studies have also concluded that it is the therapeutic relationship and client variables which have the greatest bearing on outcomes (Norcross 2002; Cooper 2008). There is a lack of evidence supporting any one modality/technique over others. Hubble *et al.* (1999) offer an explanation: clients are resourceful and can be the architects of their own change processes, using whatever healing processes are going.

We could also critique current outcomes research as reductionist and 'out' its preferential intent by asking: 'In whose interests is this research?' We could highlight the problematic nature of comparing hugely variable therapy experiences, and make the point that studying short-term gains are of limited value. Even Martin Seligman, former President of the American Psychological Association (APA), has been obliged to concede that his beliefs have changed about what counts as a 'gold standard': 'deciding whether one treatment under highly controlled conditions works better than another . . . is a different question from deciding what works in the field' (1995: 966).

Playing a different game

If we want to dialogue with the mainstream without 'selling out', we must change the game and fight for what we believe. One neat move would be to shift the focus from outcomes on to researching process. What happens in the therapy relationship? Timulak (2010) has used rigorously scientific meta-analytic methods to examine findings about process from qualitative studies, specifically exploring clients' perceptions of therapy and what they find helpful. Studies demonstrate the complex ambiguity of the field and how meanings are embedded in specific therapy contexts. Interestingly, emotional–relational aspects of significant moments in therapy are particularly valued over the cognitive aspects frequently stressed by therapists less versed in existential therapy approaches.

We could also dispense with the rulebook of the 'evidence-based practice' movement and, instead, promote practice-based evidence as the new game. This involves small-scale 'practitioner research' in everyday clinical settings, placing therapists'/clients' experiences at the core (McLeod 1999). With clinicians themselves acting as researchers, the research is integrated into the therapy. Studying the value, processes and challenges of therapy in this way becomes a natural extension of our normal reflective/analytical approach.

In practice-based research, experiential, theoretical and empirical evidence for our therapy practice enjoy equal legitimacy. Therapist-researchers might offer detailed descriptions of some aspect of their clinical case work – via a case study, say. They might describe the context and process of therapy offering supporting evidence of its effectiveness by using standardized measures, therapist observation and client self-reports. Alternatively, a therapist-researcher might just carry out a scholarly exploration of a theoretical construct/process issue drawing on practice examples.

Another way of changing the agenda would be to challenge prevailing notions of 'science'. Giorgi,[3] notably, has continually insisted on the need for a specifically and avowedly human science instead of a natural science. Here, researchers aim to hold fast to a scientific method that is rigorous and normative, where each step is carefully scrutinized and where techniques are systematically applied.

The descriptive phenomenological approach (based on Husserl's philosophical phenomenology, employing the epoché and eidetic reduction towards describing the essence or structure of experiences and the manner in which they are given in consciousness) explicated by Giorgi (1985) and others in the US is one example. In the UK, interpretative phenomenological analysis (IPA) – a hermeneutic methodology which has burgeoned rapidly over the last decade (particularly in the field of health psychology) – offers an equally structured methodical approach (Smith *et al.* 2009).

Playing in a different field

If we do not want to play on the pitch already marked out for the evidence-based practice game where 'referees' might be biased, we need to move elsewhere. Hermeneutic phenomenologists, for instance, recommend engaging modes beyond the scientific and measurable: for example, art, literary prose, dance, poetry. Jager (2010), embracing the poetics of later Heidegger, argues that researchers interested in the human condition need to think in terms that apply to our lived human world:

> Science and technology certainly lightens the burdens of our daily life, but we should remain mindful of the fact that we come face to face and heart to heart with our friends and neighbor or with a work of art only by entering into a covenant and obeying the grammar of an inhabited cosmos.
>
> (Jager 2010: 80–81)

Hermeneutic phenomenologists seek methods that allow the concrete, emotional, intuitive, imaginative, aesthetic, embodied and relational nature of experience to be revealed. They embrace the growing trend of articulating an 'aesthetic phenomenology' (or 'expressive' phenomenology) which draws on more evocative, poetic forms of writing. They encourage researchers to find words that capture ambiguity and carry textural dimensions of experience forward:

> A poetics of research makes neither research into poetry nor researcher into poet. Rather, it deepens research and makes it richer by attending to the images in the ideas, the fantasies in the facts, the dreams in the reasons, the myths in the meanings, the archetypes in the arguments, and the complexes in the concepts.
>
> (Romanyshyn 2007: 12)

In a bid to capture an 'alive' sense of the experience of caring for a partner with Alzheimer's, Galvin and Todres (2009) use 'embodied inter-pretation' – a hermeneutic way of re-presenting other people's experiences based on Gendlin's practice of drawing on 'felt sense'. They favour:

> the kind of qualitative research that communicates human experiences in ways that people can really feel and relate to. . . . Such entry into

alive meanings . . . requires the kind of receptivity of the lived body that 'lets be,' in a bodily participative way.

(p. 311)

As we shape our new 'game' on a pitch of our own making, we are free to engage with 'structure' and 'texture'; to embrace an artful component within a scientific project. Now we have the scope to use methods that resonate authentically, providing understandings that touch others' 'heart' and 'head' (Todres 2007).

Methodological choices

What does empirical research from an existential perspective look like? What kind of research would practitioners (not versed in impact-rated research) be drawn towards? Given that there are many methodological routes to choose from, which capture our imagination?

In the first place, qualitative inquiry would seem a sine qua non. As therapists we are drawn towards routes that focus on holistic experience rather on reductionist behavioural outcomes. We seek to understand the 'what' of our existence rather than analyse causal variables or whether one treatment is more effective than another. We prefer inductive and exploratory methodologies rather than hypothesis testing. We favour experiential methods that offer implicit meanings and subjective interpretations of a fluid, uncertain world: e.g. interviews, participant observation, reflection and first person writing studies. We are suspicious of the 'objectivity' claimed, when quantitative researchers employ experiments or attitude surveys. Instead of detachment and neutrality we celebrate subjectivity. We recognize that researchers are involved in co-constructing knowledge, and that knowledge is shaped by context.

We are pulled specifically towards phenomenological research that describes lived experience – what it is to be human. The research that makes the most sense to us is that which invokes everyday experience in all its ambivalence. In his celebrated rallying cry 'Back to the things themselves!', Husserl exhorted phenomenologists to go all out to capture the ambiguity of the 'thing', by which he meant the richness of life as it is given to the experiencer. The transformative power of such research is the way it offers individuals opportunities to be witnessed in their experience, allows them to 'give voice' to what they are going through, plus opening new opportunities for both researcher and researched to 'make sense of' the experience in focus (Finlay 2011).

The existential accent of phenomenological research effortlessly attracts us. Through the contributions of phenomenological philosophers such as Sartre (1969), Heidegger (1962) and Merleau-Ponty (1962), we are instinctively in tune with certain ideas: that we all have an embodied sense of self which is always in relation to others, while our consciousness is shared with others through language, discourse, culture and history. We experience time in our recollection of past joys and trauma. We also anticipate what is to come in the future. We are placed into a matrix of spatial relations in the world, surrounded by things which have meaning while we engage with ideas and activities which become our projects. We are thrown into the world in order to live: we act, make choices, strive, become. And ultimately we die. Applying these concepts to research, van Manen (1990) recommends that we use four fundamental lifeworld 'existentials' – spatiality, corporeality, temporality and relationality – as helpful guides for research.

In addition to being qualitative/phenomenological, the research which attracts is relational, reflexive and dialogic, mirroring the processes at the heart of our practice of existential therapy.

While relational–reflexive–dialogical research takes various forms, all tend to be influenced by existential phenomenological philosophers such as Buber, Lévinas, and Gendlin – specifically their work on self–other understanding, ethical relating and the healing power of dialogue. As Gendlin puts it: 'The essence of work with another person is to be present as a living being' (1996: 297).

In relational–reflexive–dialogical approaches to research, researchers try to start from an open, curious, unknowing place. Data is seen as emerging out of the researcher and co-researcher[4] relationship, co-created in the embodied dialogical encounter. These researchers believe that much of what we can learn and know about another comes through dialogue and arises within the intersubjective spaces between researcher, co-researcher and the phenomenon being studied. This dialogue (verbal or non-verbal) forms the basis for reflection on both self and other. In this opening between lurks ambiguity and unpredictability, together with the possibility of true meeting; anything can – and does – appear (Finlay and Evans 2009; Finlay 2011).

Conclusion

In this chapter I am calling us to face our professional responsibilities: to confront the 'existential predicament' at the heart of our practice, and affirm (or redefine) our professional self-identity.

I have argued the value of research as a means to combat our professional crisis. Rather than being an ivory tower option waiting politely but ineffectively in the wings, research offers us a purposeful way ahead. Let us not continue to marginalize ourselves. Armed with research rooted in the values and existential perspectives we hold dear, we can change the nature of the 'game'. Our challenge is to find ways to do our research authentically but in ways others beyond our field will accept and respect.

This is the moment to participate in the debates: Do we do 'outcome measurement' or 'process-orientated' research? Evidence-based practice or practice-based evidence? Science or art? Quantitative or qualitative? If we engage with phenomenological research, what variant should we embrace – descriptive? hermeneutic? relational? We need to own our choices.

I believe we should nurture research which we can do well, and model it for others. I value the communicative power of research that challenges, unsettles and reverberates, that strikes a chord with our everyday experience of life. I want to be touched by the captivating, allusive power of research which evokes lived experience. For me, phenomenology achieves this best when it focuses on existential issues, uses relational–reflexive–dialogical forms and when it can draw on the arts. Such a phenomenology turns doing/reading research into an experience in itself. In turning to the arts, we:

> correct the one-sideness of medicine . . . the one-sided ministrations of psychological science, but also because, thus, we can enjoy a psychotherapy [or research practice] which is a creative servant of life and laughter and love.
>
> (Wilkinson 2009: 236)

Acknowledgements

I am grateful to Wiley-Blackwell for giving me permission in this chapter to draw liberally on other published work, namely from: Finlay, L. and Evans, E. (2009) and Finlay, L. (2011).

Notes

1 Therapy knowledge thus becomes ever more dominated by research which is both policy and ideologically driven rather than theory-practice led. Arguably, policy-driven research is more about cost cutting; ideologically driven research is more about defining one group as more deserving than another.
2 More creative research approaches are blocked by various gatekeepers – including the demands from professional organizations and research ethics panels. Moreover, psychotherapy training courses in the UK are currently being restructured to appeal to external masters rather than being guided by internal congruence and professional values. In the USA practitioners are forced to 'bow' before demands of insurance companies.
3 With his experimental psychology background, Giorgi does not want to reject science, but to modify it so that it investigates the human side. Giorgi has provided the impetus for what has become known as the Duquesne tradition which has spawned thousands of phenomenological research studies throughout the world (e.g. Giorgi 1985, 2009; Wertz 2011).
4 I use the term 'co-researcher' instead of research participant to highlight the fact that relational–reflexive–dialogic research is collaborative in spirit. Existential–

phenomenological researchers often prefer to do research *with*, as opposed to *on*, participants.

References

Cooper, M. (2008) *Essential Research Findings in Counselling and Psychotherapy*, London: Sage.

Evans, K. and Finlay, L. (2009) '*To be, or not to be . . .* registered: A relational phenomenological exploration of what state registration means to psychotherapists, *European Journal for Qualitative Research in Psychotherapy*, 4: 4–12.

Finlay, L. (2011) *Phenomenology for Therapists: Researching the Lived World*, Chichester: Wiley-Blackwell.

Finlay, L. and Evans, E. (2009) *Relational–centred Research for Psychotherapists: Exploring Meanings and Experience*. Chichester: Wiley-Blackwell.

Galvin, K. and Todres, L. (2009) 'Poetic inquiry and phenomenological research: the practice of embodied interpretation', in M. Prendergast, C. Leggo and P. Sameshina (eds) *Poetic Inquiry: Vibrant Voices in the Social Sciences* (pp. 307–316). Rotterdam: Sense Publishers.

Gendlin, E. T. (1996) *Focusing-oriented Psychotherapy: A Manual of Experiential Method*, New York: Guilford Press.

Giorgi, A. (ed.) (1985) *Phenomenological and Psychological Research*, Pittsburgh, PA: Duquesne University Press.

Giorgi, A. (2009) *The Descriptive Phenomenological Method in Psychology: A Modified Husserlian Approach*, Pittsburgh, PA: Duquesne University Press.

Heidegger, M. (1962 [1927]) *Being and Time*, trans. J. Macquarrie and E. Robinson, Oxford: Blackwell.

Hubble, M. A., Duncan, B. L. and Miller, S. D. (eds) (1999) *The Heart and Soul of Change: What Works in Therapy*, Washington, DC: American Psychological Association.

Jager, B. (2010). 'About "doing science" and "contemplating the human condition"', *Humanistic Psychologist*, 38 (1): 67–94.

McLeod, J. (1999) *Practitioner Research in Counselling*, London: Sage.

Merleau-Ponty, M. (1962 [1945]) *Phenomenology of Perception*, trans. C. Smith, London: Routledge and Kegan Paul.

National Institute for Health and Clinical Excellence (NICE 2004/7) *Guidelines on Depression*. www.nice.org.uk/guidance/CG23. Accessed 21 July 2009.

Norcross, J. C. (ed.) (2002) *Psychotherapy Relationships that Work: Therapist Contributions and Responsiveness to Patients*, Oxford: Oxford University Press.

Romanyshyn, R. D. (2007) *The Wounded Researcher: Research With Soul in Mind*, New Orleans: Spring Journal Books.

Sartre, J.-P. (1969 [1943]) *Being and Nothingness*, trans. H. Barnes, London: Routledge.

Seligman, M. E. P. (1995) 'The effectiveness of psychotherapy: the consumer report study', *American Psychologist*, 50: 965–974.

Smith, J. A., Flowers, P. and Larkin, M. (2009) *Interpretative Phenomenological Analysis: Theory, Method and Research*, Los Angeles: Sage.

Timulak, L. (2010) 'Significant events in psychotherapy: an update of research findings', *Psychology and Psychotherapy*, 83, 421–447.

Todres, L. (2007) *Embodied Enquiry: Phenomenological Touchstones for Research, Psychotherapy and Spirituality*, Basingstoke: Palgrave Macmillan.

Todres, L. and Galvin, K. T. (2008) 'Embodied interpretation: a novel way of evocatively re-presenting meanings in phenomenological research', *Qualitative Research*, 8 (5): 568–583.

van Manen, M. (1990) *Researching Lived Experience: Human Science for an Action Sensitive Pedagogy*, New York: State University of New York Press.

Wampold, B. E., Mondin, G. W., Moody, M., Stich, F., Benson, K. and Hyun-nie Ahn (1997) 'A meta-analysis of outcome studies comparing bona fide psychotherapies. Empirically, all must have prizes', *Psychological Bulletin*, 123: 203–216.

Wertz, F. J. (2011) 'A phenomenological psychological approach to trauma and resiliency', in F. J. Wertz, K. Charmaz, L. McMullen, R. Josselson, R. Anderson and E. McSpadden (eds) *Five Ways of Doing Qualitative Analysis: Phenomenological Psychology, Grounded Theory, Discourse Analysis, Narrative Research, and Intuitive Inquiry*, New York: Guilford Press.

Wilkinson, H. (2009) *The Muse as Therapist: A New Poetic Paradigm for Psychotherapy*, London: Karnac.

Chapter 14

Depth and the marketplace

Psychology's Faustian plight: a dialogue

Kirk J. Schneider and Simon du Plock

DEPTH AND THE MARKETPLACE: PSYCHOLOGY'S FAUSTIAN PLIGHT

Address to the 8/08 APA Annual Convention, Boston

Kirk J. Schneider

In his recent book, *Multiple Intelligences*, Howard Gardner introduces the concept of 'existential intelligence' – an intelligence that asks the 'big questions' about life ('Why do we live?' 'Why do we die?' 'Why do we love?' and 'Why do we make war?'). He then goes on to imply that this kind of intelligence appears to be of universal value and questions why it is not more widely recognized. But then he says something rather shocking – that existential intelligence is a 'candidate intelligence' – not quite scientifically legitimate. And why? Because, and I quote, there is a 'dearth of . . . evidence that parts of the brain are concerned . . . with these deep issues of existence' (2006: 21).

What a curious field we dwell in, that has to possess physical evidence in order to legitimate one of the most time-honoured components of human thought – the quest to understand ourselves. What a strange institution we have created that cannot accept the expressions of some of our greatest artists and thinkers as legitimately intelligent in the absence of demonstrable brain activity.

It is statements like these that have got me thinking about the state of American psychology. How is it, that in the most subtle and gross ways – and *despite* often, our most elemental instincts, we continue to be in the grip of 'reductionist envy' (which is my term for the increasing pervasiveness of the original phrase 'physics envy'). In so many corners of our field, from personality to evolutionary studies, to biology, to clinical, we persist in finding the neatest, smoothest, and most expedient 'answers' to our most vexing problems. And again, *despite our best instincts!*

Increasingly, I have come to the view that the forces of what Naomi Klein (2007) calls 'free market fundamentalism' are the engines which both fuel and fool mainstream American psychology. While I am not alone in this assessment, I am attempting to clarify in a more fine-grained way than I have seen, the correspondence between mainstream theory and practice and the mania for profits. By the mania for profits, I am speaking about the rising tide, over the last 25 years in particular, of unbowed mercantilism and embrace of the quick-fix model for living. This model accentuates speed, instant results, appearance and packaging, culminating in the *illusion* of power and control. Almost every advertising, public relations, and propaganda strategy capitalizes on this model. (See the British Broadcasting System documentary film *Century of the Self* [2005] for an elaboration on the latter.)

Yet many in our profession are unaware of the linkage between free markets and psychological application, and blithely go about their business as if what they do is either comfortably premised on science, or has no major relation to any grand system or context within which they are operating. I want to vigorously dispel these assumptions.

When I hear apologists for the status quo, for example, protest that psychological methodologies (mainly quantitative-experimental) and practices (mainly cognitive-behavioural) are not geared to the market but to scientific rigor, I feel the need to step back and take another look at what they are saying. What they seem to be saying is that we now have volumes of studies on the efficacy of short-term, solution-focused therapies, cognitive-behavioural strategies (such as rational restructuring, positive self-talk, and habit formation), the neurobiology of mindfulness and meditation, the adoption of religious ritual, and psychotropic medication – and, in light of this research, mainstream psychology works, it *betters* people's lives.

Well, this is certainly true to an extent. I grant that many of these things are helpful for certain levels of living, but the question is, to what extent? For example, in the clinical area (my area of specialization), we now have a massive number of studies that go *directly against* what mainstream therapy researchers, not to mention private and government insurers at one time believed: technical dimensions of therapy (such as psychoanalytic interpretations, cognitive reframes, or behavioural strategies) are *not* per se responsible for the lion's share of effective therapeutic outcomes. On the other hand, that which is preponderantly responsible for such outcomes are *anti*-technical factors, so-called common or context factors, which are relatively spontaneous, personal and artistic (Wampold 2001; Elkins 2007). Coupled with this research, we have increasing evidence that experiential (that is, immediate, affective and embodied) levels of therapeutic contact are superior to contrived and manualized forms of therapeutic contact for a variety of client issues (Weston *et al.* 2004; Fauth *et al.* 2007; Greenberg 2007). We also have the 2900 participant consumer reports study (Seligman 1996), which upholds the value of in-depth, long-term therapy (post two years) over solution-focused short-term therapy (six months and under) by a substantial margin. And finally, lest you consider the findings in this area as relegated to the 'worried well', we now have a very strong suggestion from the highly reputable *Schizophrenia Bulletin* that 'first and second order schizophrenic patients' in the 3–5 month, existentially oriented treatment facility Soteria House (directed by Loren Mosher) fared as well and in some cases better than those in conventional psychiatric treatment (Calton *et al.* 2008).

Given these findings, I can only be forced to conclude that not only have many therapists' careful observations over the decades about personable, artfully engaged therapy been found to be accurate, but that existential-humanistic or 'romantic' therapy (see Schneider 1998, 1999) – an approach that Nick Cummings and Will O'Donohue (2008: 97) identified recently as one of the 'Eleven Blunders that Cripple Psychotherapy in America', must now be seen as a beacon. Why? Because it is an approach that not only includes but *specializes* in the dimensions (i.e. personal presence, empathy and relationship) that leading researchers now view as integral to effective therapy (Wampold 2001).

I am also forced to conclude that the key reason why mainstream therapy continues to roll on, in the face of *substantial evidence that it is suboptimal,* is that insurance companies and the prevailing socio-economic machine *require* suboptimal practices (Bohart *et al.* 1998). Now Cummings and O'Donohue may elect to capitulate to these prevailing forces requiring suboptimal (methodological and clinical) practices, and that is their right. In fact, I defend their right because this is a very complex issue that understandably puts many practitioners in a bind. The authors *do* reflect the reality out there – that many third party payers, the prevailing health-care system, will not fund what many of us know now to be optimal for our clients and that capitulation seems the only viable strategy.

However, a growing number of us question capitulation as the only viable strategy. Indeed many of us call for a wholesale reform, not only for the healthcare system, but for the socio-economic system, the system that both fuels and *demands* a suboptimal mentality. Before I make a few suggestions about how we might get out of this capitulation pickle, let me outline another area where I believe we are cutting corners (wittingly or unwittingly) to appease the powers that be.

This area is generically termed the positive psychology movement. While the positive psychology movement is now made up of a diversity of sub-divisions, many of them making laudable contributions, my concern is with the movement as a whole, which implies, wittingly or unwittingly, a kind of one-sided psychology. Moreover, this psychology disturbingly meshes 'hand in glove' with the consumerist mentality. Who, for example, isn't lured by 'steps' or 'programs' that promise 'positive' results? Who isn't seduced by overt and measurable outcomes of happiness, and the gloss of happiness? The problem of course is that happiness or positive lifestyles are rarely one-sided affairs – and the deeper questions about the vital and fulfilled life (or life well lived) is not generally the stuff of profit-driven programs or soothing formulae.

At a more subtle level, the neurobiology of emotions, and even the recent craze over mindfulness meditation has demonstrated a similar predicament. Authors such as Daniel Siegal and Roger Walsh have provided eloquent roadmaps to psychological and physiological well-being, and I think there is a great deal to what they teach, but again, their psychology tends to be one-sided. For example, Siegal characterizes mental well-being as the 'linkage of differentiated components of a system into a functional whole' (2007: 288). He also goes on to describe this system in terms of the acronym 'FACES' – 'flow, flexible, adaptive, coherent, energized, and stable,' and contrasts this with 'chaos and rigidity' on the pathological end. Walsh, correspondingly, writes of the benefits of meditation in terms of the following 'enhanced capacities' – attention, cognition, sense withdrawal, lucidity, emotional intelligence, equanimity, motivation, and moral maturity (Walsh and Shapiro 2007).

Yet nowhere in the above two descriptions of well-being or enhanced consciousness is the *poignancy* of living. Nowhere is there a discussion of the reality, and indeed, life-enhancing *value* of anxiety, or for that matter *asynchrony*, pathos, and even disability. Who knows precisely what concatenation of triumphs and vulnerabilities, difficulties and efforts must come together to form a vibrant life – the voice of artists certainly have a say here, along with the voice of neuroscientists and meditators (see, for example, the legion of creative geniuses who might well have received diagnosable clinical conditions in Kay Jamison's 1993 germinal *Touched with Fire*).

Hence, what we have here is the convergence of fashionable psychological trends that both wittingly and unwittingly fit hand in glove into the market-driven, expedience-oriented, quick-fix model for living. This model emphasizes speed, instant results, and appearance and packaging. It also stresses overt and measurable 'answers' rather than exploratory quests. While overt and measurable answers have their place to be sure, they fail resoundingly when it comes to the core questions of life – 'Who are we?' 'What deeply matters?' and 'How are we willing to live?' These questions require a psychology of complexity and depth, a psychology of freedom and ambiguity that I have elsewhere termed 'awe-based' (Schneider 2004, 2005). By awe-based, I mean a psychology that elucidates the fuller ranges of our being, from our deepest dreads to our most dazzling desires, and from our acutest experiences of smallness (fragility) to our most daunting perceptions of greatness (possibility). Awe-based psychology stresses the poignancy of life, the profundity and vivacity of life, about which classic literature has revolved for centuries. Is this not the 'take home' message, for example, of

Cervantes' *Don Quixote*, Goethe's *Faust*, Tolstoy's *Death of Ivan Illych*, Fitzgerald's *Great Gatsby*, and Woolf's *To The Lighthouse*? Do they not all speak to the inadvertent costs of expediency and the fuller, more enduring rewards of the life deeply lived? Does one really have to be a Romantic to appreciate this, or does one just need to be both practical and modestly conscious to see how an awe-based reform can benefit both the individual and society as a whole?

Given the prevailing obstacles then, what can be done to redress them? Can a viable existential model of human flourishing be offered as an alternative to the reductionist models currently in vogue? Can a life of paradox and complexity – or what I call awe-based transformation – be supported by a socio-economic system designed precisely to subvert it? I believe it can, but only if we in the existential depth community begin channelling our energy in ways that will reach the broader public. One way to do this is to 'compete' with the system at its own game, the game of profit calculus, or cost offsets. Consider, for example, all the medical, vocational, and interpersonal cost offsets that could be realized in the wake of awe-based therapies and programs. Let me highlight a few of those possibilities here – awe-based education, awe-based vocation, and awe-based democracy. These proposals are drawn from my books *Rediscovery of Awe* (2004) and *Awakening to Awe* (2009), as well as an article summarizing the topic (Schneider 2005).

Awe-based education

The general principle of this proposal is the promotion of an educational system that immerses students in the awe of both theory and action. One potential application is an 'awe-based' curriculum that challenges students to study the promotion or suppression of awe by various cultures down through history (e.g. agrarian-neolithic, Greco-Roman, African, Asiatic, European, etc.), and engages them to grapple with the relevance of those findings to their own contemporary lives. This kind of curriculum would help set the tone for the love of study, while at the same time promoting a broadening and deepening of virtually any eventual specialization or craft.

To elaborate, this form of education is very similar to other calls for educational reform, such as that of the Inquiry Learning Action Group of the Teaching and Learning Centre at the University of Calgary (ILAG 2005), with, however, a few nuances of difference. For example, awe-based discovery focuses students directly on that which inspires (i.e. evokes awe) and that which devitalizes (i.e. evokes despair) in all the major epochs of human history. Such a format not only encourages personal encounters with the problems and possibilities of given moral dilemmas, but also immerses students in the wisdom-teachings of the past, and how best to apply those teachings to present challenges. The awe-based curriculum also combines critical-reflective inquiry with 'hands on' engagements with the arts, literature, field investigation, and so on. The emphasis of an awe-based curriculum is on holistic – rather than primarily verbal/analytical – discovery and application.

Awe-based work

This reform proposes a one hour a week mental and physical well-being program designed to awaken a sense of passion and purpose about one's job. The program would be voluntary and administered by both management and employees. The mental well-being component, for example, could begin as a pilot project, and entail a variety of holistic offerings: from group explorations of the meaning and impact of work for employees' lives, to topical seminars on stress, holistic healing, spirituality, and multiculturalism. Facilitators could include psychologists, psychiatrists, counsellors and holistic health practitioners; their collective concern, however, would be experiential depth – the extent to which employees are assisted to immerse in and not just 'report about' the topics that matter to them.

While the coordination of such an operation, and the obstacles it would face, would of necessity be formidable, its potential fruits, in my view, would be inestimable. Among these would be a salutary impact on just about every major sector of society, from the motivation, engagement, and even product quality of the work setting, to the cascade effect these enhancements would bring to employees' home lives, relations with community, and outlook on life. Just a few paltry hours, in other words, could help to spark a revolution!

Awe-based democracy

The idea here is to link an experiential component (above and beyond the conventional 'rational' approach) to the proceedings of deliberative bodies, such as legislatures, diplomatic organizations and ethics panels. This experiential component, moreover, would be facilitated by highly skilled depth-experiential therapists. By 'experiential component', I mean the supplementation of both formal and informal deliberative processes with the following awe-based features: (1) an appreciation of the many-sidedness of a given dilemma; (2) a whole-bodied attunement to and encounter with that many-sidedness; (3) a whole-bodied response to and discernment of that many-sidedness, leading to a substantive action in the world (see also Tillich's 1967 notion of 'listening love'). These experiential processes could be facilitated in small group encounters of two to five legislators, where deliberations of moral import would go beyond the usual rhetorical level to a level of personal and intimate exchange. The results of such exchanges could then be passed on to the legislature at large for integration and

complementation. Who knows what the ultimate impact of such a procedure would be on the body politic as a whole? Yet one point that does
ring clear is that the democratic principles of openness, deliberation, and
voting one's conscience will all have been given their due.

These then are some glimmerings of a new pathway for psychology. They
do not preclude standardized or conventional elements – in fact each of the
reforms elucidated are likely to draw from those elements (Schneider 2008).
But the point is that they do not end with those elements. They encompass
more, far more, and they draw on a far more vitalizing science. Therefore, I
call for the following action plans within the existential, awe-based research
and practice communities:

- Begin pilot projects implementing the above awe-based programs.
- Design a study of awe-based existential therapies and programs and
  their cost offsets in terms of medical, vocational and interpersonal
  spheres of functioning.
- Design a study comparing cost offsets between cognitive-behavioural
  strategies and programs and those of existential-humanism.
- Design an in-depth, qualitative study of the consequences of awe-
  based, existential living, that is, living characterized by an inner sense
  of freedom, acknowledgment of life's paradoxes and a willingness to
  creatively engage those capacities.

If we can follow this action plan, as well as any of a variety of related plans,
we will then be in a stronger position to impact the larger world with what
my colleague Eugene Taylor has characterized as the 'New Existential Man
and the New Existential Woman' (2008) or alternatively, as my colleague
Ed Mendelowitz has put it, people of 'character' (2008).

The task before us could not be more urgent.

A RESPONSE TO 'DEPTH AND THE MARKETPLACE: PSYCHOLOGY'S FAUSTIAN PLIGHT'
Simon du Plock

It is, I believe, entirely fitting, given the title of this book, to note both what
European and North American approaches to existential therapy hold in
common, and what distinguishes them from each other. It also seems
apposite given that our title marks 50 years of existential therapy, to
acknowledge the extent to which the adaptation of European existentialism
for American consumption, as identified by Rollo May *et al.* in the seminal
text *Existence* (1958), continues to hold sway. An authentic recognition of
both differences and similarities can only be beneficial. My sense is that in
this, as in therapy, grand schemes and universal models must yield to local

conditions if they are to have any lasting impact, and genuine dialogue provides the necessary conditions for creativity and growth.

I agree whole-heartedly with the general thesis that psychology and psychotherapy are less effective when distorted and limited to fit the marketplace. Clearly, traditional one-to-one long-term ways of delivering therapy (and I use the term 'deliver' with our position vis-à-vis consumerism in mind) are increasingly dismissed on grounds of accessibility and cost-effectiveness; and, arguably, some forms of 'applied psychology' which have been developed represent a dilution of the original meaning of psychotherapy as 'attending to the soul'. I agree, as you say in an earlier paper, that our culture provides little freedom to 'suspend our resolution-mania, and dwell in the doubts, tangles, and uncertainties that lead to growth' (Schneider 2007: 36). The debate, then, about ways in which therapy is adapting to the marketplace is a vital one. I resonate strongly with much of what you say about the current state of psychology and psychotherapy; I think, though, that we differ significantly in our response to the dilemmas you outline so well. This may be rooted in the difference between European and North American perspectives on therapy recognized by May, and more recently expressed by Irvin Yalom (1980) in his response to Continental European existentialism. It is a difference, perhaps, in the pragmatic notion that we can *do* something with psychology by using it in a direct approach to change social, economic and political systems, on the one hand, and on the other a view which sees psychology as one among a number of knowledge bases which can contribute to an enhancement of our understanding of the human condition. The development of psychology in socially responsible ways may, from the latter perspective, enable people to become stronger, more resilient, more resourceful. Rather than pursue a path which will see increasing numbers of 'depth psychologists' exercising their expertise at every level of political and economic activity, I suspect there is more to be gained by a radical revisioning of psychology and therapy in ways which demystify their knowledge and make it more widely available. I suppose I am arguing for a preventative approach and in this respect I resonate with David Smail's *How to Survive Without Psychotherapy* (1996). A key element of this approach, at least as I see it, is our ability as existential practitioners (and social activists) to remind people of the many existing ways by which they can, as you express it, ask the 'big questions' about life. I am not sure that they need to find answers, but I am sure that keeping these questions in mind provides a compass for living in an active and vibrant way. I am sure it will not surprise you that the ways I think people can stay reconnected with these questions are very similar to the ideas you have proposed for rediscovering awe (Schneider 2008, 2009).

Problems are particularly evident in western democracies where the work model has changed dramatically – largely in terms of technology, and it seems to me important to ask to what extent the solutions you propose can be applied outside the US. The desire for the genesis of the 'New Existential Man' and the 'New Existential Woman' reminds me of the title of an existential-humanistic conference held in Lithuania in the aftermath of the fall of the communist regime: 'Psychotherapy and the Post-Soviet Person'. In 2009 Professor Rimas Kociunas (Professor of Clinical Psychology at Vilnius University) and I presented a dialogue at the 'East European Versus West European Mentalities' Conference in Vienna. We called our session 'Psychotherapy in the West European and Post-Soviet Space: From Control to Control' in recognition of the speed with which Soviet psychiatry, with its brutally reductionistic philosophy of human nature, was being replaced with manualized and technical 'treatments' which, in their turn, largely eschew serious engagement with what it means to be human. I regret that I am not optimistic about the future of psychology as an institution independent of the state. In any case I think it improbable that psychology will become the dominant term of reference for everything which happens in 'the larger world' in the absence of a social-political-economic revolution. If psychology can gain an enhanced political role in the US, it may indeed be a force for good, but it is difficult to see how an awe-based psychology would translate universally without such a revolution, not least since it rests on culturally specific ideas of education and democracy. To give an example, the adoption of awe-centred education in the UK would require the political will to dismantle the existing system of training, rules, regulations and 'league tables' which drives our schools. And while philosophy is a core part of the school curriculum in France, the state-imposed ethos would not be congenial to the concept of awe as a key element.

Which brings me round to the term 'awe', its religious connotation and specifically Judeo-Christian theological point of reference. (Not to mention its imperialistic use in Iraq as part of Operation Shock and Awe.) Perhaps 'wonderment' – the secular equivalent of awe – might be a more helpful, less fearful term? I am thinking here of wonderment in the sense in which it is used by Coleridge when he writes:

> Hast thou ever raised thy mind to the consideration of existence, in and by itself, as the mere act of existing? Hast thou ever said to thyself thoughtfully *It is!* Heedless in that moment whether it were a man before thee or a flower or a grain of sand . . . without reference in short to this or that mode or form of existence?
>
> (1868: 463)

There is, I think, a direct link through from Coleridge's 'wonder of all wonders' to taking existence seriously and Rollo May's 'Here-is-a-new-person' and 'I-Am' experiences.

This erosion of wonderment begins with childhood. 'Childhood' is, of course, a social construct, but in the last half-century we have all but abandoned the Romantic celebration of the child's view of the world as expressed, for example, in Wordsworth's 'Intimations of Immortality Based on Recollections of Early Childhood'. Children are increasingly required to be 'busy' as adults are – constantly engaged in some activity or other. We should stop processing children as the recipients of each new technology and reflect on what childhood might be. One of the most important things to restore is wonderment. A child raised on ready-made, often violent, computer imagery must necessarily lose out in terms of a cultivation of their own imaginative resources. Colette, I believe, was accurate:

> The style of things, the kind of things that we shall love in later life are fixed at moments when the child's strong gaze selects and moulds figures of fantasy that for it are going to last.
>
> (Phelps 1966: 498)

The rediscovery of wonderment, for both children and adults, is not just the task of therapy and therapists. Wonderment does not preclude the spiritual, but holistically encompasses mind, body and spirit. If indeed we increasingly lack the ability to experience wonderment, I would like to suggest ways of promoting it, of reminding ourselves how we can be more fully human and more aware of our existential being. These owe more to the roots of existential therapy in philosophy than to a narrowly defined psychology. In their apparent simplicity and ready availability, they may help us to revision therapy in increasingly democratic ways. They may help people in identifying the effects of the worst excesses of consumerism and materialism and support them in their efforts to find (inexpensive) ways to help themselves counter some of the more toxic aspects of contemporary life – thereby gaining a sense of mastery and agency, where there was previously a sense of helplessness or passivity.

Smail (2005) refers to the erosion of communal living and the glorification of selfishness and competition, which characterize the contemporary west. He argues that deciding what sort of world we want to live in is an ethical choice. We existentialists have a responsibility to critique technical individualistic treatment of distress and to show how mechanisms of power and interest impact upon the subjective experience of individuals.

I want to introduce some ideas of an eccentric nature. By 'eccentric' I am referring to the etymological sense of being 'outside the centre', being marginal or liminal. I find, as a practitioner, that this eccentric perspective – the stance which asks not 'why', but 'why not?' – often assists clients in their pursuit of clarity about their own way of being in the world. A liminal position enables us to throw light on to different parts of the client's world, while a central position, I would argue, tends to reinforce the normative, the status quo, sedimenting the client's sense of being in some way marginal or mistaken in their worldview, rather than allowing it to simply come into focus as fully as possible.

I think we can learn a lot from the philosophers, and not always in the most obvious ways. Kierkegaard, for instance, made several references to the therapeutic value (both physical and metaphysical) of physical exercise in his diary and letters: 'every day I walk myself into a state of well-being and walk away from every illness' (Poole and Stangerup 1989: 69). Walking kept him socially involved and was, for him, a symbol of movement itself. For Kierkegaard, as for Blake, 'Energy is eternal delight'. For Kierkegaard, physical exercise was an integral part of community life, poles apart from the modern day gym culture – let alone hours of solitary sitting at the computer.

Richard Mabey, the author of the remarkable autobiographical *Nature Cure*, reminds us that a respect:

> for the curative properties of nature goes back as far as written history. I want to suggest a greater sense of the natural world provides an ideal way of increasing our ability to experience wonderment. . . . The Romans had a saying, '*solvitur ambulando*', which means, roughly, 'you can work it out by walking', including your own emotional tangles.
>
> (2005: 223)

Mass pilgrimages were regular occurrences in the medieval world and if we know our Chaucer at all, we know the journey was at least as important as the destination. Mabey stresses the strong connection between nature, language and identity:

> We constantly refer back to the natural world to try to discover who we are. Nature is the most potent source of metaphors to describe and explain our behaviour and feelings . . . [they] are miniature creation myths, allusions to how things came to be, and a confirmation of the unity of life.
>
> (2005: 19–20)

Since movement, observation of nature and the world around us, and freedom of expression seem intimately related, we can see exercise as our first route to an enhanced sense of being.

It is also important that we experience ourselves in relation with our fellow human beings, and this itself can be a constant source of wonderment. In one of his papers, Eugene Gendlin mourns what he sees as the end of community and argues that in its absence we have to find new ways of being in relationship: 'To be in a group, one had to plead sick (therapy) or one has to have (or pretend) an interest in photography, adult education, or politics . . . *Soon it will become understood that everyone needs to be in a group*' (in Lander and Nahon 2005: 15). On this view social life has become so depleted that we all need to join some sort of 'encounter group'!

The awareness of the significance of this dimension of relationship is not a recent phenomenon. Michel de Montaigne, the sixteenth-century French essayist, recommends conversation as an intellectual sporting event that will improve the mind. Through the eighteenth century, writers, including Jonathan Swift and Adam Smith, argued that conversation promoted psychological health and intellectual development. Echoing these thoughts, Samuel Taylor Coleridge says that it helped him control his despair over his drug habit. 'The stimulus of Conversation suspends the terror that haunts my mind; but when I am alone, the horrors I have suffered from Laudanum, the degeneration, the blighted Utility, almost overwhelm me' (Miller 2006: 22).

In *The De-Voicing of Society: Why We Don't Talk to Each Other Anymore* (1998), John L. Locke argues that modern technology has had a negative effect on sociability. A number of studies, he says, make it clear that many people use email to avoid face-to-face interaction. This trend is disturbing because we learn many things from a person's voice and gestures, and much about ourselves through interaction. Kurt Vonnegut similarly problematizes the god we call 'Progress': 'Electronic communities build nothing. You wind up with nothing. We are dancing animals. How beautiful it is to get up and go out and do something' (2006: 61–62). Perhaps also one of the implications of the radical subjectivism of post-modernism is that if all ideas are personal truths, there can be no solid conversation – no interchange of ideas. Each speaker (or writer) can only recite their truths. And the audience (or reader) can say only: 'Thank you for sharing your personal truths with me.'

Finally, I want to come to reading as a source of wonderment. I have been fascinated recently to see that, as part of the struggle to reduce National Health Service waiting lists, practitioners have focused on reading – devising 'bibliotherapy' schemes whereby patients are prescribed self-help literature before, or instead of, referral to a therapist. Now, the therapeutic potential of literature has probably been known since the beginning of written communication – the inscription over the entrance of the Ancient Greek library at Thebes proclaimed it 'The healing place of the soul'. And the oral tradition of storytelling predates even this.

Technique, though, has increasingly come to the fore; bibliotherapy has been reshaped as primarily an efficient and cost-effective way of delivering cognitive behavioural therapy, which CBT practitioners, many of them clinical psychologists, have now claimed as their own and hence given 'evidence-based' status. At the most optimistic and pragmatic end of the spectrum, Stanley (1998) refers to bibliotherapy as a 'science' and provides recommendations for readers seeking guidance on subjects as specific and as amorphous as: 'Coping With a Chronic Illness', 'Addiction and Recovery', 'Self-Esteem', 'Discover Your Life's Mission'.

From an existential perspective we can see that, paradoxically, the notion of scientific bibliotherapy appears on the one hand to offer individuals a powerful way of treating themselves, without the necessity of deferring to an 'expert', while on the other hand disempowering them by implying pathology and prescribing specific 'drugs' to remove their symptoms.

The direction of UK bibliotherapy reflects the US approach in that it takes a technological view of suffering, and, like most US bibliotherapy, is delivered using one or more non-fiction CBT-based self-help texts pre-scribed from a short list of 'approved books'. These schemes are largely compatible with treatment approaches concerned with cognition and beha-viour, but are far less relevant for therapies which attempt to engage with less tangible aspects of human existence such as values, meaning, subjective truth and, dare I say, authenticity. It seems to me that the client's subjective and empowering experience of reading is getting lost in this drive to claim 'scientific status' for bibliotherapy.

I have argued that there is evidence for opening up the simplification and manualization of the National Health Service concept of bibliotherapy by returning to the phenomenon itself – clients' reading: helping patients reflect on the ways they use texts to create their sense of self, rather than prescribing books for the relief of specific symptoms. Such an 'existential bibliotherapy' can provide a way of moving beyond symptom alleviation in order to assist people to engage with problems of living: it shifts the focus of practice, inviting the client to join the therapist in a co-research of their past and current reading, thus co-constructing a 'reading history' – a description of the client's individual use of literature. This moves us beyond prescribing and into a 'being with' rather than a 'doing to' relationship – I have certainly not become a bibliotherapist!

I have only mentioned a few aids to wonderment: there are many more including writing, dance, and playing or listening to music. The specific activity is less important than the attitude of openness and attentiveness we bring to it. And it is at this point – the nurturing of people's ability to attend to existence and to themselves – that I think the continuing potential of existential psychology and therapy becomes evident. I noticed an adver-tisement for a large UK university on the Underground recently. It began: 'Thinking about the Big Questions?' and ended with the exhortation 'Just do it!' I think we need to focus on what can assist people to address the absurdity of the human condition without losing themselves in action or in contemplation of questions of existence.

KIRK'S RESPONSE

Dear Prof. du Plock
First of all, I relish this opportunity to celebrate the remarkable legacy of my dear friend Rollo May, but also, and equally, to engage in a forward-

looking and long overdue conversation with you (and by implication, European existential psychology as represented by you).

I am largely in agreement with you, as apparently, you are with me, on many matters, including aspects of your vision for responding to our 'awe-depleted' personal and cultural situation. I very much like what you say about wonderment, relational needs, the Romantic and poetic tradition of literature, and the need to 'give away' existential psychology to the people, so to speak. As you indicate, I've been chiselling away at these themes for a considerable time (Schneider 1998, 2004, 2009).

However, where I differ with you in regard to your proposals is more in nuance and tone, than nature and kind. As a general point, I find your use of certain terms and concepts helpful so far as they go, but feel, in some instances, that they don't go far enough. For example, I too prize the term 'wonderment' – I used it as an aspiration in my book *Horror and the Holy* (1993), but I have since downplayed it in favour of what I view as the richer, fuller term 'awe'. Coleridge notwithstanding, wonderment has, for me, a certain airiness which lacks what Rollo May used to call the 'punch' or muscularity that is necessitated at this time. Hence my main reason for replacing wonderment with awe is that both etymologically and experientially, the latter in my view, carries more weight. By this contention I mean that awe is one of the few transcendental terms that intensely and squarely embraces the paradox of our condition – our experience of being stumbling, struggling *creatures* as well as, at some level, soaring, swelling *gods*. (Or 'Gods who shit', as Becker 1973 once so aptly put it.) The etymology and history of the word 'awe' are reflected today in its commingling senses of wonder, dread and reverence; a multifaceted and subtly nuanced term, ideally suited to counter the aridity and hollowness of our current age (from which the East incidentally, is also not wholly immune). Briefly, while wonderment captures the soaring, emboldening side of our humanity, it does not do justice to the poignant and vulnerable side, which as existential-oriented thinkers have been arguing incessantly, is the mead of a *well-leavened* life.

With regard to relational needs, unquestionably, we are impoverished in our contemporary world. No doubt many of the ideas you suggest about social interaction would enhance our personal and collective well-being. The only point I would stress here is that it is not only relational impoverishment that besets us today, it is also the impoverishment of an inner life – of depth and character. To the extent that we can reconnect with our selves, we can also reconnect with those about us – and vice-versa.

As for the drawbacks of a society of therapeutic experts and the need to give existential psychology away to the masses for their own empowerment, I am in much agreement. However, I don't see these developments as mutually exclusive. It seems to me that we can have *both* an expanded base of depth-oriented facilitators, as I have outlined in recent books (Schneider

2004, 2009), *and* give away our practices to the public. Your examples from philosophy and literature are beautiful, but I see no reason why existentially oriented practitioners couldn't also facilitate more direct life-enhancement interventions in areas such as the educational system, the work setting, and the legislature. We have much to offer in these areas, including a very salutary check against the excesses of the existing power structure – a structure marked not by philosopher kings, but by profiteers, militarists, and technocrats (Klein 2007). The idea of shrinking from intervention is unduly reticent in my view. So it is not that I'm unwary of your concern – and indeed you have an incontestable proportion of history on your side – but on balance, and given how precarious things have been of late, I think we could *and need to* risk more activism.

References

Becker, E. (1973) *The Denial of Death*, New York: Free Press.

Bohart, A. C., O'Hara, M. and Leitner, L. M. (1998) 'Empirically violated treatments: disenfranchisement of humanistic and other psychotherapies', *Psychotherapy Research*, 8: 141–157.

Calton, T., Ferriter, M., Huband, N. and Spandler, H. (2008) 'A systematic review of the Soteria paradigm for the treatment of people diagnosed with schizophrenia', *Schizophrenia Bulletin*, 34: 181–192.

Century of the Self (2005) British Broadcasting System documentary film.

Coleridge, S. T. (1868) *The Complete Works*, New York: Harper.

Cummings, N. and O'Donohue, W. (2008) *Eleven Blunders that Cripple Psychotherapy in America*, New York: Routledge.

Elkins, D. (2007) 'Empirically supported treatments: the deconstruction of a myth', *Journal of Humanistic Psychology*, 47: 474–500.

Fauth, J., Gates, S., Vinca, M. A., Boles, S. and Hayes, J. A. (2007) 'Big ideas for psychotherapy training', *Psychotherapy: Theory, Research, Practice, Training*, 44: 384–391.

Gardner, H. (2006) *Multiple Intelligences: New Horizons*, New York: Basic Books.

Greenberg, L. S. (2007) 'Emotion coming of age', *Clinical Psychology: Science and Practice*, 14: 414–421.

Inquiry Learning Action Group (ILAG, 2005) *Action Plan*, Calgary: University of Calgary.

Jamison, K. (1993) *Touched with Fire: Manic-depressive Illness and the Artistic Temperament*, New York: Free Press.

Klein, N. (2007) *The Shock Doctrine: The Rise of Disaster Capitalism*, New York: Henry Holt.

Lander, N. and Nahon, D. (2005) *The Integrity Model of Existential Psychology in Working with the 'Difficult Patient'*, London: Routledge.

Locke, J. L. (1998) *The De-Voicing of Society. Why We Don't Talk to Each Other Anymore*, New York: Simon and Schuster.

Mabey, R. (2005) *Nature Cure*, London: Chatto and Windus.

May, R., Angel, E. and Ellenberger, H. F. (eds) (1958) *Existence: A New Dimension in Psychiatry and Psychology*, New York: Basic Books.

Mendelowitz, E. (2008) *Ethics and Lao Tzu: Intimations of Character*, Colorado Springs, CO: University of the Rockies Press.

Miller, S. (2006) *Conversation. A History of a Declining Art*, London: Yale University Press.

Phelps, R. (ed.) (1966) *Colette. Earthly Paradise*, Harmondsworth: Penguin.

Poole, R. and Stangerup, H. (eds) (1989) *A Kierkegaard Reader. Texts and Narratives*, London: Fourth Estate.

Schneider, K. J. (1993) *Horror and the Holy: Wisdom-Teachings of the Monster Tale*. Chicago: Open Court.

Schneider, K. J. (1998) 'Toward a science of the heart: romanticism and the revival of psychology', *American Psychologist*, 53: 277–289.

Schneider, K. J. (1999) 'The revival of the romantic means a revival of psychology', *Journal of Humanistic Psychology*, 39 (3): 13–29.

Schneider, K. J. (2004) *Rediscovery of Awe: Splendor, Mystery, and the Fluid Center of Life*, St Paul, MN: Paragon House.

Schneider, K. J. (2005) 'The fluid center: an awe-based challenge to humanity', *Journal of Humanistic Psychology*, 43 (3): 133–145.

Schneider, K. J. (2007) 'The experiential liberation strategy of the existential–integrative model of therapy', *Journal of Contemporary Psychotherapy*, 37: 33–39.

Schneider, K. J. (2008) *Existential-Integrative Psychotherapy: Guideposts to the Core of Practice*, New York: Routledge.

Schneider, K. J. (2009) *Awakening to Awe: Personal Stories of Profound Transformation*, Lanham, MD: Jason Aronson.

Seligman, M. E. P. (1996) 'Science as an ally of practice', *American Psychologist*, 51: 1072–1079.

Siegal, D. (2007) *The Mindful Brain: Reflection and Attunement in the Cultivation of Well-being*, New York: Norton.

Smail, D. (1996) *How to Survive Without Psychotherapy*, London: Constable.

Smail, D. (2005) *Power, Interest and Psychology. Elements of a Social Materialist Understanding of Distress*, Ross-on-Wye: PCCS Books.

Stanley, J. (1998) *Reading to Heal. How to Use Bibliotherapy to Improve Your Life*, Boston, MA: Element Books.

Taylor, E. (2008) Personal communication, August 15.

Tillich, P. (1967) *My Search for Absolutes*, New York: Simon and Schuster.

Vonnegut, K. (2006) *A Man Without A Country. A Memoir of Life in George W. Bush's America*, London: Bloomsbury.

Walsh, R. and Shapiro, S. L. (2007) 'The meeting of meditative disciplines and western psychology: a mutually enriching dialogue', *American Psychologist*, 61 (3): 227–239.

Wampold, B. E. (2001) *The Great Psychotherapy Debate: Models, Methods, and Findings*, Mahwah, NJ: Lawrence Erlbaum Associates, Inc.

Weston, D., Novotny, C. M. and Thompson-Brenner, H. (2004) 'Empirical status of empirically supported psychotherapies: assumptions, findings and reporting in controlled, clinical trials', *Psychological Bulletin*, 130: 631–663.

Yalom, I. (1980) *Existential Psychotherapy*, New York: Basic Books.

Chapter 15

On reading Irvin Yalom's *Staring at the Sun: Overcoming the Dread of Death*

Maurice Friedman, Havi Carel, Judith Hassan and Donna Orange

As befits a founder of dialogical psychotherapy, Professor Friedman's choice of topic emerged from out of our dialogue and involved a personal dialogue with Irvin Yalom's book *Staring at the Sun*. Yet it was not until we had read his essay that we realized how well it could lend itself to being opened up beyond a dialogue of two into a 'roundtable'. This idea seemed to capture the imagination of the three contributors whom we then contacted, Dr Havi Carel, Judith Hassan OBE and Professor Donna Orange, and we are grateful to all four authors for the way in which they chose to engage with this novel format.

CONFRONTING DEATH: REFLECTIONS ON IRVIN YALOM'S *STARING AT THE SUN*

Maurice Friedman

This essay brings with it a sense of closing a number of circles. I first encountered Irvin Yalom when he led a day's workshop on his book *The Theory and Practice of Group Psychotherapy* in 1972 for the Carl Rogers' Center for the Study of the Person in La Jolla of which I was a Visiting Fellow. I did not meet him again until he came to be the speaker at the annual conference of the Institute for Dialogical Psychotherapy of which I was a co-director. At that time he read us the chapter on the fat girl from his forthcoming book *Love's Executioner*. Not long after that he published his book *Existential Psychotherapy*. He was interested in Jean-Paul Sartre at the time. My colleagues and I were very interested in existential psychotherapy, but because of my work on Martin Buber, we were closer to Buber than Sartre, and it was under the influence of my book *Martin Buber: The Life of Dialogue* (1955) that we coined the term 'dialogical psychotherapy'. Irvin Yalom is a prolific writer, and we were fascinated to see how in book after book he moved ever closer to dialogical psychotherapy – although it is not a term that he himself would use to describe his theory and practice.

I laid out the foundations of dialogical psychotherapy in my 1985 book *The Healing Dialogue in Psychotherapy* and have unpacked its meaning in several of the essays that I have written since, as has my fellow co-director Rich Hycner in his book *Between Person and Person: Toward a Dialogical Psychotherapy* (1993). In 'dialogical psychotherapy', what is essential is not what goes on in the minds of the partners in a relationship but what happens between them. For this reason dialogical psychotherapy, or 'healing through meeting' as it is also called, is opposed to that psychologism that wishes to remove the realities of relationship into the separate psyches of the participants. 'Dialogical psychotherapy' is the central healing mode whatever analysis, role playing or other therapeutic technique may be involved. If the psychotherapist is seen as an indispensable midwife in bringing up what was not yet conscious, this is not 'healing through meeting'. Only when it is recognized that everything that takes place within therapy – free association, dreams, silence, pain, anguish – takes place within the context of the vital relationship between therapist and patient, do we have what may properly be called dialogical psychotherapy. The deciding touchstone of reality is the therapist and the relationship, not the methods. Healing through meeting is a two-sided event that is not susceptible to techniques of willing and manipulating in order to bring about a certain result. What is crucial is not the technical skill of the therapist but what takes place between the therapist and the client. To be aware of another person means to perceive the dynamic center that stamps on all utterances, actions and attitudes the recognizable sign of uniqueness. Such awareness is impossible if, and as long as, the other is the detached object of my observation, for that person will not thus yield his or her wholeness and its center. It is present only when he or she becomes my partner in dialogue. In genuine dialogue we relate to others in their uniqueness and otherness and not just as a content of our experience. From this standpoint, the psychological is only the accompaniment and not the touchstone of reality in itself. The basic element of healing, when it is a question not just of repair work but of healing the atrophied center, is healing through meeting. The many individual cases that Irvin Yalom describes for us in *Staring at the Sun* enable the reader to see for himself or herself the remarkable extent to which this is true of Yalom's practice. Yalom recognizes fully the power of presence: 'One can offer no greater service to someone facing death . . . than to offer him or her your sheer presence' (2008). This is a fine example of Martin Buber's 'I–Thou' relationship of openness, immediacy and reciprocity. It is truly dialogical in Buber's sense of the term, yet no word needs to be spoken. To Yalom connection is paramount:

> Whether you are a family member, friend or a therapist, jump in. Get close in any way that feels appropriate. Speak from your heart. Reveal your own fears. Improvise. Hold the suffering one in any way that gives

comfort. . . . The more you can be truly yourself, can share yourself
fully, the deeper and more sustaining the friendship. In the presence of
such intimacy, all words, all modes of comfort, and all ideas take on
greater meaning.

(2008: 130–131)

The real heart of *Staring at the Sun* is revealed by its subtitle – *Overcoming the Dread of Death* – and this is what most people will read the
book for. *Staring at the Sun* contains many powerful anecdotes about
the reality that we all share – that sooner or later we shall die and that
before that takes place we shall undoubtedly awaken to this fact. The fear
of death, Yalom writes, 'is the paramount and pervasive factor underlying
so much of our emotional life' (p. 275). Yet he sees awareness of death as
an awakening, a great advantage: 'A confrontation with death arouses
anxiety but also has the potential of vastly enriching life' (p. 75). Furthermore, he argues, 'the way to value life, the way to feel compassion for
others, the way to love anything with greater depth is to be aware that their
experiences are destined to be lost' (p. 147). So, far from accepting the idea
that his concern with death is in any way morbid, Yalom stresses that it is
the very center of life and of healthy living. What Yalom is seeking in this
book is an awakening of consciousness to one's own mortality as the
beginning of an overcoming of the terror of death. Such awakening, Yalom
claims, can often be facilitated by the help of another – a friend or a
therapist – with a greater sensibility to these issues. Throughout human
history the awareness of transiency has always been the key element in such
awareness. The pain of transiency may be tempered by the awareness of
what Yalom calls 'rippling': 'Rippling reminds us that something of each of
us persists even though it may be unknown or imperceptible to us' (p. 92).
Rippling can also be expressed in modelling: 'I can set a model for my
friends and family by facing death with courage and dignity' (p. 138).
Yalom concludes:

> We should confront death as we confront other fears. We should
> contemplate our ultimate end, familiarize ourselves with it, dissect and
> analyze it, reason with it, and discard terrifying childhood death
> distortions. . . . Let's not conclude that death is too painful to bear. . . .
> Anxiety will always accompany our confrontation with death.
>
> (p. 276)

The last of my 24 published books is *The Affirming Flame: A Poetics of
Meaning* (1999). The conclusion of this book is entitled 'Confronting
Death'. In writing this essay on Yalom's *Staring at the Sun* I have asked
myself to what extent his desire to face death and at the same time
overcome its terror is similar to my 'confronting death'. I therefore want to

add here a few of my own thoughts on confronting death, not as a criticism but as a supplement to Yalom: when we overcome the terror of death, we are left with the task of confronting death and that is what I shall address here. Yalom recounts for us many individual cases where he has helped a patient wake up to and become aware of this emotional undertone and undertow. What I deal with are the many factors that fuse together to make us and our contemporaries conscious of a pervasive death anxiety that is perhaps unique to our time.

The human being is the only creature who knows that he will die and who can make of this knowledge a foundation for his life and even for his joie de vivre. For Psalm 90, the knowledge that all flesh is as the grass which grows up in the morning and withers in the evening leads to a desire not to escape from the mutable to the immutable, as with Plato, but to 'number our days so that we may get a heart of wisdom'. To the native American, every man must learn in this world enough of the meaning of life to be ready to die. The Hasidic rabbi Simha Bunam said to his wife that his whole life was only that he might learn how to die. Martin Buber planned to have a chapter on death in his philosophical anthropology *The Knowledge of Man* (1965), but then decided against it because, as he told me, we do not know death in itself as we know the concrete realities of our existence. This is true, but what we do know is the anticipation of death – the imagining of death – one's own and others, and the attitude one brings to this somber and unavoidable future. For both Martin Buber and the poet Rainer Maria Rilke, death and life formed together one reality. Rilke called death 'friendly' because he saw life and death, the visible and the invisible, as a seamless whole.

The human attitude toward death has always been bound up in the closest way with the human posture vis-à-vis nature, time and community. Although he is aware of the seasons, the modern person hardly lives in the time of nature. His time is abstract, calendrical, and conventional, and his relations to nature are more and more detached – whether nature be the object to be exploited, the scene to rhapsodize over, the terrain for a holiday from the city, or the great Earth Goddess celebration every Year on Earth Day to ward off the threat of pollution and ecological imbalance. We have lost contact with real nature altogether because we have robbed it of its otherness and made it over in our image. As a result, it is hardly possible for us moderns to see our own death as a part of the natural rhythms and cycles of nature, to be accepted with the wisdom of nature itself.

Our relationship to time has also become distorted. Every moment of our lives is a gradual submergence into death. Yet neither in our own lives, which have a beginning and end, nor in the beginningless, endless movement of time itself can modern man find a meaning. To live as persons we have to have a sense of meaning in our personal life and in history. Yet there is nowhere in time itself that meaning can be found. Our attempt to find a foothold in present reality cannot succeed because we are always using the present as a means to some future end. This functional relation to time is caused in turn – and reinforced – by that sense of isolation, restlessness and exile that makes us feel, in moments of awareness, that we know no real life.

Similarly, we are cut off from the nourishing stream of community in such a way that the prospect of our own death takes on an overwhelming importance that robs life itself of meaning. Death is that uttermost solitude of which every other abandonment is only a footnote, as Martin Buber suggests. So often, what should be the very height of mutual presence – sex and love – has become the opposite. In *Love and Will* (1969), Rollo May has vividly shown how our culture uses sex as a way of not facing age or death – more or less adequate sexual functioning as a sign that we are still alive and not threatened by death.

With loss of a healthy relationship to nature, time, community and intimacy, Death becomes the Absurd precisely as Camus has defined it in *The Myth of Sisyphus* (1975). It cuts us off from a meaningful relationship to past and future and from a meaningful relationship to each other. It is one thing to recognize, with 'Everyman', that no one else will go for you or that, like Jesus, 'You gotta walk that lonesome valley, you gotta walk it by yourself'. It is another to carry around one's general expectation and one's specific fears about death as an invisible barrier that gets in the way of any directness of relationship and of any present immediacy. How many of us can really say with the Song of Songs: 'for love is stronger than death', or with Martin Buber that 'a great relationship throws a bridge across the abyss of dread of the universe', the abyss of death (Buber 1985: 116)? Death has always been the foremost advocate for the absurdity of life. 'This too shall pass away.' 'All things change, all things perish, all things pass away.' 'Vanity of vanities, all is vanity.' And our clients tell us: 'What's the point, if anyway I'm going to die?'

But there is much in our day that has heightened the absurdity of death that we must confront, to the point where it is qualitatively different. The assassinations of John F. Kennedy and Martin Luther King, Jr., the riots in Los Angeles, the Vietnam war and the wars in Iraq and Afghanistan have brought to the surface that terror and violence which seethes beneath the seemingly most successful civilization in the world's history. This is echoed throughout the world: Iraq's genocidal destruction of its Kurds; Bosnia's death camps for the 'racially impure'; the growing racist violence in France, Germany, and Russia; and the systematic starvation of its people by the rival tribal chiefs of Somalia. Hiroshima, with its sudden death and long years of slow death by radiation, has created, as Robert Jay Lifton has shown, a 'death-culture' in which even those who live are weighed down by the conviction that they too will be stricken, as well as by the 'survivor guilt' of those who seem senselessly spared from a common doom. The atomic bomb survivors, *hibakusha*, 'seem not only to have experienced the atomic disaster, but to have imbibed and incorporated it into their beings, including all of its elements of horror, evil, and particularly of death' (Lifton 1968: 201). Their own identities merge not only with the dead relatives but with the anonymous dead. 'With both Hiroshima and Nazi concentration camp survivors,' writes Lifton, '*the grotesqueness surrounding the death imprint* . . . conveyed the psychological sense that death was not only everywhere, but was bizarre, unnatural, indecent, absurd' (p. 480). Even the seeming recovery of the atomic bomb victims became a 'lifelong sense of vulnerability to the same grotesque death' (p. 481). Their '*jarring awareness of the fact of death*' and their own mortality issued into a 'vast breakdown of faith in the larger human matrix, and in the general structure of existence' (p. 481).

> This death anxiety was concerned not just with dying itself but with *premature death and unfulfilled life.* The *hibakusha* and the Nazi concentration camp survivor witnessed mass death that was awesome in its randomness, in its inclusion of small children quite new to life and young adults at their prime, as well as old people . . . The anxiety-laden imprint retained by both groups of survivors was of death that has *no reasonable relationship to life span or life cycle, of profoundly inappropriate death.*
>
> (p. 487)

The starvation of the children of Biafra, the devastation in Indochina of millions of people by napalm, burning, bombing, disease, starvation, and outright murder, the genocides in the former Yugoslavia and in Rwanda are illustrations of the readiness of dictatorships and democracies alike in our day to create vast death cultures as instruments of national policy. More than illustration – prototype – is the Nazi death camp in which six million Jews, one million gypsies, and four million other people were exterminated. 'Auschwitz' stands not only for death and death culture, but for a systematic dehumanization such as the world had never known, a scientific undermining of the very foundations of social existence. In the world of Auschwitz, social mistrust and existential mistrust are interwoven into the greatest assault on man as man that human history has known. However much death has challenged human meaning in the past, death for modern man, disconnected from nature, time, community and meaning, is preeminently an encounter with the absurd.

Martin Heidegger takes the half-truth of separation that the knowledge of our unique and individual death imparts to each of us, and makes it into the specious whole truth of our existence being 'ultimately non-relational'. Actually the anticipated reality of death is present in love and gives it its special poignancy, when the love is real, without destroying it. Our awareness of death enters both into our situation and our response, but it does not dominate it. Only when we are not focusing on the future negation of life by death do we have any presentness and immediacy. That self-preoccupation that makes suicide the only philosophical question of any importance, as Camus claims in *The Myth of Sisyphus*, is mostly laid to one side in our actual lives, in which what is central is our response to what is not ourselves.

The memory of death and the anticipation of death is often a calling to account, as in Tolstoy's *The Death of Ivan Ilyich* and Kafka's novel *The Trial*. 'This door was intended only for you. I am now going to shut it,' says the doorkeeper in Kafka's 'Parable before the Law' (Kafka 1976: 121). We are called to account for the uniqueness of our lives and of the lives of all those with whom we have been intertwined – not in some Last Judgment or moralistic, idealistic superego standard, but in the simple perspective of that moment when life and death are simultaneously present. 'Why is man afraid of dying?' asked the Hasidic rabbi of Ger, and answered, 'What man fears is the moment he will survey from the other world everything he has experienced on this earth.' In therapy after a confrontation with death (e.g. after a diagnosis of cancer) clients may voice this sense of being called to account: 'When I look back on my past, I have so many regrets'; 'The cancer is an indictment of my life'; 'I need to take stock of my life, rethink my priorities.'

Franz Rosenzweig begins *The Star of Redemption* (1971) with the reality of the fear of death and ends it with the phrase: 'Into Life.' Death is not of the future at all, nor of the past; it is an inescapable reality of the present. It is inescapable because it colours our existence at its far horizons. Yet all we ever know is the present, and all we know in that present is life itself. Living life one day at a time is something that clients almost invariably speak of after a diagnosis of cancer. However, while this is accompanied by a sense of the preciousness of time and life, it is usually conjoined to a feeling of anxiety about the future and the pointlessness of planning ahead. There is seldom the philosophical acceptance implied in the Talmud's injunction to regard each day as if it were the one before our last or in the kindred attitude embodied in T. S. Eliot's meditation on the Bhagavad Gita in *Four Quartets*.

Rollo May

I was delighted when I discovered that Irvin Yalom devotes a whole segment of *Staring at the Sun* to his relationship with my old friend Rollo May. I was never a patient of Rollo's as was Yalom, but we had a friendship and a rich association that lasted 40 years until Rollo's death. My relationship with Rollo began in 1959 when he asked me to write a review article on his book *Existence*, although he must have known me before to have made such a request. I read the book carefully; *Existence* confirmed my identification with existential psychology and psychotherapy. Rollo invited me to become a member of the Executive Council of the Association of Existential Psychology and Psychoanalysis – which I remained until I left New York. For years, together, we edited the *Review of Existential Psychology and Psychoanalysis*. Because I really cared for Rollo, I was very pleased when I heard that I had been given two Rollo May awards after his death. The first, in 2000, was from Division 32 of the American Psychological Association, where I delivered a long paper on 'Martin Buber and Dialogical Psychotherapy', with a half-hour of questions and discussion afterward. The second was given me in 2009 by Saybrook – a graduate school mostly concerned with psychology with which Rollo had a long association. It carried with it a handsome honorarium. There, I gave a half-hour lecture on 'The Outreach of Dialogue', which has since been published in the *Journal of Humanistic Psychology* (2009). I began this lecture by saying how pleased I was to have an opportunity to express my thanks to Rollo, as I am pleased now to end this essay with a section on him: he has been compared by many to the great American psychologist William James.

The Association for Existential Psychology and Psychoanalysis also held a number of important conferences. The one I remember best was when both Gabriel Marcel, the French Catholic existentialist, and Paul Tillich presented their views of existentialism. We also had a conference that centered on Medard Boss, as well as one around Ronald Laing. These conferences were well attended. Rollo was chairman of the Executive Council, until my friend Leslie Farber of the Washington School of Psychiatry succeeded him. It was Leslie who brought Martin Buber to America in 1957, during which visit Buber's now famous dialogue with Carl Rogers took place. I was then the dialogue moderator, and a young man. Now some 50 years later, and exactly 50 years after writing a review of *Existence* for Rollo, I find myself contributing an essay to an anniversary tribute to that book and, if not 'staring at the sun', very much in my 'sunset years' – and grateful that the sun has not yet set on me and that, even if my memory is a little impaired, my thinking is not.

I am pleased to be ending this essay with a section on Rollo. He and I became good friends, and I also got to know his wife Ingrid and his last wife Georgia May (but not so well). When I sought Rollo's advice about taking a position in California, he advised me to stay in the East, the intellectual center of America. But in the end neither of us did. Rollo moved to Tiburon in Marin County, north of San Francisco, where I often visited him. Once, he gathered a number of psychologists to meet and talk with me at his home. He also once gently reproved me, with good reason, for always coming around to Martin Buber in our discussions. I had done so much work on Buber, including a three-volume and later a one-volume biography of Buber, that I suppose it was inevitable that I overdid it.

I did not know Rollo at the very end of his life as did Irvin Yalom, who became Rollo's friend after being his patient. I did not know until I read *Staring at the Sun* that Irvin Yalom was so close to him at the end of his life – even preparing his body for the crematorium, a task which I did not envy and which understandably depressed Yalom. However, I was particularly touched by the last time I stayed with Rollo, when we had an in-depth talk about my life – from his advising me to write more slowly to his concern about my losing weight.

I am now 88 years old, older than Irvin Yalom. I am Emeritus Professor of Religious Studies, Philosophy and Comparative Literature at San Diego State University, have practised psychotherapy for a quarter of a century and am ready to still do so. I have published 24 books, including four on psychotherapy (1972, 1984, 1985, 1992); however, another four remain unpublished: *All Real Living Is Meeting: My Friendship with Martin Buber*; *Abraham Joshua Heschel: Awareness of the Ineffable: Our Thirty-Year Friendship and Dialogue*; *Building Genuine Community*; and *Down in My Heart: A Conscientious Objector in the Second World War*. I very much hope to see these books published before I die.

When I phoned Irvin Yalom and told him I was writing this essay springing from his book *Staring at the Sun*, I asked him whether he would be willing to respond to it briefly. He replied that he had put everything he knew into that book – as any reader of *Staring at the Sun* can see. Besides, he added, he had put everything else aside to finish a novel on Schopenhauer that he was halfway through writing. So I am sorry that this is a circle that we shall not be closing together.

* * *

Havi Carel, a Senior Lecturer in Philosophy, was diagnosed at the age of 35 with lymphangioleiomyomatosis (LAM), a rare, life-threatening illness. Here she offers her response to reading Yalom's Staring at the Sun, *reflecting on her confrontation with her own mortality and the help that philosophy has afforded her.*

NON, JE NE REGRETTE RIEN: LESSONS FROM FINITUDE
Havi Carel

> For there is nothing fearful in life for one who has grasped that there is nothing fearful about the absence of life.
>
> (Epicurus, 'Letter to Menoeceus')

How should I face the fact of my death? This is perhaps the most fundamental question reflective human beings have asked themselves. It was also one of the first and most serious questions philosophy had to encounter. Socrates said that those who pursue philosophy 'study to die', or use their wisdom in order to learn to accept their finitude. Indeed, 'to them of all men death is least formidable' (*Phaedo* 67D). On this view, philosophy can provide tools with which to come to terms with our death. Philosophical debates of death are rich and fascinating, but are at their best when supporting a genuine existential exploration, such as Irvin Yalom's in *Staring at the Sun*.

For Yalom the question is: How can I help my patients live well with the knowledge of their impending death? For me the question became: How can I live well with the knowledge of my illness and poor prognosis? Of course, death can be impending even if the person concerned with it is not terminally ill or very old. Death can be existentially present, indeed impending, for anyone, even a child. As Yalom illustrates through the case studies described in the book, the fear of death (and other existential concerns) can be at the heart of seemingly disparate kinds of psychic suffering. At the heart of dissatisfaction with life, sexual promiscuity, Oedipal engagement and so on, there is an existential concern with our place in the world, in the natural order of things. And part of that natural order is also death.

The existential terror of annihilation is not always directly expressed. Sometimes it requires recovering from within other experiences and themes. At other times, such as bereavement or illness, the fear of death itself is explicitly the source of concern. The symptoms Yalom describes – waking up in the night, failure to commit, repeated dreams, anxiety, dissatisfaction – seem to be very general, but at the same time also utterly specific to the sufferer. What this captures is the fact that many of our existential concerns are highly unique to us in our idiosyncratic way of living them, and yet are universally shared by people from all walks of life, all historical periods, all ages.

It is this universality that philosophy captures and explores with a set of analytic and reflective tools. It provides arguments and thought experiments with which to unpick our fear of death. In this sense philosophy is complementary to psychotherapy, as it provides a general philosophical framework that can then be applied to a unique individual's situation (as existential therapy so aptly demonstrates). But how successful is philosophy in providing us with tools to think through our own death? In my own experience of serious illness, the answer is: extremely successful.

When I was first diagnosed with LAM, I went through a dizzying array of emotions. I was told by an evasive radiologist that my life expectancy was ten years. That figure – ten years – initially stunned me into complete paralysis, and later haunted me for many months. The destruction to my life was total: I literally did not know what to do with this perverse glimpse into my future that medical technology had awarded me. I did not know what to do with my death, how to relate it to my life.

I instinctively turned to philosophy. I thought: I spent all these years studying philosophy and then teaching it. Surely it has something to offer me in my plight? And indeed, my search was richly rewarded. Philosophy did have useful, insightful and important things to say about death. It has been an enormous help to me in my struggle to come to terms with and live happily with the knowledge of my possibly all too early extinction (Carel 2008). It has been particularly useful for me in exploring the fear of death, how death is linked to life, and how to live well with the knowledge that we are mortal and have little control over our time and way of dying.

The fear of death is very real to us, as animals who wish to live on; as Yalom rightly observes, it is a major source of suffering. But the philosopher Epicurus examined this fear and deemed it irrational. He thought that all suffering arises from destructive unhealthy ways of thinking, in this case thinking about death. Epicurus argued that death should not worry us, because we should only worry about things that bring us pain or suffering, namely, things we can experience. And because he saw death as complete annihilation and denied the existence of the soul after the death of the physical body, there is no need, he argued, for us to fear death, as we will not be there to experience our death. As Epicurus writes: 'For all good and bad consists in sense experience and death is the privation of sense experience' (Inwood and Gerson 1994: 29). In such a situation, there is no danger of suffering, there is no loneliness, no pain – there is nothing. So at the very least one should appreciate the release from pain and suffering that may be brought about by death.

One may retort that that is precisely what is so scary – the thought of our own annihilation. But Epicurus presses us further on this, asking why, exactly, is it scary? We do not feel anxious or sad about our nonexistence before our birth, so why should we feel sad about nonexistence after our death? Yalom adopts this line of argument in his attempt to unpick his clients' fear of death. He further addresses this fear with his notion of rippling – the ongoing and unpredictable effects one's actions and words may have beyond their lifetime. So a part of us lives on through rippling, the myriad ways in which we touch others' lives. Rippling does not offer false metaphysical comfort, through notions of an afterlife, but simply provides another way of thinking about our heritage and lasting impact on the world (Yalom 2008: 133). Even if we only help build a playpark for children, like Akira Kurosawa's protagonist Watanabe (1952), our ripples may be felt for many years.

I think Yalom's notion of rippling manages to capture something that is important to many, without resorting to any notion of afterlife, or soul outliving the body. In this respect he succeeds in offering genuine consolation in the form of one's continuity through rippling. When I worry about not being able to see my son grow up, I do genuinely believe that the love and happiness I give him now will be a substantial part of his future life, even if it is lived without me.

The second insight that philosophy provided me with is that death is not some distant event that has nothing to do with life. Rather, it is part of life and affects it at every moment. And indeed, Yalom's clinical vignettes show the many ways in which death is constantly present in life, even if sometimes unconsciously. For me it was the German philosopher Martin Heidegger who captured death's relationship to life in the most systematic and convincing way. Heidegger argued that knowledge of mortality is a constant presence in life, and renamed human existence 'being towards death'. What is human existence, he said, if not a limited stretch from birth to death? Human existence is marked by finitude and limitation, and those of us who ignore this fact are engaged in a futile pursuit, trying to escape the inescapable. To understand life fully, Heidegger argues, you must understand yourself as finite (Heidegger 1962: 294; 250; Carel 2007: 547).

Indeed, for Heidegger the only way to live authentically, fully, is by understanding every moment as an irreversible step taking us closer to our death. Thus our death is not merely some external event that will delineate life from the outside, as it were; rather it is what gives meaning to life by making each moment unique, and each choice a critical contribution to who we are and how we live (Heidegger 1962: 310; 265).

Life, for Heidegger, is a constant movement towards death. His formulation of human existence as 'being towards death' captures the temporal essence of human existence. This temporal essence condemns us to be constantly propelled through time towards our own annihilation. This annihilation is not culmination or achievement. Unlike a fruit ripening, or writing a novel which culminates in the final published book, human life ends in nothing. Human life lacks the final goal, or *telos*, that the ripe fruit and the finished novel have. We propel ourselves through life; but to what end? None, says Heidegger. There is nothing at the end. This is what we need to make sense of: the bare nothingness of death (Carel 2006). Our mortality is at once a key fact about human existence, a structuring element of human life and consciousness, and something that has no meaning. So why should we think about it?

Heidegger thinks that although we cannot defeat mortality we are nonetheless obliged to understand ourselves as finite, to grasp our mortality in order for us to be able to live authentically. Living authentically relies heavily on understanding ourselves as finite, limited creatures that are first and foremost temporal. We exist in and as time: we change with time, our past existence makes us who we are in the present and we make future plans towards which we project ourselves. Humans strive to achieve goals and aims and the limited opportunity to do so can drive and motivate, rather than lead to despair. As Heidegger writes: 'Anticipation reveals to

Dasein its lostness in the they–self and brings it face to face with the possibility of being itself [. . .] in an impassioned freedom towards death' (1962: 311; 266).

On this view, which seems in complete harmony with Yalom's, death is a source of edifying meaningfulness. 'Can you find a way to live without continuing to accumulate regrets?' asks Yalom (2008: 101). The knowledge of the unique and non-repeatable nature of each moment of our lives can help generate meaning, not destroy it. Instead of ruining my life, I found out that my illness has helped me sharpen my sense of responsibility for my well-being and life. Because the future became uncertain, I clung to the sense of well-being I found in the present moment. Thus focusing on the beauty and significance of the present can shift the weight from our obsession with future plans and achievements to a simple appreciation that the greatest achievement lies in living well now, in this moment. This sense of ongoing responsibility for one's well-being at any given moment captures the significance death has for life. This insight is echoed in Yalom's words: 'Staring into the face of death [. . .] not only quells terror but renders life more poignant, more precious, more vital. Such an approach to death leads to instruction about life' (2008: 276).

I have now spent just over four years of my ten living more vitally than ever before. I remain alive, but also suspended in mid-air, mid-life, constantly negotiating and rethinking the existential concerns that have become my daily bread. Like gravity, a force whose influence we always live under, my mortality is with me on a daily basis. But this knowledge is not unique to me, nor is my condition singular. We all live with our mortality, as a shadow of nonexistence contouring every moment of existence, imbuing each moment with creativity and choice.

As Heidegger wrote, we should not brood about death, but we should anticipate it. And what I understand him as meaning by 'anticipation' is living with the mindfulness of the irreversibility of time, the power of nature over us as organisms, the temporal axis that underlies our existence. As thinking organisms, we can also live well with this knowledge, harness it to fuel and make vital our every day. It is living as mortal, or 'being towards death' that is the greatest lesson existential philosophy has taught me.

* * *

Judith Hassan has been listening to Holocaust survivors and refugees for over 30 years, learning from them how to help them to live with their memories of severe trauma. The survivors have inspired her to pioneer innovative and creative responses that have formed the bedrock for the therapeutic services founded over 20 years ago at Jewish Care's Shalvata and the Holocaust Survivors' Centre (HSC) in London. (Hassan 2003.)

SPIRITUAL LIBERATION FOR SURVIVORS OF GENOCIDE

Judith Hassan

Professor Maurice Friedman, quoting Lifton 1968, writes: 'the Nazi concentration camp survivor witnessed mass death that was awesome in its randomness . . . The anxiety-laden imprint retained by . . . survivors was of death that has *no reasonable relationship to life span or life cycle, of profoundly inappropriate death*' (p. 214). Those who were there looked death full in the face. They were, as Irvin Yalom puts it, 'staring at the sun'. I would like to focus on the impact that past traumatic reality is having on survivors' lives as they get frailer and closer to the end of their natural lifespan. I shall address the particular fears and anxieties survivors may have about growing older and once again confronting death. I will balance this focus against the positive responses that can be made to ensure that the last part of the survivors' lives is as comfortable, peaceful and dignified as possible.

What are some of the fears that survivors have about ageing? Despite the fact that survivors have, on the whole, led fulfilling lives and contributed so positively to society, the emotional vulnerabilities related to their severely traumatic experiences in the Holocaust remain just beneath the surface of the skin and tend to erupt with increasing age. If we remember that the old and infirm were amongst the first to be gassed in the death camps, it is hardly surprising that many survivors fear their failing health. The survivors' loss of control over their physical and mental deterioration as they age can reactivate memories of their earlier victimhood when they were at the mercy of the Nazis. For example, severe weight loss in illness may take survivors back to that other time when their bodies were similarly emaciated. For a few survivors, illness may also be their first confrontation since the camps with doctors and tests, and their horrific associations. It follows that, for ageing survivors, the practical and emotional ramifications of growing old are magnified many thousands of times compared with the elderly generally.

One of the survivors' deepest concerns as they get closer to the end of their lives is that their memories of severe suffering will die with them. After their physical liberation in 1945, many survivors have devotedly and courageously carried the memory of those murdered in the Holocaust. The dead have resided in them, and they have 'carried' them for 65 years. For many survivors, that has been a crucial part of their raison d'être. At the same time, their duty to remember meant that they never felt truly free. As survivors grow frailer, many find it increasingly difficult to continue travelling to schools, universities and prisons to pass on their eye-witness accounts, and this causes them distress.

Some survivors had hoped that their children and grandchildren would carry their memories into the future, and so ease their anxieties about future remembrance. However, many of their children are not able or willing to do so, having heard the detail of their parents' suffering all their lives. They are now older themselves and may have additional stresses of being carers for their frail survivor parents.

Despite the fact that there is a National Holocaust Memorial Day, that there are museums which record the detail of the Holocaust experience, and that there is a wealth of testimony recordings, many survivors still feel that, with time, their experiences will be watered down and ultimately forgotten. Not surprisingly, therefore, as they draw closer to the end of their lives, many ask: 'Who will remember us when we are gone?' They fear that if they and their murdered families are not remembered, it would be as though their suffering had been in vain – as though they had never existed. The ensuing anxiety makes it more difficult for them to let go of life peacefully; I feel passionately that I/we must not let that happen.

My aim is to help survivors by lifting some of the emotional weight of remembrance from them and their families, and by ensuring the trans-mission of their legacy to others who will carry it to future generations. If we are able to do this, survivors may then feel free to continue to positively maximize the time they have left in their lives, to find creative talents they never thought they had, for example, through art or writing in the HSC's social programme, to take a 'loan on life' (Yalom 2008: 104), and generally to celebrate their lives. Survivors, whose freedom was once so inhumanely restricted, need the freedom to choose how they wish to live their lives into old age. This freedom they seek is what I call 'spiritual liberation': it includes helping them to feel that they matter, and that they will not be abandoned as they once were; it involves the commitment of those who will live on after them to carry the survivors' memories, so that the survivors can peacefully let go.

What does this mean and how do we put it into practice? I believe there can be such a thing as a 'good end'. I tend to see the end of life as part of a continuum that links the past and present to the future. Perceived in this way, the end can be seen as a new beginning in which we are all the potential baton carriers in the fight against forgetfulness and indifference. At the core of my perception is hope. It is a hope that springs from deep inside me based on my personal beliefs, the influence of my home and background and my spirituality. It is a hope echoed throughout Yalom's moving and uplifting book about 'overcoming the dread of death'. I also see hope in the survivors who, even at a very advanced age, can still enjoy themselves, have fun, tell jokes, and be positive. Knowing that there are things we can do, practically, emotionally and spiritually before the sur-vivors have all died, feeds that hope.

Working towards a 'good end' depends on planning with survivors, both collectively and individually, how they want the end of their lives to be. We must consult with them as we have done throughout our work with survivors. Even though time is finite for the survivors, it is never too late for them to make changes, or as Yalom puts it, to minimize feelings of regret (p. 145).

For instance, we have now developed, in consultation with survivors, a new scheme of Independent Living Apartments (Jewish Care). At the root of the scheme is the survivors' wish for independence and to maintain control over their lives; this is in direct contrast to their memories of imprisonment which are often triggered when they enter institutional care, however benevolent it might be. Every detail had to be scrutinized: the colour scheme (no yellow or stripes); the amount of light needed for the well-being of those who had been incarcerated; whether showers were appropriate for those who had been in death camps; and how catering should be offered to people who have suffered starvation. The new apartments will offer adequate practical services day and night, so survivors can be free to live their lives to the full.

The scheme also addresses the survivors' emotional need to be with other survivors in a mutually supportive community in order to counteract, as far as possible, the reality that dying can be a lonely experience (p. 119). The centrality of the survivors in the scheme gives them a sense of being valued and empowered. The survivors' voice, which had been silenced in the Holocaust, now speaks clearly about what they want and need. This exciting new project helps to breathe new life into our work and gives us the impetus to do more.

Perhaps the greatest challenge for those of us who work with survivors emerges from the individual encounters we have with them as death becomes a regular visitor. We have built relationships with them over many years, and for some we have become like their replacement family. The blurring of professional boundaries, which has proved so essential in building up trust with those whose trust was shattered in the Holocaust, exposes us to feeling the survivors' loss more deeply and personally when they die. To stay close to survivors at this crucial time, we work together as a team, we support and talk to each other. We share the responsibilities of being with survivors at their funerals and houses of mourning. We also enable them to support each other. For example, I have seen survivors propping each other up at the graveside, bringing back glimpses of earlier times when they may have been too weak to stand during the endless hours of *appel* (roll call) in the death camps. *Their* survival strategy helps to inform our responses.

The practical and emotional aspects of our work are only part of the equation. Spiritual liberation for survivors may involve a wish to return to their Jewish roots. Having been persecuted as Jews they may have a complex relationship to religious and spiritual matters. We talk with some survivors about giving their murdered families a Jewish burial. For example, a hidden child I worked with was able to mourn for her mother who was murdered in Auschwitz after she had arranged to have her mother's name inscribed on her sister's gravestone who was buried in London. Together with a rabbinical colleague we recited Kaddish (mourning prayers) at the graveside. This helped us to work on the 'unfinished business' from her past, and for her to move on in her life.

Without any pressure to do so, we offer members of the Centre opportunities to connect or reconnect to their Jewishness and cultural past by linking them to positive memories and rituals from before the Holocaust began. For some survivors, coming to a Jewish Centre, eating food that tastes of 'home', or speaking Yiddish is enough. For others, it is through attending the celebrations of the Jewish festivals or the monthly Friday night (Sabbath) dinners at the Centre. I have seen some survivors, who were initially hesitant to join in the prayers and songs, then begin to warmly embrace familiar memories that were in danger of being lost. That matters to me and touches me. Once the practical preparations such as funeral arrangements and wills have been made, it seems to help survivors to let go of life more peacefully.

The survivors' peace of mind at the end of their lives also rests on the transmission of their legacy, as mentioned earlier. The key to the success of our legacy project lies in the personal links that are made to survivors, particularly by young people. It is what Yalom calls 'human connectedness' (p. 117) that helps to mitigate the fear of dying. In practical terms it includes: engaging survivors' families as volunteers or fundraisers; encouraging school groups that visit Poland to debrief with survivors at the HSC; exchanging skills – for example, schoolchildren teaching survivors IT skills in exchange for language tuition by survivors. By reshaping the legacy to include the survivors' rich cultural heritage and post-Holocaust successes, we hope to make its transmission more akin to an honour rather than a burden.

The survivors' legacy is also 'rippling' (Yalom) through my teachings and consultations with others who work with war trauma, and through my direct work with a group of Bosnian refugees. Their legacy will continue to be transmitted through my networks with other organizations concerned with future remembrance and fighting 'Holocaust fatigue'. I am committed to continue on my journey with survivors until I begin to hear them positively say 'We will be remembered' before they die; then I will know they are closer to a more peaceful end and nearer to their spiritual liberation. *I will then be free to let go.*

* * *

Finally, it remains for Professor Donna Orange, the Intersubjective Systems Psychoanalyst, to weave together the three previous contributions with her own personal and professional response to reading Yalom's book, thus bringing this 'roundtable' to a close.

STARING AT MEANING: OUR OWN DEATH AND THE DEATHS OF OTHERS[1]

Donna Orange

> There is a radical difference between *the suffering in the other*, where it is unforgivable to *me*, solicits me and calls me and suffering *in me*, my own experience of suffering, whose constitutional or congenital useless-ness can take on a meaning, the only one of which suffering is capable, in becoming a suffering for the suffering (inexorable though it may be) of someone else.
>
> (Lévinas 1998b: 94)

'Death is always an outrage!' responded a compassionate friend of a bereaved person whose mother had just died in her late nineties. The mourner had heard so many already say, 'Well, she had a good long life' and other such familiar platitudes. This one, instead, had understood that every death ruptures complex and important emotional ties, and defies generalization. His humanity shone out, unmistakably and unforgettably.

But let us return to his words themselves, in the context of the three responses to Yalom that I am asked to discuss. Is every death an outrage? And in what sense? Irvin Yalom's *Staring at the Sun: Overcoming the Dread of Death* intends to show us not only that we and our patients can live better if we learn the existentialists' lesson about taking our finitude seriously, but also how we can, in our older years, prepare less evasively for our own impending deaths.[2] Like the philosophers who have been so helpful to Yalom and to Havi Carel, we can discover that to philosophize is to learn how to die (Critchley 2009). Carel's moving and motivating per-sonal story, and what she has made of it, speak for themselves. Shocking and traumatic as one's own death may be when we first face it full on, it may not remain outrageous or even tragic for oneself. It can become, instead, our personal version of the inescapable human condition. Every-thing that Yalom and Epicurus, Socrates and Epictetus, have taught us about fearing to do wrong more than to die can help us.

The death of the other, however, should assault me, especially violent and avoidable death. It ruptures the dialogic encounter that Maurice Friedman so treasures, and exiled his (and my) beloved Martin Buber to Palestine, destroying his world and his people. Friedman alludes to many other recent holocausts as well. Such devastation leaves a remainder that Judith Hassan, and others of us who work with the profoundly traumatized, recognize as belonging to a kind of death and suffering that should be no part of the human condition. For such travesty we should not be preparing by accepting our finitude. In the face of Darfur and similar horrors, we need not 'terror of death', but outrage. This outrage includes the sense of indignation and offense, but also, as we shall see, absurdity and meaninglessness.

But what about the intermediate case, the one with which we began? Here we have a 'normal' death, like so many others in old age. Often the elder says: 'I am ready to go', while the family and the medical establishment seek to prolong life. Does the existential therapist, or the philosopher, help us to understand this problem? Yalom's focus, like Heidegger's, is on one's own non-evasive being-toward-death which frees us for a life more genuinely lived. As a psychoanalyst, I might say that this approach may work for me, but, for those who love me, what about the attachments, the intricate involvements we humans have with each other? What about the feeling that something is being ripped apart? Or even for me, even if I become able to accept that my own time is coming to an end, how much must I harden my heart to leave those with whom I have been so intertwined?

There is also the possibility that there are no 'normal' deaths. As I write this, my younger sister, in her early sixties, after an aneurysm and complex surgeries last year, faces another life-threatening brain surgery within this month. She has 'put her affairs in order' and I will fly across the country to see her before the surgery. She is grateful to have seen both her sons grown, married and doing well. She accepts, but I cannot. For me, it is an absurdity, an outrage in this sense.

Perhaps the philosopher and Talmudic teacher Emmanuel Lévinas can help us. Born in Lithuania in 1906, he studied in Strasbourg and, in 1928–29, in Freiburg with Husserl and Heidegger. From Husserl he learned the relentless focus on lived experience (Lévinas and Nemo 1985), and remained himself a lifelong phenomenologist: 'The phenomenological method enables us to find meaning *within* our lived experience' (Cohen 1986: 14). Caught up, like many other philosophers of his generation, in the fever generated by Heidegger's early philosophy of being-in-the-world, Lévinas valued Heidegger's account of affectivity or *Befindlichkeit* (Heidegger 1962; Gendlin 1979) for its worlded relationality and for the understanding of the human being as temporality. He compared Heidegger's *Being and Time* to the work of Plato and Hegel, but, shocked and horrified, he threw away his own book-in-progress on Heidegger when that philosopher joined the Nazis and, as rector, tried to impose their program on Freiburg University in 1933–34 (Stolorow *et al.* 2010).

In 1940, Lévinas was imprisoned in a labour camp near Hannover for five years until the end of the war, while his wife and daughter were hidden by nuns. His status as a French officer protected him from transfer to the death camps, but like the other Jewish inmates, he was made to work much harder than the others. Only the camp dog, Bobby, he later wrote, welcomed the Jewish prisoners as much as the others (Lévinas and Robbins 2001: 92). His entire Lithuanian family was murdered. His life, he later wrote, 'is dominated by the presentiment and the memory of the Nazi horror' (Lévinas 1990: 291).

In the face of such horror, Lévinas questioned the philosophy of those who had supported all this death. What good, he wondered, was the ontology (the study of being itself) or epistemology (the study of the nature of knowing and what justifies our claims to know) if this could be the outcome. He concluded, in his magnum opus, *Totality and Infinity* (Lévinas 1969), that totalizing – treating others as something to be studied or comprehended, leads to murder. Then, having taken into account Derrida's critique (Derrida 1978) – that he was using Heidegger's language to refute Heidegger, he produced his second magnum opus, *Otherwise than Being or Beyond Essence* (Lévinas 1981). Many books and lectures later, he died in 1995. Interest in his work has grown immensely since his death, in part because an ethical void was left by postmodernism, in part because Habermas and Rawls had developed generalized theories of equal treatment justice, without an ethics of the infinite value of every individual human being (Rawls 1971; Habermas 1984). The much-needed work of Lévinas addresses this gap.

Traditionally, metaphysics (the study of the nature of the real), or ontology (the study of being itself) had been thought the primary or foundational matter of philosophical concern. In recent centuries, epistemology took first place. No, protested Emmanuel Lévinas, ethics comes first, just as Socrates had taught and died for it. Lévinas's 'big idea' was, in the words of Simon Critchley,[3] 'that *ethics is first philosophy,*[4] *where ethics is understood as a radically asymmetrical relation of infinite responsibility to the other person*' (Critchley 2002: 6). In Lévinas's own words, 'the ethical relation is not grafted on to an antecedent relation of cognition; it is a foundation and not a superstructure' (1998a: 57). To understand this idea, we must remember that Heidegger, for whom ontology, the study of being, was everything, had explicitly used his philosophy to support the regime that imprisoned and enslaved Lévinas for five years, and murdered all his family. Though Lévinas continued to regard Heidegger as 'a philosophical intelligence among the greatest and fewest', he always also commented on 'the irreversible abomination attached to National Socialism in which the brilliant man could have, in one way or another, it does not matter how, taken part' (Malka 2006). Lévinas became convinced that something 'otherwise' than being or knowledge must be fundamental. His title, *Totality and Infinity*, contrasted what he called 'totalizing' with responding to the face of the other. This irreducible 'face' always infinitely transcends our concepts, representations and ideas: 'The way in which the other presents himself, exceeding *the idea of the other in me*, we here name face' (Lévinas 1969: 50). The other (*Autrui*, the human other) presents me with an infinite demand for protection and care. The face says: you shall not kill (*tu ne tueras point*). You shall not allow me to die alone. In other words, the death of the other can never be a matter of indifference to me, nor even of acceptance, as my own can be. It is useless, like useless suffering, unforgivable.

In Lévinas, we find a striking contrast in his attitudes toward death and suffering in the self and in the other. The other's suffering, he wrote, is 'the purest evil' (1998b: 93). It removes all meaning, drowns the naked face of the other in vulnerability and pain. Only in what he called 'substitution' does suffering become meaningful:

> Once again . . . there is a radical difference between *the suffering in the other*, where it is unforgivable to *me*, solicits me and calls me and suffering *in me*, my own experience of suffering, whose constitutional or congenital uselessness can take on a meaning, the only one of which suffering is capable, in becoming a suffering for the suffering (inexorable though it may be) of someone else.
>
> (Lévinas 1998b: 94)

When I accept some of your suffering or hospitably relieve it, my suffering for and with you then becomes meaningful; suffering in the stranger, without response, remains absurd, the very definition of absurdity, of meaninglessness.

My response to the face is simply '*me voici*' (*hineni*), not 'Here I am' as it is usually translated. Rather, as Paul Ricoeur pointed out, 'it's me here' (Ricœur 1992) renders the meaning better without so much 'I'. Subjectivity is minimal here: it consists in the hospitable and welcoming response to the widow, the orphan and the stranger. (Lévinas frequently in a quiet way invited lonely and hungry students to dinner with his family, and unobtrusively paid their expenses.) The face of the other calls me, demands from me, takes me hostage, persecutes me. The ethical response is my refusal to be unmoved, or indifferent, to the face of the other, to the other's 'useless suffering' (Bernasconi and Wood 1988). Sometimes Lévinas implied that one cannot be indifferent, that one is held hostage, but he knew very well that many did not respond. The bystanders watching their neighbours taken to concentration camps continue to haunt. This 'cannot' must refer to the unavoidable ethical demand. What I am or need, or how I feel toward the other, is, for Levinasian ethics, not in question (Orange 2010).

Now we can return to our original question: whose death is outrageous? If I stare at the meaning of my own death, I must agree with Yalom and with Havel, that there are ways to make peace: Eriksonian generativity, Socratic serenity, Yalom's rippling, Havel's Epicurus. Speaking of the necessary passivity of my own death, Lévinas says that 'the point that death seems to mark in our time . . . is a pure question mark' and this ignorance 'writes checks on an empty account' (Lévinas 2000: 21). But so it is. If I look with Hassan and Friedman and Lévinas at the death of the other, it is an outrage, an insult, an absurdity, unthinkable, not situatable. In between, in the meantime, I am called to an ongoing dialogue between accepting my own death and realizing that my death is an outrage for those to whom I am dear. Perhaps the Levinasian 'hospitality imperative' becomes a responsibility to hear the perspective of the other's loss, even while I engage and accept my own finitude. The inevitably different meanings of our own death and the death of the other challenge our existential convictions, our compassionate intentions, our dialogic attitudes, everything.

Notes

1 I am grateful to Donald Braue and Hilary Maddux for very helpful readings of this piece.
2 Probably the book that most influenced my 1980 decision to leave academic philosophy and to become a psychotherapist was Irvin Yalom's *Existential Psychotherapy* (1980) (his personal kindness was also a huge help at that time). I have also needed meanwhile the inspiration of people like Hassan, and in psychoanalysis, Sandor Ferenczi, D. W. Winnicott, Frieda Fromm-Reichmann, and George Atwood, to work with the deeply devastated.
3 I am more than grateful to Simon Critchley for his hospitality in making Lévinas accessible to me. It is a response that leaves the neighbour changed.
4 The expression 'first philosophy' comes from Aristotle, who used it to refer to his metaphysics, the study of those principles that underlie and transcend the contents of the particular sciences. Lévinas's point was that ethics is even more fundamental.

References

Bernasconi, R. and Wood, D. (1988) *The Provocation of Levinas: Rethinking the Other*, London, New York: Routledge.
Buber, M. (1965) *The Knowledge of Man*, trans. G. S. Smith and M. Friedman, New York: Harper and Row.
Buber, M. (1985 [1947]) *Between Man and Man*, introd. M. S. Friedman, trans. R. G. Smith, New York: Macmillan.
Camus, A. (1975 [1942]) *The Myth of Sisyphus*, trans. J. O'Brien, Harmondsworth: Penguin.
Carel, H. (2006) *Life and Death in Freud and Heidegger*, New York: Rodopi.
Carel, H. (2007) 'Temporal finitude and finitude of possibility: the double meaning of death in *Being and Time*', *International Journal of Philosophical Studies*, 15 (4): 541–556.
Carel, H. (2008) *Illness*, Durham: Acumen.
Cohen, R. A. (1986) *Face to Face with Lévinas*, Albany, NY: State University of New York Press.
Critchley, S. (2002) 'Introduction', in S. Critchley and R. Bernasconi (eds) *The Cambridge Companion to Levinas*, Cambridge: Cambridge University Press.
Critchley, S. (2009) *The Book of Dead Philosophers*, New York: Vintage Books.
Derrida, J. (1978) *Writing and Difference*, trans. A. Bass, Chicago: University of Chicago Press.
Friedman, M. S. (1972) *Dialogue and the Human Image, Beyond Humanistic Psychology*, Newbury Park, CA: Sage.

Friedman, M. S. (1984) *Contemporary Psychology: Revealing and Obscuring the Human*, Pittsburgh, PA: Duquesne University Press.

Friedman, M. S. (1985) *The Healing Dialogue in Psychotherapy*, New York: Jason Aronson.

Friedman, M. S. (1992) *Religion and Psychology: A Dialogical Approach*, New York: Paragon House.

Friedman, M. S. (1999) *The Affirming Flame: A Poetics of Meaning*, Amherst, NY: Prometheus Books.

Friedman, M. S. (2009) 'The outreach of dialogue', *Journal of Humanistic Psychology*, Routledge, 49 (4): 409–418.

Gendlin, E. (1979) 'Befindlichkeit: Heidegger and the philosophy of psychology', *Review of Existential Psychology and Psychiatry*, 16: 43–71.

Habermas, J. (1984) *The Theory of Communicative Action*, trans. T. McCarthy, Boston: Beacon Press.

Hassan, J. (2003) *A House Next Door to Trauma: Learning from Holocaust Survivors How to Respond to Atrocity*, London: Jessica Kingsley Publishers.

Heidegger, M. (1962 [1927]) *Being and Time*, trans. J. Macquarrie and E. Robinson, London: SCM Press.

Hycner, R. (1993) *Between Person and Person: Toward a Dialogical Psychotherapy*, Gouldsboro, ME: Gestalt Journal Press.

Inwood, B. and Gerson, L. P. (1994) *The Epicurus Reader*, Cambridge: Hackett.

Kafka, F. (1976) *The Trial, and Other Works*, trans. W. and E. Muir, London: Secker and Warburg/Octopus.

Lévinas, E. (1969) *Totality and Infinity; An Essay on Exteriority*, trans. A. Lingis, Pittsburgh, PA: Duquesne University Press.

Lévinas, E. (1981) *Otherwise than Being or Beyond Essence*, trans. A. Lingis, Boston: Nijhoff, Kluwer.

Lévinas, E. (1990) *Difficult Freedom: Essays on Judaism*, trans. S. Hand, Baltimore, MA: Johns Hopkins University Press.

Lévinas, E. (1998a) *Collected Philosophical Papers*, trans. A. Lingis, Pittsburgh, PA: Duquesne University Press.

Lévinas, E. (1998b) *Entre nous: On Thinking-of-the-other*, trans. M. B. Smith and B. Harshaw, New York: Columbia University Press.

Lévinas, E. (2000) *God, Death and Time*, trans. B. Bergo, Stanford, CT: Stanford University Press.

Lévinas, E. and Nemo, P. (1985) *Ethics and Infinity*, trans. R. Cohen, Pittsburgh, PA: Duquesne University Press.

Lévinas, E. and Robbins, J. (2001) *Is It Righteous To Be?: Interviews with Emmanuel Lévinas*, Stanford, CA: Stanford University Press.

Lifton, R. J. (1968) *Death in Life: Survivors of Hiroshima*, London: Weidenfeld and Nicholson.

Malka, S. (2006) *Emmanuel Lévinas: His Life and Legacy*, trans. M. Kigel and S. M. Embree, Pittsburgh, PA: Duquesne University Press.

May, R. (1969) *Love and Will*, New York: Norton.

Orange, D. (2010) *Thinking for Clinicians: Philosophical Resources for Contemporary Psychoanalysis and the Humanistic Psychotherapies*, London and New York: Routledge.

Plato (1942) 'Phaedo', in *Plato: Five Dialogues*, trans. H. Cary, New York: Everyman's Library.

Rawls, J. (1971) *A Theory of Justice*, Cambridge, MA: Belknap Press of Harvard University Press.

Ricœur, P. (1992) *Oneself As Another*, trans. K. Blamey, Chicago: University of Chicago Press.

Rosenzweig, F. (1971 [1921]) *The Star of Redemption*, trans. W. Hallo, Notre Dame, IN: Notre Dame Press.

Stolorow, R., Atwood, G. E. and Orange, D. (2010) 'Heidegger's Nazism and the hypostatization of being', *International Journal of Psychoanalytic Self Psychology*.

Tolstoy, L. (1981 [1886]) *The Death of Ivan Ilyich*, New York: Bantam.

Yalom, I. D. (1970) *The Theory and Practice of Group Psychotherapy*, New York: Basic Books.

Yalom, I. D. (1980) *Existential Psychotherapy*, New York: Basic Books.

Yalom, I. D. (1989) *Love's Executioner, and Other Tales of Psychotherapy*, New York: Basic Books.

Yalom, I. D. (2008) *Staring at the Sun: Overcoming the Dread of Death*, San Francisco: Jossey-Bass.

Conclusion

Laura Barnett and Greg Madison

The collected essays of *Existence* (May *et al.* 1958) offered the world an introduction to the possibilities of psychotherapy based upon philosophies of human existence rather than primarily upon theory and technique. In *Existential Therapy: Legacy, Vibrancy and Dialogue*, we see how that initial offering continues to inspire therapists to challenge conventions and orthodoxies that separate us from an open phenomenological exploration of our own being. Paradoxically, though this book is part of the 'Advancing Theory in Therapy' series, it challenges the place of psychotherapeutic theory itself, offering the twenty-first century a practice and understanding of therapy that is still phenomenologically derived and grounded in philosophical reflection. In this brief conclusion, we shall not attempt to summarize the preceding 15 chapters to arrive at a formal definition of existential therapy. Rather, we would like to highlight themes and offer a few impressions regarding past concerns, present issues, and future challenges of existential psychotherapy that arise out of our reading of this volume.

The emergence of an existential tradition in psychology, psychotherapy, and psychiatry, was in part a rebellion against the dualisms and reductionism of psychoanalysis. The philosophical thought of Dilthey, Husserl, Heidegger and others provided a conceptual basis to this rebellion, which for some therapists seemed as much to do with their own discomfort with the impersonal analytic stance in the consulting room as it was with arguments regarding causality and unconscious processes. Some early existential practitioners may have needed, as much as their patients, a type of engagement that was less one-sided, the ebb and flow of real interaction as it emerges between therapist and client explicitly in dialogue and implicitly in the feeling of being-together. Other existential therapists maintained features of psychoanalytic practice, while shifting the focus of interpretation on to the client's being-in-the-world. Whatever the initial reasons for parting company, they do not necessarily justify remaining estranged. Over the last 50 years more existential and phenomenological forms of psychoanalysis have developed, such as the relational and intersubjective schools; so perhaps it is time for both traditions to consider leaning across the historical divide to reassess where each is today in terms of practice. Our inclusion of various authors who traverse this divide may hopefully contribute in some way to this potential dialogue.

As well as paying more phenomenological attention to the 'real relationship', psychotherapy is increasingly attending to the importance of 'the body'. Existential philosophy consistently points out the need to attend to 'the body' as concretely experienced, not as abstractly conceived by medicine and science. A number of contributors in this volume argue strongly that existential therapy needs to incorporate experiential interventions which allow clients to find the changes that existential philosophy suggests are possible. Todres and Cannon illustrate this with case studies and show how we learn from what we spontaneously enact and embody, more than from expert interpretation of hidden 'content'. Such inquiry, similar to qualitative research, is uncertain, never conclusive, yet goes straight to the quick and as such reveals the nature of human existence itself.

Many existential therapists welcome an unpredictable, democratic dialogue between therapist and client. The therapist must be willing to take off the cloak of professionalism and expose himself or herself to being personally challenged and changed by the encounter. This also raises questions about the place of self-disclosure and the boundaries that are necessary for a relationship founded upon these values. The therapist's attitudes go beyond objectifying the client, beyond the mere external manifestations of behaviour. In the words of Maurice Friedman, this is a 'healing through meeting'; not based upon separate psyches, techniques targeted at specific symptoms, or fitting a person to a theoretical mould.

The existential therapist focuses on the client's uniqueness as well as his or her openness to the shared realms of relationship. How we relate to ourselves and how we relate to the world are not two separate processes. Our personal problems often connect to our efforts to wrestle free from the burden of our human situation; change results when these situations are adequately described, understood or interpreted. Yet any interpreting comes not from abstract psychological theories, but from the ground of human existence in its lived ontic-ontological forms – where philosophical generalities are released into the specific two-person process in order to be elaborated and explicated concretely. The client's meanings unfold within a therapeutic dialogue that encourages connection and intimacy.

Existential therapy thus offers a respectful and reflective space to ask fundamental questions which involve bringing as much of oneself as possible into existence and into relationship. Much psychotherapeutic technique and theory can obscure the mutual aspect of such a meeting. We are all, therapists and clients alike, human beings living this life, struggling with problems of existence. It can be a relief for clients to name with an other, who responds from this human position, what they have been living, alone. And for the therapist, too, resonating with the client's insight can enhance their own understanding as well as a felt sense of mutual intimacy. An existential approach does not offer a quick-fix manual for specific diagnoses. Rather, as many chapters of this book have highlighted, it encourages creative reflection upon how to live the ethical demands of a human life in a world that is rapidly changing.

Today we have entered an era where the pervasive medicalization of suffering has nearly eradicated its meaning: we see antidepressants routinely prescribed to the bereaved and the suffering, and not always with their consent. We live more and more bereft of a sense of ourselves as responsive, meaning-creating human beings and the crises and pain this may at times involve. Despite mounting pressure to conform, the existential tradition remains critical of the disease model of diagnosis and the threat of clinical manipulation that can at times place medicine in the role of agent of social control. Medical explanations of psychological suffering do not provide an understanding worthy of any person's meaningful experience. We lose ourselves if we use technology to treat life and its challenges as problems to be solved.

Existential psychotherapists ignore the current state of the world at their peril: for example, we need to take seriously the relational ramifications of globalization and the revolution in technological advancement. How do we respond if the socio-economic system itself pushes us to relinquish aspects of our human potential in order to 'function healthily' within an increasingly superficial world? We cannot afford to assume that where we have come from will help us prepare for where we are going. What does the future hold for humanity generally and for existential therapy in particular? What role, if any, will we have amid the technological and ecological changes to come? In another 50 years, will there still be interest for a new anniversary collection of existential therapy? Indeed, will there still be psychotherapy, as we understand it, at all?

The reflections of a mortal being must at some point turn to confront the anxiety of non-being, and the suffering and 'outrage', which the death of a loved one highlights. The round-table discussion of Yalom's text *Staring at the Sun* (2008) illustrates the personal engagement that each of us must have with mortality if we are to avoid the pretence inherent in an objective discussion of death. Here our impressions as co-editors differ, coloured by the way we ourselves engage with the issue of our own mortality and the 'question mark' that is death; so we offer you our interwoven impressions.

A number of perspectives are highlighted in that chapter, including the idea that something of us remains after death ('rippling'), that there is meaning in modelling courage in the face of death, and the idea that we were not bothered about our nonexistence before birth so why be anxious about nonexistence after death? Much food for thought, but maybe not for comfort: for each of these carries a sting in its tail. For example, there will be no 'I' there to know if my impact on the world 'ripples'. In addition, the nothingness before I existed may be irrelevant since there was no 'I' then, but once I exist, there is an 'I' to compare *being* with the imagined *infinity* when I will never *be* again. So a few questions: as existential therapists, do we look for consolations in the face of death, for ourselves as well as our clients, try to manage our own fears and reduce our anxieties? Certainly facing our finitude with Heidegger's 'sober anxiety' (1962: 358; 310) can help manifest the 'vitality of death' (Koestenbaum 1971), as Carel movingly describes. But does it always? Can we be certain that vitality is not the response of half-seeing through the camouflage of life and that seeing clearly, if that were ever possible, would not have consequences quite different from 'vitality'? How would we ever know? And what if we do not experience any great anxiety as we reflect on our mortality? Are we necessarily deluding ourselves?

It is astonishing to think that every unique world will dim and vanish forever; yet equally astonishing to think that some lives have touched others, often unknowingly and down the generations. In that sense, we carry the legacy of millennia and hand ours down the ages. Indeed, part of our own existence consists of bearing these losses and wondering at those possibilities. The existential therapists in this book have taken up the legacy of *Existence* and offered their thought-provoking responses. Their own legacy now is in your hands.

References

Heidegger, M. (1962 [1927]) *Being and Time*, trans. J. R. Macquarrie and E. Robinson, Oxford: Blackwell.

Koestenbaum, P. (1971) *The Vitality of Death, Essays in Existential Psychology and Philosophy*, Westport, Greenwood Publishing Company.

May, R., Angel, E. and Ellenberger, H. (1958) *Existence: A New Dimension in Psychiatry and Psychology*, New York: Basic Books.

Yalom, I. D. (2008) *Staring at the Sun*, New York: Basic Books.

Index